THE WELLS OF IBN SA'UD

D. VAN DER MEULEN

The Wells of
Ibn Sa'ud

FREDERICK A. PRAEGER
NEW YORK

Published in the United States of America in 1957 by
Frederick A. Praeger, Inc., Publishers, 15 West 47th
Street, New York 36, N.Y.

DS
244
M4

PRINTED IN GREAT BRITAIN

38940

To the memory of my wife,
my counsellor and best companion
in the writing of this book

Contents

Author's Acknowledgements

FOR those parts of this book that lay beyond his personal knowledge and experience the author has relied on three writers: H. C. Armstrong and his *Lord of Arabia*, H. St. J. B. Philby and chiefly his *Arabian Jubilee* and Ameen Rihani and his *Muluk ul Arab*. Without them, and most particularly without Armstrong, this book could not have appeared in its present form.

In acknowledging his deep indebtedness to these writers the author takes the opportunity of expressing his admiration of their work and his gratitude for the help it afforded him.

The author also wishes to express his grateful thanks for the help he has received in preparing his text for the English reader: its idiosyncrasies are all his own.

Illustrations

From photographs by the author, except where otherwise acknowledged

*Photos: * By courtesy of Professor Dr. C. Rathjens
† By courtesy of ARAMCO*

Introduction

I HAD never dreamt of going to Arabia. Roaming the fields and woodlands of that part of Holland where I was born and now have my home, near to Sir Philip Sidney's Zutphen and not far from the Arnhem sacred to later British soldiers, I, as a boy, thought of distant lands. But the lands I thought of were not of the Middle East but of the Far East where we Dutch had had a footing for many centuries. It was the lush green isles of Java, Sumatra, Celebes and Borneo that first called me, not the steaming coasts and the scorched, arid plains of Arabia Deserta. I came from a home of devout parents and might well have felt the call to be a missionary. As it turned out I ended up as Netherlands Minister in Jedda but the career I actually embarked on, when the time came to make a choice, was in the Dutch Colonial Service.

It was thus in the second year of World War One that, fresh from the lecture-rooms of Leyden University, I found myself in the interior of northern Sumatra as a District Officer. My post was on an island in the middle of a large lake. We thought ourselves remote from war in that distant outpost but were mistaken. Muslims in the backwoods of Djambi in southern Sumatra felt the moment opportune to attack their Christian rulers, and before long the movement had spread to the then still heathen part of the Batak country in the north.

Dutch rule had penetrated that part of the Batak jungle for only a score of years or so and although it had opened a new era there and established peace and security and justice, even for the very poor, it had, inevitably, upset existing ways of life. The people resented being upset and the resulting unrest outweighed the good we had brought them. When they found that they were not to be left alone with their old beliefs and customs they

I

revolted and a contributory cause to their revolt was fear of neglected gods.

The outbreak was sharp and sudden and the administration was quite unprepared for it. For me personally it was like a lightning flash that illumines a whole horizon. I saw the storm that was gathering over Asia and I realized that in nearly the whole of the Dutch East Indies Islam offered an obvious rallying point for a nationalist movement. It was my consciousness of the importance to us of Islam and of my lack of understanding of what was moving in its mysterious depths that led me, when on my first home leave in 1923 after eight years' service, to put my name forward for inclusion in a picked group of civil servants who were to be given a two-year course of special study at Leyden University under Professor Snouck Hurgronje. Alas! the Colonial Office told me that my rating of my capacities was higher than theirs and that seemed to be the end of my aspirations.

Then the unexpected happened. Once every five years a Colonial Official was earmarked for the post of Consul at Jedda, the post, at that time, being of much more interest to our Colonial Office than to our Foreign Office. The man selected was given three years' training under Snouck Hurgronje's personal supervision to prepare him for his task. Many applied and when I saw my name at the bottom of a list that included the names of many older, abler and, particularly, more senior colonial officials than myself I felt that my chances were poor indeed. But to my surprise and, I fear, that of the Colonial Office, it was I whom Snouck Hurgronje selected. I was the youngest and, possibly, physically the fittest of the applicants and this turned the scale in my favour but, as I afterwards learnt, Snouck Hurgronje also told the Colonial Office that he preferred me because I faced the prospect of Jedda with a smile.

I thus returned to my old university for three years and bowed under the severe rule of my great master. Snouck, as he was familiarly called, was a world-famous Arabic scholar and expert on Islam. He had become a Muslim in early manhood, made the pilgrimage to Mecca, stayed eight months in the Holy Cities of

Islam and written the book *Mekka*, which is generally accepted as the standard work on the subject. An abridged English version appeared in 1931 under the title *Mecca in the Latter Part of the Nineteenth Century*.

To learn Arabic is in itself a major undertaking but I soon found that knowledge of the language was but a first step to the study of the *Qur'an*, the Traditions of the Prophet and the vast world of the Spirit of Islam in which I was expected to move if not at ease at least not uneasily. From being a hard taskmaster Snouck Hurgronje gradually changed into a fatherly friend. How he would have loved to change places with me and visit again those lands he had seen fifty years before! But as, because of his great age, that was no longer possible he did everything he could to help me. He wanted to make me more than a good Dutch Consul. He wanted to make me a man with an open mind so far as Muslims, their Holy Land, their religion and its problems were concerned. Apart from pouring out to me the riches of his mind and of his experience, it was he who introduced me to the prominent Arabists of Europe and America and who paved the way to my meeting leading Muslims in Arabia, all of whom had known and trusted him under his Muslim name of 'Abd al Ghaffar (The Servant of the Forgiver), whose studies and articles, written in immaculate Arabic, they had all read. No sooner had I arrived in Jedda than a regular correspondence developed between us. My problems and my queries had his immediate personal attention and I know that he must often have sat through the night so as to reply to me by return of post in long, long letters written in his own fine, precise hand. May he rest in peace!

In the days before World War One Arabia was—with few exceptions—under the nominal suzerainty of the Sublime Porte and the chief interest of the European Powers in the part of the country that comprised the Holy Land of Islam—the Hejaz— was to see that protection, in the shape of consular representation, was available during the months of the pilgrimage for those of their Muslim subjects who undertook the journey to Mecca and Medina and to ensure that no infectious diseases were spread by returning pilgrims. This attitude of almost exclusively benevolent interest in the sacred territory continued to a large extent, certainly so far as my Government was concerned, for some time after World War One. The consular representatives who went to Jedda for the pilgrimage season left as soon as it was over and when I was first selected for appointment to the Hejaz it was to fill the purely temporary post of Consul of the Netherlands.

World War One had, however, brought about very considerable changes in the Arabian scene. With the end of the war all the Turks disappeared. The French and British were installed as Mandatory Powers (under the then existing League of Nations) on the Mediterranean seaboard and in Iraq, and two indigenous families had emerged from within Arabia to become rulers. One was the Hashimite family of the Grand Sherif of Mecca, which, although expelled later from the Hejaz as it had been earlier from Syria, was to found dynasties in Iraq and Jordan and the other, the Saʿudi family from Nejd which, after expelling the Hashimites from the Hejaz, was to found the new kingdom of Saʿudi Arabia covering the rest of the peninsula with the exception of the Yemen, the southern coastal fringe and various tracts on the shores of the Persian Gulf.

The House of Saʿud was very closely identified with that reformed and austere form of the religion of Islam associated with Abd al Wahhab and called, from him, Wahhabism, and the war saw the rise in Ibn Saʿud of the greatest of the House of Saʿud. My arrival in Jedda coincided with his eviction of the Hashimites from the Holy Land of Islam, with his introduction there of the tenets of ʿAbd al Wahhab and with his own arrival on the political scene as a world figure. Wahhabism, together with his own genius and the circumstances of the war, had brought Ibn Saʿud to the front. But at the same time Ibn Saʿud had brought Wahhabism to the front and both were now to be tested on a world-set stage. More than that: Islam itself, through Wahhabism, was to be subjected to a severe spiritual crisis. Would that crisis be its last? It was my task to help find the answer to that question.

4

But my appointment to Jedda, in bringing me into close touch with Arabia, also gave me a very much nearer view than I had ever had before of the workings of British policy. In the course of time this view also covered American activities, but when I first went to Jedda there were no Americans there and my only contacts with the British had been in the Far East. In the Far East Dutch and British colonial administrations had for various reasons—not least geographical—been quite apart, not to say aloof, but here in the Hejaz I found myself right in the middle of a British sphere of political—as distinct from colonial—influence. The experience was as unfamiliar to me as it was illuminating.

Someone ought to write a study of the impact of Arabia on individual Englishmen—and women. From Doughty to Glubb they include a number of exceptional figures not excluding Lady Hester Stanhope although her sojourn—I almost wrote performance—much preceded that of Doughty. A large number took to writing and what writers some of them were! Is it the empty desert, where the horizons spell infinity, that stimulates the written word? Does the knowledge that this is the land that traditionally saw the birth of the human race lead to literary creation? Are the writers inspired by the fact that it was from here that our greatest spiritual treasures flowed to the ends of the earth? Or are there just books in the air that one breathes in Arabia, for I, too, have breathed that air?

Doughty seems, beyond question, to have been the finest figure of them all, for in dark and dangerous days he did not hesitate to travel about the interior as a confessed Christian. Of Kinglake I know very little. Burton showed enviable courage and an intrepid spirit of adventure but his greatest achievement, that of performing the pilgrimage to Mecca in disguise, is open to the serious objection of being founded on deceit. Two of the more recent figures, Lawrence and Philby, appear in this book, not altogether to their advantage. During the course of thirty years I met many, although obviously not all, of the leading British who were in Arabia as officials or have for various reasons been associated with that country. I cannot, of course, speak of those I did not know, but most of those I knew seemed, as I enviously noted, to be capable and intelligent and often men and women of exceptional qualities. But it always appeared to me that, whatever their professional talents and individual gifts, they had, with two particular exceptions, both mentioned in this book, one of them by name, no sense of mission. They were not dedicated persons and certainly not shining examples of Christian virtues.

So far as her nationals abroad are concerned, it is all very well to say that a modern western state does not choose its servants for their moral worth, but it is none the less true that in Muslim countries, at least, that is the standard by which we members of nominally Christian nations are judged by the local peoples, official and lay alike. This is their Muslim tribute, doubtless unintended as such, to Christianity and to the Western powers, perhaps especially to Britain as the most familiar of those powers. But that tribute is also a challenge and a challenge that ought to be met.

Arabia is a land with a great historic and, particularly, a great religious tradition. When I first went there it was just emerging from a torpor of centuries. After years of penury it was to acquire economic freedom and great wealth, thanks to American development of the country's tremendous oil resources. We shall see how oil and the Americans radically changed the face of the country for good and all or, as I would rather put it, for bad and all. But more about that later. In my early days there the country was quickly acquiring political consciousness. Within the peninsula relations between the various states were bedevilled by the quarrel between the two ruling families of the Hashimites and the Sa'uds. Of that quarrel I was to acquire first-hand acquaintance. I came to the country with a knowledge of its language, a keen interest in its people, a sound grounding in the history and tenets of its faith and in the problems that confronted that faith if it were to survive as a religious, and not merely a political, force. I came as a Consul to look after the needs of poor pilgrims, I stayed to become a Minister to talk with Kings. Here, then, is the setting of my book.

I

I Meet Wahhabi Arabia

THE decrepit mail steamer dropped her anchor in the inner harbour of Jedda and it rattled down through the blue water into a doubtless familiar resting-place in the dim coral world below. It was the beginning of February 1926 and I stood on the Captain's bridge recovering from the welcome of the local pilot. He had stared for a moment at the Dutch Consul-to-be, the man whose favour he wanted to win because of the big pilgrim ships from Java that were a source of livelihood for him and his large family. Then, in a voice used to roaring orders above the noise of wind and waves, he welcomed me half in English, half in Arabic. His sinewy arms he flung around me and he pressed a kiss just below my astonished right shoulder. His short wiry beard pricked through my shirt and tickled me almost to laughter. But how good was that first Jeddawi welcome! Self-interest or not, how comforting, how reassuring that the first to greet me in an Arab land should be an Arab.

For the world I looked out on was new to me. It belonged neither to the noisy crowded world of the West, nor to the world I had got to know in the Far East, a damp, warm, lush green world, heavy with vegetation and swarming with animal life.

This world before me was older, much older than the two I came from. Here where the sea ended the desert began. Here there was no sign of life or motion, but a shimmering emptiness as of a land waiting for something to happen. Like the pilgrims who year after year follow the injunction of the Prophet of Mecca I had come to this Holy Land. This was the same land where to the north God had spoken to Abraham as a friend and Moses had led a people guided by the God of Israel. It was in Arabia that voices from Heaven had spoken to man, and in this part of the world guidance had been given to mankind. How barren and poor this desert and these rocky hills looked in the haze that enveloped them, yet this was the land where spiritual fountains had flowed to enrich the whole world. Here it was that prophets had lived and spoken, where men had eked out a hard existence in the sight of eternity, where no essential changes had taken place since Old Testament days.

A mile or so away from me stood the town called Jedda or 'grandmother'. The town where 'Ummina Hawa—our Mother Eve—had been buried, according to Muslim belief. Her tomb lay hidden behind a low wall in the desert to the north of the town wall. Behind it, in the distance, there arose blue rocky hills and to the south the town itself stood out like ivory in the heat of a scorching sun and the wind-blown desert dust. With her protecting walls around her Jedda looked like an old cameo in a gold and turquoise setting.

The spell was broken when I walked ashore. Seen at close quarters the town was neither serene, lifeless nor clean. It seemed to be crumbling into ruins and overhung by a penetrating odour. This smell, peculiar to Jedda, arose chiefly from the sewage which was allowed to seep through the walls of the houses. The streets, too, were dusty and unswept and used as a common latrine by both man and beast. Jedda had an age-old smell. Was it the dirt from the camping-grounds of generations and generations of pilgrims visiting the sanctuaries of Islam, for the greater part of whom Jedda was the port of entry and departure?

As I walked through the narrow lanes of the town and inhaled its odorous dust I looked admiringly at the decaying houses and my eyes feasted on the carving of its powdering, crumbling doors and its hundreds of wooden balconies, all different in style and most of them near to falling to pieces. Nowhere in the world, I felt, could one get so near to the sufferings and longings of the human heart as in this gate to salvation where hope and deception

8

met, and where the unselfish and god-fearing rubbed shoulders with those whose shameless livelihood was to fleece pilgrims to the sanctuaries of Allah.

My coming to Jedda marked a fresh stage in my official life. It was no chance appointment that brought me here but a move planned to advance me in Islamic studies and to lead me nearer to the Muslim, and especially the Muslim in Indonesia, in which country my career had hitherto been spent. My qualifications for the appointment were nearly eight years in the Civil Service of the Dutch East Indies and a period of study of Arabic and Islam under the guidance of Snouck Hurgronje in Leyden University. Snouck Hurgronje was famous the world over as an Arabic and Islamic scholar and as a young man he had rounded off his studies by embracing Islam, going to its holy city and collecting there material for his standard work, *Mecca*.

Up to the time of my arrival in Jedda my life had been occupied with the problems of Western administration of Eastern countries, in my case the Dutch East Indies. Independence was on its way to these Eastern nations but only few of us were then aware of, and possibly none prepared for, it. Jedda was not for me an escape from colonial problems. On the contrary it was an attempt to get me nearer to the heart of them. In Jedda the welfare of the pilgrims from Indonesia would be a chief responsibility. By daily contacts I might get a chance to fathom what was going on in the mysterious core of that faith which is not only a spiritual but also a political religion. Jedda meant for me an opportunity to get closer to understanding the riddle of Islam.

In 1926 the Hejaz, as the kingdom of which Jedda was the chief port was then called, was at a turning-point in its history. The first World War had brought Turkish domination to an end thanks to British policy as personified in the redoubtable Lawrence. The Grand Sherif of Mecca, Husain ibn 'Ali al Hashimi, had become king of a liberated Hejaz but his newly-acquired subjects soon discovered that their conditions of life were not much improved by the change. King Husain was hungry for power and thirsty for wealth. When British policy denied him the first beyond the limits of the Holy Land of Islam and when his kingdom could not satisfy his greed for the second he became a morose and embittered old man and as narrow-minded politically as his forebears on that particular branch of the Prophet's family tree. Had Lawrence and the British Arab Bureau in Cairo studied the first, that is the historical, part of Snouck Hurgronje's *Mecca*, they might have learnt the lesson of history, not to look for political wisdom in the Qatada house, which was that of this Grand Sherif of Mecca.

The Jedda I first knew was heartily grateful for King Husain's flight from the country. His son 'Ali, who took over, had shown himself to be a kindly man of clean character but it was soon clear that he was not the man to push back the Sa'udi invader and in fact he put up only a token resistance. Thus it was that the next disaster the men of Jedda were preparing for was the rule of Ibn Sa'ud and his Wahhabi followers. The Jeddawis had no sympathy for Wahhabi puritanism. To them it seemed a most dangerous creed for a country whose sole source of income was the annual pilgrimage. What they wanted was a tolerant, liberal régime that would welcome pilgrims of every type who brought money into the country. Austerity, religious zeal and reform certainly would keep away many Muslims who had no taste for extreme orthodoxy. But the Jeddawis had no choice. Allah in His wisdom had allowed these fanatical wild men from the desert to conquer His Holy Places. *Allahu a'lam*—God knew best! And closer acquaintance showed the Wahhabis to be less forbidding than had been feared.

I saw a Jedda that had just escaped the rigours of a siege that had meant starvation, disease and death for thousands of its normal inhabitants and of those Beduins who had fled before the invader to the protection of the town. By the time I arrived the population had thinned out considerably. Those who had survived were enfeebled. Fear had not yet left them and they spoke with hushed voices. On evening walks along the lagoon outside the town and in the neighbouring sand dunes one walked through newly-formed graveyards that remained as a record of recent sufferings.

Soon these headstones would topple over in the loose sand, gently and noiselessly the desert wind would lay a mantle over them, dust would cover dust and all trace would be lost.

Face to face with their new rulers the Jeddawis wondered what life had in store for them. These Wahhabis from the desert did not laugh. They were deadly serious. Their law was the divine command, directly taken from Allah's revelation to the Prophet. Strict obedience would be the only rule in the country singled out by God as His Holy Land. So life from now on was to be hard. The five daily prayers were to be strictly performed in the mosque. Smoking tobacco, drinking alcohol, dressing up in fine attire: all that would belong to the past. Music was banned. Men would no longer shave but have beards like the Prophet. Disobedience would be followed by the punishments laid down in the Prophet's own book the *Qur'an*. Thus a new, and hitherto remote, fear lay on the town: the fear of the Wahhabi.

The only ones that laughed and ventured to speak aloud and show good-humoured interest in this new fate of the country were the foreigners, the Christians who were free from Wahhabi interference provided their behaviour in public was seemly. For them it was a relief to be able, at long last, to venture outside the town walls that had been their prison for more than a year and the men competed, sportingly, in growing beards. But the Jeddawis silenced their music and stopped their dances to the beating of drums for fear they might be overheard by passing Wahhabi patrols or by untrustworthy neighbours. At the hours of prayer shops were shut, the streets emptied into the mosques and silence, except for the loud murmur from the crowded mosques, fell on the town. Jedda had at last been gathered into the great Wahhabi fold. The rhythm of its public life slowed down to that of the nomads of the desert and religion governed it again as in the early days of Islam.

Who was the man who had done this, who had been able to force a nation into this total, this political and spiritual surrender? It was Ibn Sa'ud, the undisputed leader of the second Wahhabi movement, and it was my good fortune to become an eyewitness of this second attempted puritanical reform of Islam by the Wahhabis. I was not unfamiliar with the later problems of the world of Islam. Who indeed in the present century could fail to be impressed by the leaven that has clearly been working in Muslim minds? Political freedom was one aim they had but by itself that was not enough. What answer had their faith to give to the pressing problems of the modern age? Could Islam adjust itself to the passage of time? That is the great Moslem problem. The Al Azhar University of Cairo had sought an answer in its Modernist Movement. In India the Ahmadiyya had presented a typically Indian if unorthodox Muslim way of escape. Mustafa Kemal Pasha had roused great expectations, but in his modern Turkey he soon showed that though he had a genius for building a state he had no conception of what religion meant to a nation.

Ibn Saʿud's solution was to point the way back to the original sources of Islam. Could he do more than point? Would he be able to give a lead that would avoid the errors of the past and restore the faith of Islam as a living inspiration for its adherents? It seemed possible. In Arabia, amid these bare rocky hills and deserts, Islam was born. When the Arabs had first accepted the faith they had conquered and led the world. Could not this rebirth at least redeem its own world?

I could not help thinking that Ibn Saʿud stood a fair chance of success. Even more did I think so after I met the man and heard the personal message he gave to me as representative of my Queen then ruler of the second greatest Muslim nation, that of the Dutch East Indies. Ibn Saʿud immediately struck me as an exceptional man in appearance, in his actions, and even more in his word. He had then, at the beginning of 1926, reached the summit of his career, He had rounded off his conquests and, except for ʿAsir which was added later, ruled over the greatest indigenous state built in the Arabian Peninsula since the time of the Prophet.

Would this prove enough for him and be his limit? Or was there a chance that this second Wahhabi surge would not stop here but be an inspiration for the outside world of Islam? That is what I was to see and hope to tell.

2

The Town of the Consuls

I BEGAN this Arabian interlude in my career hoping to gain from it a deeper understanding of Indonesian spiritual life and so return to the Colonial Service better prepared for the nationalist movement that was then dawning in the Dutch East Indies. But I was also attracted to the spiritual and geographical centre of Islam as a proud rival of Christianity in its claim to provide the remedy for the ailments of this world. To be in Jedda meant to me not only meeting the real Arab, but it also meant contact with Muslims from all over the Muslim world. It meant especially contact with Indonesians and peoples I had never seen before and would never see again as a Colonial Civil Servant. Last, but not least, it meant contact with colleagues representing nations quite unfamiliar to me. The Western colonial powers had attached to their staffs Vice-Consuls and Pilgrim Officers from the important Muslim countries of their dominions. I think that my European colleagues—with whom my wife and I had such happy relations—will forgive me if I say that it was in their Pilgrim Officers, rather than in themselves, and in the colleagues of non-European powers that I was particularly interested.

European colleagues, if I may say so without offence, tend to run to a type and I had met the type many times before in the deadly monotony of hotel life, in the boring confinement of passenger liners and in those places where Westerners out in the East inevitably meet. Jedda gave me the opportunity of meeting the others, the men who had a humbler, a secondary sphere of action in a world still ruled by the white men from Europe. In Jedda I met men who resented the nations to which they belonged being rated as second class. They were proud of their nationality, convinced that the future could not fail to do them justice and restore them and their spiritual assets to former glory and influence. The men of India, Afghanistan, Indonesia and Malaya felt attracted to the representatives of Persia, Iraq and Egypt and all of them realized that Islam and the bar between white and coloured were the cause of conflicts and prejudices. The largely Muslim nations belonging to the coloured, and at the same time underdeveloped, part of the world, were represented in Jedda by men differing from those of the West, who often felt that difference a painful thing. In their contacts with the local authorities they felt equal and free. I realized that in the colourful pattern of Jedda I had, as never before, a chance of contacts with that part of humanity I was most interested in, and that I might never have it again.

In those days not only was Jedda going through an historical change which gave promise of great consequences, but many of the visitors that passed through its gates lived in a mood of suspense. There was unrest in the atmosphere of the town, rising with the influx of pilgrims from countries in conflict with their Western overlords, and ebbing away when this excited type of visitor went home again. The tension between East and West, between Muslim and Christian, was to be felt, as it had always been felt, in the immediate proximity of Islam's holy places. It was less than a hundred years before that this latent sentiment had exploded in the murder of Christians in Jedda and the desecration of the graves in the Christian cemetery there. There still persisted the feeling that Jedda belonged to the holy territory which should be forbidden to all non-Muslim believers. As it was, these latter were denied the right to own real estate and their cemetery had been placed near the town's refuse dump. The Prophet had not ordered this. He had proclaimed Mecca a holy city and a place from which only polytheists should be expelled and never admitted again. It was later practice that extended the ban to all non-Muslims, although the educated Muslim of our day knows that the Prophet did not exclude believers in the one God from the Holy Land of Islam.

I remember that about a year after my arrival I had a private conversation with Ibn Sa'ud and asked him his opinion on the question of the exclusion of Christians from Mecca and Medina. The King said to me: "Real Christians were allowed by the Prophet to be in Mecca."

I was very astonished to hear so moderate a statement from the Wahhabi leader. Seizing my chance I said: "So Your Majesty would allow me to go to Mecca?"

"I said real Christians. You don't pretend that you are one?"

"I do try to be one."

"Do you mean that you are doing what is written in your Book?"

"I earnestly try to."

"But you drink whisky, you play at cards, you dance with the wives of your colleagues?"

"No, Your Majesty. I have no taste for those things."

"Then I would have to allow you to come to Mecca."

"That is what I hoped you would do."

"But I am not going to give you my permission. If your colleagues heard that you had gone, they would insist on being given equal rights, and I would never want to have them in Mecca. Besides, my beduin followers are unlearned fanatics. You would get into trouble with them and before I could help you, you might be killed."

No Muslim, and certainly no Muslim leader, had ever before spoken to me like that.

Ibn Sa'ud's strong right arm was stretched protectingly over the foreigners in Jedda. But the town, as such, even in those days was not free from its feeling of superiority over Christians. Foreign consular representatives had been admitted into the town by the lax Turkish authorities and the Western powers had strong reasons for being there. They wanted to be represented where thousands of their subjects went and were known to suffer from dangers and hardships. The ubiquitous Greek merchant and a few Jews succeeded in slipping in under the protection of some of the consulates and Western trading firms and shipping agencies followed. Together these elements formed the small non-Muslim group that lived in the land of Islam. But it was only Jedda that suffered this foreign intrusion. This gave her the name *Bilad al Kanasil*—the Town of the Consuls—and every inhabitant of the Hejaz understood it meant the unclean town in a pure land.

Where people are allowed to live they have to be allowed to die, and so Jedda got its Christian cemetery. Inside it I found several rows of tombs, some covered with an inscribed stone sent from Europe by loving relatives. The tombs had been damaged by roving fanatics or robbers during the century of its existence. There lay the mortal remains of Huber, the French explorer who had been killed by beduins while he and his German companion Euting were making for the coast after having discovered the famous stone of Taima with its three inscriptions that gave the key to ancient Arabic. The writing on his gravestone said that the French Government had ordered his body to be buried there but that his heart had been taken to Paris for burial in the Pantheon. I remember another grave, the last resting-place of a young explorer of the sources of the Nile who had died aboard ship on his way home and had been buried there. A French consul was in this for ever silent company. In a fit of madness he had leapt from the roof of the four-storeyed French consulate. A honorary Netherlands consul also lay there. He too had found life too hard and had voluntarily parted with it.

Gradually the fear of the Wahhabis that had weighed heavily on Jedda during that long year of the siege passed away and budding confidence took its place. Rich citizens who had escaped to the other side of the Red Sea, to Eritrea, came trickling back to their abandoned houses. The town returned to her old trade and settled down to wait for the arrival of pilgrims, praying Allah that fear of the Wahhabi would not keep the devout away.

I began to pay a few local calls. I first went to the ruling classes: they were small in number and in self-confidence. There was the *Raʿis al Baladiya*—Head of the Municipality—to be visited, the Chief of Police, the Commander of the local garrison, the Chief of the Customs and a few more. At their head was the *Qaʿim Maqam*

—the Governor of the town—Hajji 'Abdullah 'Ali Ridha, a merchant of Persian origin. Hajji 'Abdullah was a fine old gentleman with an attractive face framed in a white beard and turban. He had withstood the storms raging round three régimes. The Hashimi one had proved to be the most dangerous for him because old King Husain had made him taste the inside of his *qabu*—prison—of evil reputation. The imprisonment had not been for long and had been shared with a number of leading men in Jedda who, the King thought, had not contributed enough to the spoils he was preparing to take with him when he fled the country. Hajji 'Abdullah enjoyed the confidence of the poor and the envy of the rich who were jealous of the trading advantages he acquired as Governor. All agreed that no man could have done better than he under such widely different masters. Ibn Sa'ud was not slow to appreciate his worth for not one of Ibn Sa'ud's Wahhabis could handle foreigners and traders or had ever met such people before. Hajji 'Abdullah was therefore confirmed in his appointment and his advice had weight with the King, who, having no Department of Foreign Affairs of his own, was able to profit by the good relations established by Hajji 'Abdullah with foreigners and his skill in handling them.

Soon an atmosphere of mutual trust developed between us and his office became a place where I liked to dally. The Governor handled official and private business at the same time and callers never for a moment stopped dropping in to pass the time of day and indulge in short snatches of conversation. Hajji 'Abdullah was very deaf so I could hear everything that was said and in this way I learnt much about the way the town and the neighbouring beduins were ruled. When we were alone he would invite me to sit close to him and then he would explain to me the background of what was happening. He was a rich man and had lived many years in Bombay. He understood the foreigner, and especially the British, well. He had had long experience of Turkish rule. He had withstood King Husain and quickly gained Ibn Sa'ud's confidence, and throughout it all had never lost his sense of humour. His smile prevented one from feeling too depressed when

17

listening to his stories of the everyday happenings of the country.

A friendship grew up between us. When his son and his cousin came home on holiday from school in Bombay Hajji ʿAbdullah asked me to take them out in the desert for a ride on horseback or by launch to the quarantine island. Muhammad and Saʿud were fine boys and I was doubly pleased at being able to render this service to the *Qaʿim Maqam* because of the pleasure I got out of these excursions. Whenever I left Jedda on leave, Hajji ʿAbdullah would see me off on the quay and when I came back he would be found standing at the same place to embrace me as my old father would have done. Then hand in hand we would walk towards the gate where he would offer me the horse that was waiting there for him and I would courteously refuse. Did he ever realize what his fatherly sympathy meant to me and how far he relieved me of that feeling of not belonging to the town?

Behind the local officials stood that all important guild of pilgrim guides, a unique institution of the Hejaz. This organization was established by long tradition and it had its own governing rules. The leaders lived in Mecca, where the pilgrims went to stay during the greater part of the *hajj*. In Jedda the guides had their *wakils*—agents—whose task it was to receive the pilgrims as they arrived by ship, to send them on to Mecca and after the *hajj* to ship them off home again. All these pilgrim guides are called *sheikh* which means an old man, a leader, a man to whom respect is due.

The guild of pilgrim sheikhs has strictly partitioned its hunting-ground. Every sub-guild is allocated a Muslim country with the exclusive right of sending its representatives there to induce believers to perform the *hajj* without delay. They gather as many pilgrims as they can muster and make all arrangements for their journey, often travelling with them on board special pilgrim ships. On arrival in Jedda, the *wakils* used to sit in a long row at the landing stage loudly calling out the name of the sheikh in Mecca they represented. The pilgrim hearing the name of the sheikh he had chosen in his country of origin lined up behind the *wakil* and with others of similar choice was taken to the pilgrim quarters in town.

Pilgrims do not normally understand a word of Arabic and so are entirely dependent upon their sheikh who speaks Arabic and who often cleverly exploits that feeling of being completely lost that many pilgrims seem to bring with them into the holy country. The pilgrimage to the Hejaz was the only foreign voyage the Indonesian used to make and for the sheikhs who were allocated Indonesia the sympathy of the Dutch authorities in Java and of the Consul in Jedda was a *sine qua non* of their calling. And how cunning they were! The job was handed down from father to son through generations and it seemed as if in the course of time they had developed special qualities for their task.

From the beginning of my stay in Jedda I had continuous contact with these *wakils* of the sheikhs in Mecca and their co-operation was important for the success of my efforts on behalf of the Jawi pilgrims. Most of them spoke Malay and many of them had travelled all over the islands of Indonesia. Had they been really interested in religious life in Indonesia contact with them might have been rewarding, but for them, alas, religion was only a means of livelihood and their chief aim was gain. Nearly all of them had fallen victims of their own acquisitiveness and although their talk was devout enough their hearts were of stone. When first I met them they had been through hard times. World War One had been a severe blow to them but it was worse when the Turks departed because the new ruler was far more knowledgeable about, and greedy for, the pickings of the trade. The *wakils* might gladly have welcomed the Wahhabis had these not been such fanatical puritans and many doubtless sighed for the easy-going corruption of the Turkish administration.

There was one further class of Jedda society that must be mentioned: the men of learning. They were a very conservative group, for their studies were exclusively directed towards Islam by the old traditional methods and following the beaten path of the school, the *mazhab*, to which they belonged. The great majority of them were anti-Wahhabi, but they all well realized that they must remain silent, hoping for the speedy end of the power of the extremists. Once before the Wahhabi flood from its source on the Central Plateau had swept over the whole of the Hejaz, but had receded again.

One among them had a different outlook. His dogma was that of the school of Muhammad ʿAbd al Wahhab, and he believed in the purifying influence of the Wahhabi creed on the diseased body of Islam. He, the most learned of the men of learning in Jedda, Sheikh Muhammad Nasif, had not only followed the traditional paths of religious knowledge. He had also gone beyond them into the great domain of learning to which the Arabic language is the key, giving preference to the study of theology. He had come in contact with many scholars of other countries and became the traditional friend of all Dutch Arabists from Snouck Hurgronje onwards. This great compatriot of mine, called ʿAbd al Ghaffar in the Hejaz, had led the way in the eighteen-eighties when, having written his doctor's thesis, he made his momentous trip to Jedda and on to Mecca. Following after Snouck Hurgronje, the Dutch Consuls in Jedda, most of whom had been his pupils, received, as I did, a warm welcome from Muhammad Nasif. He, too, had been one of the Jedda notables imprisoned by King Husain in Mecca. For that reason he was one of the very few Jeddawis who were unperturbed when the town fell to the Wahhabis. His house became Ibn Saʿud's place of residence during the King's first visits to the town and it was thus in his house that I first met the man who was then reshaping the history of Arabia. Here my colleague and I listened to the long and instructive discourse in which the King told us what he wanted us to know of himself, his methods, his aim and the source of his strength.

It was, again, in Sheikh Muhammad Nasif's house that I later met many men of distinction who, if they were Muslims, came to Jedda on their way to the Holy Cities or if not Muslims came to see Ibn Saʿud or his representative outside the forbidden cities. Among these was the writer Ameen Rihani who, up to then, had written the best general book on Ibn Saʿud, his adversary King Husain, on the Imam Yahya Hamid ad-Din, the ruler of the rugged mountains of south-west Arabia, and on other picturesque potentates of the Arabian Peninsula. It was Rihani's book *Muluk ul Arab*—the Kings of the Arabs—that first made me aware of the fact, which Philby was to stress later, that in Arabia a great man had begun to make history. I had already learnt from Snouck Hurgronje that in the field of modern Arabic literature Rihani was an author of quality and it was in Nasif's house that I met again that remarkable American, Charles Crane, whom I had first seen in Snouck Hurgronje's house in Leyden and who, with the faithful help of his able technical adviser, Karl S. Twitchell, became a true friend in need for Ibn Sa'ud.

In Sheikh Muhammad Nasif's house I used to be a frequent visitor during all the years of my stay in Jedda and many were the learned men from different parts of the Muslim world I met there. Welcome exceptions for him and his friends, and for me, were the rare visits of Arabists from Europe such as Massignon from Paris, Strothmann from Hamburg, Wensinck and Pijper from Holland and others, non-Muslims, who found sympathy and a warm welcome in this place where the language and study of Islam brought us together. Soon after Ibn Sa'ud's conquest of the town Sheikh Rashid Ridha, leader of Al Azhar modernists, appeared in Muhammad Nasif's guest-room. Though little was said about the object of his visit to Ibn Sa'ud we all understood that Sheikh Ridha was seeking to establish whether there was any common ground, apart from their both being movements of reform, between Wahhabism and the Modernist movement. As nothing was ever heard about any further development of this cautious approach it became clear that Ibn Sa'ud had given his guest from Cairo a cold shoulder. Doubtless the diversity was too great, between ar-Riyadh and Cairo, between Ibn Sa'ud and Rashid Ridha. I also saw representatives of Muslim nationalist movements who resented my presence in Muhammad Nasif's house where they expected to find only Muslims and took no trouble to disguise their feelings.

Thus in Jedda I lived in two worlds, an Arab Muslim one and the Western Christian. Though this latter was often of the greatest interest the story of this book lies in the former. There were in Jedda some remarkable men who belonged to both worlds and of these the man who impressed me most and who later moved more fully into the Arab Muslim world, although he was never really welcome there, was Philby. Philby arrived in Jedda only a few months earlier than I. He had been there before, at least once, when he rode on camel-back into the town with his Arab companions who had come with him across the breadth of Arabia. He had been able to do that because he was English but he was not at all welcome to King Husain who had no love for visitors coming from his Sa'udi rival. That visit was short and not a success.

For me H. St. J. B. Philby was new. I had only known him as the author of *The Heart of Arabia*, but I was ready to meet him with respect, the man of such outstanding achievement as an explorer of unknown Arabia. I gladly took every opportunity to talk with this provocative person who seemed to go out of his way to oppose everything British and indeed, wherever Arab interests were concerned, openly scorned everything Western. Philby had begun his career in Arabia from the Indian Civil Service, proceeding by way of the British forces in Iraq to Nejd where he had met Ibn Sa'ud, the man he learned to admire and in whom he soon saw the maker of Arabia's and of his, Philby's, own future. After the war Philby served first in Iraq and later in 'Amman, the capital of Transjordan, where he held the post of Resident Adviser to the Amir, who later became King 'Abdullah ibn Husain al Hashimi. Philby cannot have been happy in this official position. His heart was with Ibn Sa'ud and he believed neither in the right nor in the capacity as ruler of the man it was his duty to assist. So Philby resigned his post and, a free man again, went to Jedda where it was clear that its siege by the Wahhabis was coming to an end. Having satisfied himself about the situation in the town he withdrew to wait for the inevitable surrender. As soon as the Wahhabis had entered the town he came back and was welcomed on behalf of Sultan 'Abd al 'Aziz as an old friend.

When I met Philby he had just embarked on a triple career.

OLD JEDDA. THE RUSSIAN LEGATION, 1926

OLD JEDDA

First he set out to serve the Wahhabi cause with all the means at his disposal. This would then pave the way for him to explore the unknown parts of Ibn Sa'ud's expanding domain, and thirdly he was anxious to lay a solid financial foundation for his future.

The activity of Philby that intrigued me most, as indeed all the Western onlookers in Jedda, was his propaganda in written and spoken word in favour of the great Sa'ud. This entailed his criticizing British policy that had long supported the Hashimi side and was still behind the Hashimis in Iraq and Transjordan. The tide of events was with Philby and made him bold. He was blessed with more conviction than is usually shown by official England. His open attacks, the retorts they provoked in the British press and the attitude of the British official representatives in Jedda provided a most interesting spectacle for me, a neutral witness. The men who represented England in Jedda were no match for him. He was a very capable student of Arab affairs, and had seen more of Arabia's two leading contestants than any-one else. No English diplomatist knew more than Philby of that new source of power which had spread from the heart of Arabia until it reached the western shore of the Peninsula. Philby was the only one, too, who also had knowledge based upon long personal experience of the other, the now retiring power. And Philby had freed himself from the shackles of officialdom. In the Jedda of those early days I saw him in full strength, a man free to speak and to write, armed with a wealth of information about the two-sided problem, and apparently determined to outrage English convention in dress, appearance and general social behaviour.

The contrast between Philby and the official British represen-tatives was most marked. They still lived in the glory of the declining light of British predominance in the Arab world. He, a former colleague, had quit the privileged ranks. What was he, that red-bearded Englishman, who was much too familiar with Arabs of all walks of life, who lived and traded among them in Fords and imported perambulators? Philby, although outspoken in his criticism of the British policy in Arabia and of the British in an oriental environment, was very British himself. He probably did not realize it and perhaps his compatriots were too aggrieved by his critical talk to realize it too, but Arabs and we foreigners were agreed that Philby remained fundamentally very English although he tried hard to appear publicly in Jedda as a man who had cut loose from all those conventions and racial weaknesses he so insistently exposed. He doubtless convinced himself but did not entirely succeed in convincing us that he practised what he preached. Philby remained, however, an attractive companion and a very interesting object of study. He was one of the few who were really interested in Arabia, he knew many historical and geographical facts about the country and he had made his choice in the man who would shape Arabia's future. Philby fought against prejudice but was a most prejudiced man himself. He was a born controversialist who loved contradiction and opposition. Not understanding himself, he lacked the gift of understanding others and that may well be the reason why he was always in conflict: with the Arabs of his caravan, with the Government, with its policy, with his own personnel and, I think, most of all with himself.

When I met him he had not left the turning point in his life far behind him. By breaking with his official career he felt himself to be superior to his former colleagues. He had dared to be independent and assumed the role of the lone Westerner. He took to what others might think to be the wilderness but what for him was freedom. He had the good fortune to find a man who was undoubtedly exceptional and when Philby decided for Ibn Sa'ud there is little doubt that he was convinced that with Ibn Sa'ud he could get his chance as an explorer and perhaps even be permitted to help build a Wahhabi Arabia. To secure freedom of speech and the right to follow his own convictions Philby sacrificed his official career. He had only his pension to support himself and his young family, then growing up, but he did not doubt that he would soon be able to better himself financially. In Arabia he had seen traders prosper when they allied sound political judgment with a flair for backing the winning side. Under Ibn Sa'ud's protection why should not even so inexperienced a trader as

Philby succeed? Yet it was as a business man that Philby was weakest and his business activities that did the greatest harm to his reputation. He paid for his trading with the sympathy of his Arab competitors and all serious-minded Arabs judged Philby the trader by Western and not Eastern standards. For me Philby was far from convincing on British shortcomings and Western egoism in the Middle East when I saw him so intent on the success of his own Company, Sharqiya Ltd.

England had been late in recognizing Ibn Sa'ud's importance and in recognizing it seemed reluctant to give it due weight. The first representative the British Foreign Office sent to Jedda held no higher rank than that of a Vice-Consul. He was an Australian who entered the service straight from the army and so had no consular, let alone diplomatic, background. Such a choice can hardly have been anything but a disappointment for Ibn Sa'ud who by then had some experience of British officials of a high calibre, including none other than Sir Percy Cox. In due course a number of other British consular officials took over the post, all mostly young or youngish and it was not until the Russians had set the example that Great Britain decided to raise her local establishment to the rank of a Legation. For Philby who had done his utmost to bring about this change it was a day of achievement when a British cruiser entered Jedda harbour having on board the first British Minister to Ibn Sa'ud. For Jedda society the occasion was a great one and all were invited to a reception held on board. The party assembled under double awnings on the gaily decorated after-deck in the best of spirits. Philby was there and before long he came to the fore with a proposal to the Captain.

"This is a great occasion, Captain, an historical event, should not we have a speech?"

"Oh no, Philby, for God's sake no speeches."

Philby was silenced and the Captain doubtless much relieved. But after a short while Philby's voice was heard again.

"Well, Captain, in any case we ought to hear something about the historical importance of this occasion, let us have some explanation of it."

"No, Philby, we don't want that, we know all about it."

"Captain, if we know all about it, you will allow me to put three questions to all who are present."

Philby was not to be repressed and in complete silence he formulated his first question. I have forgotten what it was exactly. He asked the name of a midshipman on board a British warship who had been the first to establish official contact between his country and Arabia, or something of that nature. There was dead silence among the English guests and the officers of the ship and the foreign guests looked amusedly on.

"If nobody knows, I will tell you," said Philby, producing a nice little historical anecdote. Then he continued: "My second question," and he again formulated a question about the history of England's contacts with Arabia. Again a complete silence. Having given the answer to his last question Philby waited no longer for the Captain's permission. He continued: "It is quite evident that we ought to have some comment on the historical importance of the occasion we are celebrating here." He then took a paper out of his pocket and started to read a poem he had written for the occasion, the swan song of the last British Consul as *chef de poste* in Jedda. His name was Bond. We all liked him, Philby did not. And now he made good, or shall we say bad, use of the occasion by reading some verses he had written expressing lack of regret that we would be freed of this 'bond' of slavery. The Minister who had arrived on the cruiser was Sir Andrew Ryan and the exuberant welcome Philby extended to him sharpened the sting of the farewell to Bond.

Ryan, 'the British lion' as Philby styled him, was fully equal to the occasion. He was a man of wit and an accomplished speaker. He was above all a very deliberate speaker and he knew how to talk at a snail's pace to great effect. The assembled company was all excitement to see how the Minister would handle what was after all a situation as discourteous to himself as it was unpleasant to Bond and to the Captain of the ship. Sir Andrew completely ignored the attack on Bond, he made no response to Philby's enthusiastic reception of himself but in a calm, matter-of-fact manner, at an assured but well-nigh funeral pace he completely damped down all the excitement, lowered the temperature of the party and reduced the proceedings to an appropriate, sober level. Philby amused us and Sir Andrew's handling of the situation commanded our complete admiration. But what a sidelight it gave us on the workings of British character.

It was occasions such as this that led many onlookers to believe that Philby was playing a double game and was in effect a secret British agent. Albert Londres, a celebrated French journalist, who visited Jedda two years later, wrote for the *Petit Parisien* an article in which he referred to Philby as the mystery man of British Near East diplomacy, the man with the double face. And all this talk was precisely what suited Philby.

The second aim that Philby had set himself in Jedda was the pursuit of exploration in Arabia. He applied himself to this great task with characteristic thoroughness and achieved deserved success with the help of the one man who was able to give him the run of the country and to place local resources at his disposal. A mutual interest in Arabia, the known and unknown, formed a bond between Philby and me.

His third aim of securing for himself a share in the fortunes that were to be made in trade in the Jedda of those days appeared to me as something incompatible with his political and scientific aims. I could not help seeing this part of his activity as below the standard of a man with his background. Trade in Jedda had a queer tang to it. To the uninitiated it savoured of gambling but actually it depended much on the goodwill of officials and so sowed the seeds of corruption. The agencies of solidly established Western firms found it difficult to survive in Jedda and Philby's own company of Sharqiya would certainly have suffered shipwreck if, from time to time, an official rope had not been let out to keep it afloat. Was it wise of this passionate student of Arabs and Arab policy, this scholar-explorer, to risk his reputation in financial transactions? Did he never realize that among the Arabs and Muslims of Arabia he could only lose?

It was a new experience for me to live in the Jedda of those days. As a consul and later as Minister I was never of the *carrière* and so did not regard myself as completely identified with the small Western Christian part of the town. I lived with them but apart, on a sort of dividing line, and I watched Philby (who incidentally lived away at the eastern end of the town) and others struggling and sometimes lightheartedly stepping over the line and trying to find a welcome on the other side. I was never tempted to cross that line but Philby, when the decisive moment in his Jedda life drew near, once came to me and proposed that we should take the step together.

"Let us become Muslims," he said, "you too want to see more of the other side. We shall not lose anything and may gain by it."

"You are right, Philby," I replied, "you will lose nothing for you were never a Christian and I do not understand why you did not become a Muslim long ago. For me it is different, if I went over I should lose something that I am unwilling ever to give up.'

So there I stood, on the border of the forbidden land. Wahhabi security and the motor car extended the walls of our Jedda prison; but I never got any further in the direction of Mecca than the *'alamain*—the two signs—the white stone pillars that marked the boundary of the *hima*—the forbidden territory, round Mecca. I should certainly have liked to go further but the wish was not much more than a childish urge within me: it was not necessary for a better understanding of the Arab or the Muslim. Jedda in the first place offered me an ideal opportunity for that, later supplemented by many journeys in the Arabian Peninsula. For the time being I was well satisfied with Jedda, the sea gate to Mecca, the ideal vantage-point for studying the pilgrimage and Ibn Sa'ud's political and religious activity. And that is what chiefly held my attention: Wahhabism and Ibn Sa'ud's great experiment with it.

3

The Desert Plant of Wahhabism

'ABD AL WAHHAB, the man from whom the Wahhabi movement derives, was born in 1700. But before studying his influence
on the Sa'udi family and dynasty, and so the political developments of the Arabian Peninsula, let us see what happened in the
eleven hundred years between the death of the Prophet
Muhammad and the birth of 'Abd al Wahhab.

The heavenly message the Prophet preached was in the Arab
tongue and intended for the Arab nation. Although by the end of
his life he succeeded in extending his belief through persuasion
and militarism over the greater part of the Peninsula and began to
look beyond the borders of Arabia, he kept his creed insolubly
linked with its land of origin by obliging all believers to go to
the Holy Land of Islam once in their lives. This pilgrimage, the
so-called *hajj*, made the holy places in and around Mecca a spiritual
centre for all Muslims. In Mecca was the *Ka'ba, Bait Ullah*—the
House of God—built by Abraham in accordance with divinely
dictated instructions. Ten miles to the south-east lay the plain of
'Arafat where on the great day of the *hajj* all pilgrims had to
gather round its central rocky hill, the *Jabal ar-Rahma*—the
Mountain of Mercy. Yathrib, the pre-Islamic town two hundred
and fifty miles to the north, which had been the first to receive
the Prophet after his *hijra*—severing of relations—with Mecca,
became *Medinat an-Nabi*—the town of the Prophet—afterwards
to be known to the world as Medina, *the* town. The Muslim
calendar dates from the year of the *hijra*.

The other tie by which the Prophet kept his followers in close
relation with Arabia was that of language. The revelations God

29

sent down to His *Rasul*—Messenger—had been formulated in Arabic. Muhammad used to recite repeatedly this steadily growing treasure in the presence of his friends. They stored the holy word in their memories and after his death, during the reign of his third successor, all was written down in Arabic as the *Qurʾan*, the Holy Scripture of Islam. Thus Arabic became the language of Islam and every Muslim must understand it if he would grasp the true spiritual guidance his faith can offer him.

Later, according to ʿAbd al Wahhab, the two Holy Cities had forsaken the true belief and the observance of Allah's commandments. Not only Arabia but the whole of Islam had strayed into heretical by-paths. Strict monotheism, the profession of the simplest conception of God, on which Islam had prided itself as compared with Judaism and Christianity, had been overlaid with saint-worship and the cult of tombs, characterized by the building of so-called *qubbas*—domes. The man of the desert had even reverted to the old heathen practices of worshipping holy rocks, stones and trees.

Once before, in about the twelfth century, Islam had run into a danger. Communion with God was being lost and an exact observance of the law tended to become an end instead of a means. Imam Al Ghazali (1058-1112) had foreseen this danger. In his great work *Ihya ʿUlum id-Din*—The Quickening of the Sciences of Religion—he restored law and formality to their proper place as subsidiaries to belief and to mystical contact between Allah and the human soul. Al Ghazali is one of the great if not the greatest of the reformers of Islam. His voice is still heard even today wherever seekers after God in Islam struggle with the problem of a living faith.

The reform that ʿAbd al Wahhab started was quite different and was directed against worldliness, materialism and reversion to heathen practices. Whereas Al Ghazali had voiced the longing of the heart for contact with a God who is a Forgiver, a Saviour, six centuries later ʿAbd al Wahhab called for a return to the word and example of the Prophet and to a renewal of the discipline laid down for ever in the *Qurʾan*.

The history of Islam had been one of expansion until its third century and then of decline and disintegration. Islam began to fear for its faith, and no one was to be allowed to draw his own conclusions from the Qur'an and the words spoken by the Prophet. Where interpretation was concerned only the 'ulama—learned men—who had lived not later than the first three centuries after the Prophet might be quoted. And so Islam slept. Realization of its torpor began only with the penetration of Western influence through political expansion and Christian missionary effort.

The emergence of 'Abd al Wahhab was contemporary with this awakening. He was born in Nejd into a family of prominent theologians. They belonged to a well-known Arab tribe of poets, the Banu Tamim, and lived in the village of 'Uyaina, in the Wadi Hanifa in southern Nejd.[1] His grandfather was Sheikh al Islam— the religious leader—of Nejd and one of the most learned and prominent men of his time. His father 'Abd al Wahhab, also a learned man, was judge of 'Uyaina and the author of some treatises on religious matters. With patience and devotion he himself taught his son. The boy proved to be very gifted and by his tenth year knew the Qur'an by heart. He married at the age of twelve and thus, according to the law of Islam, became 'aqil baligh—a full man—with the rights and duties of an adult Muslim. He could now perform the hajj and decided to do so. Young Muhammad 'Abd al Wahhab set out for Mecca.

One can imagine how deeply his tender, religious mind must have been shocked by what he saw in the Holy Cities. When he came back he returned to his religious studies and travelled to Basra, Damascus and Baghdad. By conviction as well as by tradition he adhered to the mazhab—school of religious doctrine— of Ahmad ibn Hanbal, to which all the people of Nejd belonged, at least in name. He studied the writings of the great Hanbali scholar Ibn Taimiyya. It is reported that in Basra he started preaching openly against shirk—polytheism—and exhorting to tauhid—the essential oneness of Allah. "Allah alone has the right to be worshipped," he said, "Walis—pious men, nearly saints—

[1] Some Arab historians say it was in Huraimala, to the north of ar-Riyadh.

31

are only entitled to respect, not worship. We can be led by a *Wali*, we can follow his example, but we pray only to Allah."

In 'Uyaina the Governor sided with him. Together they first publicly appeared as iconoclasts, for Muhammad ibn 'Abd al Wahhab knew that to convince Arabs, not words alone but violence would be necessary. Therefore, in accordance with the precepts of early Islam, a holy tree near the village was cut down and a woman caught in adultery stoned in the market-place, and the Governor himself threw the first stone. But then the Amir of Al Hasa to whom the Governor was subordinate ordered him to put to death the zealot who had disturbed the peace of the whole province. The Governor chose the safest way for both of them. He gave warning to Muhammad ibn 'Abd al Wahhab who fled to Dhar'iyya where he sought the protection of the Amir Muhammad ibn Sa'ud. At first the Amir was not favourably disposed towards him but his brothers succeeded in persuading him probably with the help of his wife who, according to the story reported by Armstrong, said to him: "This man is sent to thee by Allah." Thus began a great period of revival and reformation of the religious and political life of Arabia.

Muhammad the Sa'udi made a momentous decision when he proposed to Muhammad the Wahhabi that they should join forces. This happened in 1744. Both Muhammads made their pact for a lifetime. Little could they have thought of its extending beyond those limits. Less still that they were founding an alliance that would compass many generations and be of cardinal historical importance for Arabia up to the twentieth century. Muhammad 'Abd al Wahhab, ash-Sheikh—the spiritual leader of the movement—became, after the Amir, the most important man in Nejd. The daughters of the Sheikh were to be the wives of the Amirs of the *Al*—family—Sa'ud and the sons would marry the daughters of the ruling house.

Was Muhammad ibn Sa'ud convinced of the truth of the Wahhabi doctrine, was he really converted when he decided to put his sword at the disposal of the Sheikh? Perhaps not at first. Political ambition and expedience may have led him to embrace the reformer. 'Abd al Wahhab on the other hand was confident that his word was supported by divine command. He knew moreover that the beduin of Central Arabia must be driven by force into the path of true belief. Once this was achieved their dormant fanaticism would awake, and their most popular sport the *ghazu*—raiding—might then be turned into a Holy War. If that succeeded there would be a renewal of the great days of Islam when the early followers of the Prophet had carried a victorious Islam on the edge of their swords into the wide world.

But those who joined the ranks of the Wahhabi host were not to fight unbelievers but Muslims. They were to purify, not extend, their religion. Were they not then very different from those early zealots who went out to convert *kafirs*—unbelievers? Were not they, the Wahhabis, turning their swords against their fellow Arabs? For these new fanatics from Nejd there was no difference. For them the Muslim who had strayed from the right path was no longer a brother Muslim. They called them *mushrikin*—polytheists—and considered that they did not share the belief in the one true God but required conversion. Muhammad ibn 'Abd Wahhab was the spiritual and Muhammad ibn Sa'ud the military leader of the hosts of Wahhabism. Together they unleashed a surge of puritanism that cleansed the mundane heart of Arabia till it became irresistible.

Muhammad ibn Sa'ud died in 1764. He did not live to see the glory of his house for it was not until 1773 that ar-Riyadh, the true capital of Nejd, was taken by his son 'Abd al 'Aziz Al Sa'ud. In 1801 the war on idolatry was carried far beyond its country of origin. Najaf and Kerbala were captured and cleansed, which in their case meant destroyed. Situated in Iraq, these towns were, and still are, places of pilgrimage of the great Shi'a division of Islam whose adherents are idolators in Wahhabi eyes because they pay a deference that is nearly divine to 'Ali the son-in-law of the Prophet and to his martyred sons Hasan and Husain. A year later, in 1802, the Shi'is had their revenge when 'Abd al 'Aziz was murdered by a Shi'i assassin as he prayed in the mosque of his own town of Dhar'iyya.

33

This incursion of the iconoclasts into Iraq, however, was to have graver consequences. In stepping beyond the bounds of Central Arabia the Wahhabis brought themselves to the notice of the outside world and in particular to the Turkish Government which had Arabia under her nominal sovereignty. The Sublime Porte could not tolerate such outrages and gave orders to her Governors in Syria and Iraq to check the fanatical Nejdi hordes. But as no Governor dared march against them the Wahhabi went on with their work undisturbed.

Now indeed they turned to what should have been their first objective: the towns called holy, those that ought to have been, but were so far from being, examples for the whole world of Islam. First they attacked Mecca which was conquered in 1803. In their merciless way they swept the place clean. Everything that savoured of the glorification of man was dashed to the ground. Even the *qubbas* built over the graves of the *Ansar*—the first Companions of the Prophet—were demolished. Then it was the turn of Medina. The town was conquered by 'Abdallah, a son of 'Abd al 'Aziz and with its fall all the holy places of Islam were in the hands of the Wahhabis. The ceremonies of the *hajj* were put under their control and discipline. The Holy Cities again became holy.

But Wahhabism had inspired horror in the pilgrims who came from the whole of the Islamic world and its crisis now drew near. Soon it would be seen whether this puritanical attempt to drive Islam back to its sources would spread beyond Arabia to Islamic lands over the sea or whether the unrepentant majority would try to force it back to the deserts whence it came. It was the majority who won. Far from being welcomed as guides to the one true pure Islam, the iconoclasts were regarded as wild nomads, backward men and even heretics who cherished ideas for which the wider world of Islam had no use. To this there was one remarkable exception. In Mecca some pilgrims from the fanatic-ally Muslim highlands of central Sumatra, the Menang Kabau, were converted to the Wahhabi creed. They went home inspired with the zeal of puritans. The propaganda they made at home was successful and soon armed bands began to attack the heathen

Batak nation living to the north of their country. They sacked the villages of the Bataks, killed many of them and forced the rest to accept their Wahhabi creed. The Dutch East Indian Government was called upon to restore order and so began one of the fiercest colonial campaigns Dutch troops ever had to face.

But how were they to be got back to their deserts? Although responsible for the Holy Places the Sublime Porte in Istanbul was too weak to repel the Wahhabis by force. The task was therefore given to Egypt, then a vassal state of Turkey. The Khedive Muhammad 'Ali had built up a strong army and in 1812 he sent into Arabia an expeditionary force that reconquered Medina. Jedda and Mecca then fell into his hands. The Wahhabis retired into the desert and the Egyptians were not strong enough to pursue them. 'Abdullah ibn Sa'ud made his submission and admitted the suzerainty of Turkey but feeling safely distant from the seat of Turkish government he soon resumed his activity. Egypt then again came into action. This time it was the son of Muhammad 'Ali, Ibrahim Pasha, who commanded the expeditionary force. He decided to do the job thoroughly. His fiercest enemy was the six hundred miles of desert between the Red Sea coast and Dhar'iyya, the stronghold of the Wahhabis. He first attacked the Wahhabis in the rest of the Hejaz and in 'Asir before he went north and east. Eventually he came down from the Qasim in the north and began the siege of Dhar'iyya.

That was March 1818. A series of fierce engagements that were to last for six relentless months, developed in the Wadi Hanifa around the defensive positions of the Sa'udis. With field-guns the Egyptians, strengthened by thousands of Turkish troops, shattered the mud walls and the fort and houses inside them. When in September of the same year the Sa'udis surrendered, Dhar'iyya was reduced to one great ruin. The Wahhabi leader, 'Abdullah ibn Sa'ud, was made prisoner and sent to Istanbul. There 'Abdullah, fourth Amir of Nejd of the House of Sa'ud, was publicly beheaded in front of Aya Sofia. Many members of the House of Sa'ud lost their lives in this bitter campaign but Ibrahim Pasha's expedition had itself had to pay a high price for the defeat of the first Wahhabi movement. Philby, in his *Sa'udi Arabia*, gives the losses on the Egyptian-Turkish side as 12,000 killed of whom probably 10,000 fell in the fighting for Dhar'iyya. He also gives the losses of the Wahhabi defenders as about 13,000 among whom were three brothers of the ruler, 'Abdullah, and eighteen other members of the Amir's family.

The first Wahhabi movement thus came to an end, at least as far as outward appearances were concerned. But the spirit of the movement could not be extinguished with material weapons and would again emerge from the desert when it found for itself a new leader.

Dhar'iyya was never rebuilt and only a part of their territories with ar-Riyadh, as the new capital, were returned to the Sa'udis. So in ar-Riyadh the Sa'udis lived hoping that one day they would set out to recapture what they had lost. But for long they were engrossed in tribal rivalries and in struggles for power in Central Arabia and up to the advent of a second 'great' Sa'ud everything went wrong for them. They lost many fights against the Ibn Rashid dynasty of Ha'il in the neighbouring territory of the great Shammar tribe. Their house was visited by assassination from without and treason from within. The age-long tragedy of Arabia was their portion now. The history of the houses of both the Rashidis and the Sa'udis is a monotonous tale of jealousy, blood and poison.

What had happened to the faith and vision, to the strong arm and the clear political leadership of the house of Sa'ud? Was it never to have another chance? The outlook was not promising. But Wahhabism was not dead. Its *mutawwas*—missionaries—were still active among the tribes. They taught the boys to read and write so that they might be able to study the *Qur'an*. Second in importance came the study of the Prophet's life and sayings as recorded in the *hadith*—tradition. Wahhabism had been forced back to the deserts whence it started, where it fitted in the daily life, where it strengthened moral standards. There it smouldered on, just alive and waiting for a quickening wind to kindle its smouldering ashes.

4

The Emergence of Ibn Sa'ud

'ABD AL 'AZIZ (or Ibn Sa'ud as he is commonly known) was born in circumstances of little promise. He was the fourth child of 'Abd ar-Rahman—two brothers, Faisal and Fahd, and one sister, Nura, being older than he. The exact date of his birth is not known as his mother could not read or write but it must have been about the 20th of Dhul Hijja 1297 A.H. corresponding to 26th of November A.D. 1880. His father was the youngest son of Faisal, the seventh Wahhabi ruler in ar-Riyadh, who reigned during the Egyptian occupation. Faisal was once expelled from ar-Riyadh by the Egyptian Governor and sent to Egypt. Five years later he was reinstated and returned to rule over Nejd for the next twenty-two years. He was renowned as one of its great and successful Sa'udi Amirs. It is small wonder that Ibn Sa'ud and his sons used to mention with pride that they belonged to the *Al Faisal*—the branch, the family group descending from the great Faisal, who only two centuries ago had held the leadership of Central Arabia.

In the days of 'Abd ar-Rahman the genius of leadership seemed to have deserted the Sa'udi clan. Setbacks had not united Ibn Sa'ud's forebears. On the contrary, bitterness had increased between various members of the family as each sought in his own way to regain power; disappointment and mutual jealousy had led them to treason, poison and bloodshed. Not the least of the Sa'udi troubles was that they were now subject to the House of Rashid whose centre was in Ha'il in the north where the great tribe of the Shammar lived. 'Abd ar-Rahman was heir to the endless intrigues of his elder brothers with their conflicting

37

struggles for power and their vain attempts to free their country from this overlordship. When his eldest brother 'Abdallah ibn Faisal died in ar-Riyadh in November 1889 he was then about forty. The other brother, Muhammad, was still alive but seemed without ambition. So he took over the responsibility of ruling. But 'Abdullah during the twenty-four years of his reign had so mismanaged his inheritance that at the end of his life there was little more left of the Sa'udi state than a semblance of authority over the home district al 'Aridh and Washm and Sudair. 'Abd ar-Rahman determined to do what he could to regain the lost power of his dynasty.

Although Ibn Rashid met this new heir to the Sa'udi inheritance with an outward show of friendliness there was soon a clash when the Rashidi Governor of ar-Riyadh went on a ceremonial visit to 'Abd ar-Rahman. They were attacked. The Governor himself escaped but this act of treachery was the signal for open conflict. Treason is common enough in Arab history and it is not easy to say who was responsible on this occasion. 'Abd ar-Rahman, however, maintained that he acted only to forestall the murderous designs of his official visitor.

Ibn Rashid immediately prepared to march against ar-Riyadh. Meanwhile 'Abd ar-Rahman had not been idle. The fortifications of the town were in good repair and the look-outs were manned when Ibn Rashid appeared. There was no question of taking the town by storm. Days of siege began, the date groves near the town were cut down and so the ruler in ar-Riyadh was induced to negotiate. Included in 'Abd ar-Rahman's deputation that went to Ibn Rashid's camp was his ten-year-old son 'Abd al 'Aziz who thus appeared for the first time on the Arabian political scene. Peace was re-established, Ibn Rashid went home and 'Abd ar-Rahman was allowed to continue occupying the Sa'udi throne in ar-Riyadh. It might have ended worse for him, yet this first effort to regain the former Sa'udi power had failed.

At the end of 1890 or the beginning of 1891 'Abd ar-Rahman again joined the enemies of Ibn Rashid and again they were beaten in the field. He rushed back to ar-Riyadh convinced that

ʿABD AL ʿAZIZ BIN ʿABD AR-RAHMAN AL FAISAL AL SAʿUD

THE AUTHOR ON HIS VISIT TO THE YEMEN, 1930
PILGRIMS IN A JEDDA COFFEE HOUSE

this time the game was definitely lost for him. The men of ar-Riyadh grew tired of his repeated unsuccess and so the inevitable happened. Forsaken by his own men, ʿAbd ar-Rahman had to leave the town and take to the desert hoping to find hospitality there, and if need be to seek it with the Banu Murra in the south, on the border of the great sands of the Rubʿ al Khali—the Empty Quarter.

It was in the month of January 1891, when in the darkness before the dawn the temperature on the Nejd plateau is disagreeably low, that he who seemed to be the last ruler of the Saʿuds abandoned his mud palace. The caravan moved out and iron-studded heavy wooden doors were shut behind him. The people of ar-Riyadh must have thought that they had seen the last of this once-glorious family.

ʿAbd al ʿAziz then was ten years old. Philby says that he rode on one camel with his elder sister, Nura, each in a saddle-bag with bundles of luggage that had hurriedly been slung on top of the animal.

I myself saw ʿAbd ar-Rahman in 1926 when he visited the Hejaz to perform the pilgrimage in a then purified holy land. It was difficult to think of him as the former fugitive from ar-Riyadh. The boy, then ill with rheumatic fever, was now a man of massive proportions, King of a state vaster than Saʿudi power had ever before encompassed. Yet in the presence of his father he was still the dutiful son who bowed to serve him as master and, ceding to ʿAbd ar-Rahman the place of honour, took the lowest place in every assembly at which they were both present. All who saw this were deeply impressed. I could not help thinking of the mother, Sarah bint Sudairi. What share had she had in building the foundation of her son's greatness? She came from the family third in importance in the Saʿudiyya—the Saʿudi state—of our days, from the Sudairis of Wadi Dawasir and it is said that Ibn Saʿud inherited his imposing stature from her. As women are never seen in Arabia the only way to form an opinion of their qualities is to judge by the male members of their family. I had the good fortune to meet several of her cousins who were Governors of Provinces of Sa'udi Arabia and what a fine class of men, what born rulers they were! Philby has noted that some twenty-one of Ibn Sa'ud's sons and grandsons have, through their mothers, Sudairi blood in their veins.

But on that early morning at the end of January 1891, only a small group of loyal followers went with 'Abd ar-Rahman to ward off the attacks of the Shammar, Ibn Rashid's tribe. They sought the hospitality of the 'Ajman tribe in Al Hasa but not for long. The 'Ajman, later, were never of much use to Ibn Sa'ud and here he may have got his first warning of their unreliability. 'Abd ar-Rahman decided not to expose the women and children to further desert hardships. 'Abd al 'Aziz was still suffering from his rheumatic fever and was too weak to follow his father. The isles of Bahrain were nearby and under British protection. There the family would be safe and Western medical help was available and there it was that 'Abd al 'Aziz had his first contacts with Christian foreigners from the West. American medical missionary activity in Bahrain had not then begun. If the Sa'udi boy received treatment from a European physician, it must have been from an Englishman. In Bahrain the women and children of 'Abd ar-Rahman found what they had hoped for and quite possibly this early contact at the tender age of ten lay at the basis of the friendly relations that were to be established in later years between the vast Sa'udi kingdom and the little Bahrain Sheikhdom.

There came a day when 'Abd al 'Aziz, then King Ibn Sa'ud, was in urgent need of treatment for an affection of the throat. His private doctor, a young Syrian, realized that an operation was necessary but not being a surgeon did not dare to undertake the operation. It was then that the King thought of the medical mission that had been established in Bahrain by the Dutch Reformed Church of America and an urgent request for help was sent to the American doctors in Bahrain. Dr. Paul Harrison, who later told me the story, was soon on his way to the mainland. Having seen the King he, too, came to the conclusion that an immediate operation was necessary. "I knew it," the King said, "and you may do it. But first say your prayer in your Christian way as I am told is your custom." Dr. Harrison said his prayer in the palace of the Wahhabi ruler and then performed the operation. From then on regular contact was kept up between the palace and the mission hospital of Bahrain. The King used to ask a doctor to come twice a year to treat the whole family. And a very great family it was. The doctors were asked to bring their wives and their assistants with them. The relationship developed and Dr. Storm and Dr. Dame could, thanks to the King's initiative, make the first survey of health conditions in the outer provinces of the country, giving special attention to the incidence of leprosy.

While 'Abd al 'Aziz as a boy was being cured of his fever in Bahrain his father made one last despairing attempt to retake ar-Riyadh and drive the Rashidis back to Hail, the Shammar stronghold. It was a surprise attack and it failed. 'Abd ar-Rahman then fell back on Hufhuf, the well-fortified oasis town where the Governor of Al Hasa province lived. There the Turks made him an unexpected proposal. They maintained only a nominal supremacy over Central Arabia, playing off one ruler against another, and the ascendancy of the House of Rashid made them uneasy. They therefore decided to approach 'Abd ar-Rahman offering him money and arms on condition that he would again attack ar-Riyadh and, if successful, admit a Turkish garrison and accept the suzerainty of the Sublime Porte. In his proud rejection of this offer the Wahhabi curtly expressed his refusal to link his fortune with those who were Muslims in name only and whom he and most Arabs of those days disliked and often hated more than Nasranis—the followers of the Man from Nazareth—and Yahudis—Jews.

He then went southward to the Banu Murra, a poor primitive tribe of rough beduins who lived in the border regions of the great sand desert, the Rub' al Khali. This was a land of hunger and thirst where the struggle for life was hard indeed, but for him it meant security. No enemy would follow him there. 'Abd al 'Aziz, now recovered in health, was allowed to join him. While the father suffered under the hard conditions of life with the

Banu Murra, a people who spiritually were scarcely emancipated from their former animistic beliefs, the son took to this new way of life and grew to like it. The Banu Murra gave him his education in the struggle for life in the desert without which he could never have succeeded in reconquering Nejd in desert guerrilla. He saw the hardships the desert nomad had to overcome. With them sheep, goats and camels came first, men last.

For ʿAbd al ʿAziz, who was born in a palace, although a mud palace in a primitive town, the desert had, up till then, mostly been a hunting- and play-ground. Now he saw its grimmer side. In the tents of the Banu Murra he tasted the prose and poetry of this way of living. Here he understood the fears that surround the beduin, the need and misery that are his inseparable companions. He began to realize how indispensable and wise the old laws and customs of the desert were: those laws of hospitality handed down from pre-Islamic times, the rights of grazing and the possession and use of wells. With the Banu Murra he learned of the greed of marauding neighbours as poor as themselves and the eternal verity that survival lay in the unity of the tribe and that security demanded absolute loyalty. This nomad desert life could never bring prosperity, never escape the exclusiveness of tribal organization, never lead to an increase of population, never be a basis on which to build a nation but for ʿAbd al ʿAziz the sustained contact with desert life was exhilarating.

Being very big for his age ʿAbd al ʿAziz was soon allowed to ride with the men on their *ghazus*. His father disapproved, but as a guest scarcely liked to offend his hosts. They looked upon the *ghazu* as a virile occupation. For them it provided not only pleasurable excitement but a means of support and the only way in which they could make themselves feared by their enemies. In the desert the accumulation of lifestock was proof of supremacy. Did ʿAbd al ʿAziz also see that the *ghazu* was a two-edged weapon that cut the hand of him who handled it? Did he see that it was the father of the blood feud, itself the root of ever-present fear, a never-ending source of wailing in the camps of the nomads and that it bred hatred and banished human happiness? Did he see all this? If not his father could have shown him. His young and receptive mind certainly found much that was attractive in the vigorous desert life. He must have listened with all the attention of his young soul when, sitting round the camp fire, the sheikhs of the tribe discussed their problems or told stories of their own and of their forefathers' experiences. I myself have sat round camp fires in the open, in desert or wadi or even in the hall of some mud fort. Darkness would close in upon us but there would be a friendliness in the light and warmth of the fire. When, after endless discussion, I had to fight against sleep my Arab companions would still be wide awake and inevitably a singer with a rough voice would start singing a *qasida*—ballad. This would go on for hours while the audience would join in repeating a last word. Here they would be as happy as children, sitting together in a small world of light surrounded by darkness, the light warding off the menace of the limitless, empty desert.

Ibn Saʿud was very young when he sat with the Banu Murra around their camp fires, but he was old enough to realize that the beduin's treasure are his stories and the songs that he stores in his memory and carries with him into the emptiness of his days when, lonely, he sits watching the herd and stares into a hostile universe of heat and light and silence.

With the Banu Murra were laid the foundations of a later mastery of desert metaphor and of the accomplished oratory that so well became an imposing presence, a melodious voice and a ready tongue. Not only Arabs but Westerners too would sit entranced at Ibn Saʿud's brilliant conversation, the ease with which he expressed his ideas and the conviction he was able to carry to the very hearts of his listeners. If stress has been laid on this particular accomplishment of ʿAbd al ʿAziz it is because his mastery over unruly tribes was undoubtedly one of his outstanding qualities. For the ageing ʿAbd ar-Rahman his stay with the Banu Murra brought no such compensations. He doubtless longed to be united with his wife and children, to have the company of people more rigorous in their observance of the ritual worship of Islam. For him it must have been a relief when word came from the tiny state of Kuwait on the north-west tip of the Persian Gulf suggesting that he should settle there with his family and servants as guests of the ruler Muhammad Al Sabbah. The state of Kuwait was then little more than a town of traders, shipbuilders and seamen. It was also a town for pearl-fishing where wretched divers bartered their lives for the loans they took from their employers.

ʿAbd ar-Rahman had no suspicion that Turkish policy, active again, was behind this offer and that not his host but the Turkish treasury was to pay the expenses of his stay. It was not until later that the truth became clear to him when the Turks once more approached him with an offer of help in driving Ibn Rashid from ar-Riyadh. His second refusal of this proposal was embittered by a realization of the source of the subsidy paid him, a subsidy that in truth had been small enough, and most irregularly paid, so that the family which ranked as princely in ar-Riyadh had to live in a house of only three rooms. How they must have longed to be back in the pure desert of Nejd, in the dry, light atmosphere of its high plateau, 3,000 feet above sea level, within the ampler confines of their palace of ar-Riyadh.

In the fifteenth year of his age ʿAbd al ʿAziz's mother found him a beduin bride, but there was no money for even a simple wedding and so the ceremony had to be postponed for several months. His father's dependence on the Sabbahs can scarcely have weighed heavily on him. With other boys of his age he must have roamed the town and gained his first notions of the great world outside.

Meanwhile Mubarak Al Sabbah, a half-brother of the ruler of Kuwait, with whom relations were strained, had recently returned as a 'prodigal son', having squandered his resources in the great cities of India. Generous, warm-hearted and able, he had become a man of the world. A friendship quickly sprang up between him and young ʿAbd al ʿAziz. This unexpected contact introduced him to a world of political intrigue on a far greater scale than that of Arab tribal rivalries. In Kuwait a battle was being fought between Germany, who hoped to build there the terminus of her Baghdad railway, and Russia and Great Britain who were strongly averse to the entry of any new competitor in the Middle East. Turkey on the other hand was only too happy to find in Germany a third nation she could use to play off against the other two. The inexperienced newcomer could be used against British and Russian imperialism without becoming inconvenient for the Turkish suzerainty over Arabia.

When he was seventeen years of age the situation developed with dramatic suddenness for 'Abd al 'Aziz for his admired friend Mubarak leapt into the arena, murdered the ruling Muhammad, took his place and then, playing a clever hand, started to take part in the game of international politics. 'Abd al 'Aziz must have heard and doubtless taken part in much of the political talk in Kuwait and Sheikh Mubarak is said to have given him an explanation of the game he himself wanted to play. Mubarak had a natural antipathy towards Turkey because he was nominally subject to Turkish sovereignty. He knew of the corruptness of their administration, of their extortions and of the weakness of the central power in Istanbul. Turkey's siding with the German *Drang nach Osten*—Drive to the East—led Mubarak to look for support from the British. In this he was no doubt more guided by dislike for the Turks than by any liking for the British. May we not conjecture that 'Abd al 'Aziz, who as an adult in Kuwait saw British representatives for the first time and Mubarak's dealings with them, began to think and hope that the British might serve his purpose too?

The Germany of Kaiser Wilhelm II, impatient to make progress, pressed the Turks to impose their plan on Mubarak as the ruler of a subject state. But the Turks decided to encourage the Rashids to attack the Sheikh of Kuwait because he was harbouring the Sa'uds. The Rashids agreed and started to make preparations. Sheikh Mubarak, however, was not to be caught unawares and he gathered together, for a surprise attack on the Rashidis, the Banu Murra, the 'Ajman and the Mutair, all eager to share in a really great *ghazu*, with its promise of much booty. Any action against the Rashids had the sympathy of the Sa'uds although 'Abd ar-Rahman himself had little confidence in the leadership of a loose-living man like Mubarak. But 'Abd al 'Aziz was all afire. He admired the political astuteness of his older friend and he expected him to be as clever in the field.

Before Ibn Rashid was ready and even before he could bring himself to believe that a small town like Kuwait, with no trained fighting force, could ever think of attacking him, Mubarak's troops were marching on Ha'il in considerable force. He himself commanded the main body. 'Abd ar-Rahman he kept with him. 'Abd al 'Aziz to whom he had entrusted command of an independent group was ordered to march to the south, to conquer the small Rashidi outposts and, as he went, spread revolt in the oases and tribal settlements and so divert Ibn Rashid's attention. If he were successful he might even try to push on towards ar-Riyadh. This perhaps was to be his first real chance. Once before, too restless to sit and wait in Kuwait with some friends, he had attempted a raid on ar-Riyadh. It had proved to be the feckless idea of an inexperienced youth and ended in complete failure, for one cannot fight with inadequate resources. Now that he had the means he would give a better account of himself. Good luck was with him. As he and his men advanced and took the fortified Rashidi posts by surprise, the villages and tribes welcomed him. His army grew, for hope of booty was, as ever for desert folk, the lure.

The main body in the north was less successful. Mubarak had been unwise enough to meet Ibn Rashid and his men in the open desert. How could he with his handful of loosely co-ordinated troops expect to withstand the frontal attack of a well-trained fighting body under the command of a man like Ibn Rashid? When Mubarak's ranks broke the 'Ajmanis fled precipitously and were not above trying to loot the camp of their own side as they went. The encounter ended in a complete defeat for Mubarak and if a heavy rainstorm had not prevented pursuit the fleeing remnants of his troops could not have avoided massacre. As it was they fell back in disorderly haste on the town of Kuwait. But Kuwait was no sure protection. The mud walls had not been kept in repair for years and in any case there was no garrison to man them. They would prove no barrier to a victorious army eager to loot a trading centre. A last attempt, near Jahra, to stem the onrush ended in complete failure so with the panic-stricken townsmen the beaten army awaited the final disaster.

Meanwhile Ibn Rashid, sure of his prey, first turned on the villages and tribes that had sided with the enemy and their disloyalty was cruelly punished. 'Abd al 'Aziz, or to give him from now on the name relating him to his house by which he became known to the outside world, Ibn Sa'ud, warned in time of the disaster in the north, was able by forced marches to avoid the danger of being cut off and wiped out by the crushing superiority of Rashidi troops. One gets the impression that from that day on his friendship with Mubarak cooled. 'Abd ar-Rahman may well have blamed himself for following the lead of a man who had no reason to hope for Allah's blessing. Now it was too late; there was even no possible escape from Kuwait. It was a doomed place. But then the unexpected happened. Great Britain stepped on to the scene and stretched out her protecting hand over the town. If Kuwait had fallen to Ibn Rashid the Turks would have got their way, and behind the Turks stood Germany. So the British sent word to Ibn Rashid warning him not to go any further and a cruiser was despatched to Kuwait as a token that England was in earnest.

This was for the time being the end of the German dream of a railway terminus in the Persian Gulf and Sheikh Mubarak was saved by Great Britain's determination to stop Germany from establishing herself astride strategical routes. The Sa'uds were saved too. This was Ibn Sa'ud's second experience of Great Britain's policy in Arabia and doubtless it made its mark on him. Both Mubarak and he had learned an important lesson and one that in later years Ibn Sa'ud showed he had understood. It was that from now on desert Arabia impinged on world politics. In Kuwait Ibn Sa'ud got a glimpse of the rivalry of Western governments in their efforts to become the masters of the international trade routes which had their most vulnerable crossings around and inside Arabia. Great Britain was the leading power. She had long-standing experience and had explored these countries more than anyone else; and she best understood the Arabs and their historical background. Sheikh Mubarak had learnt what Great Britain at that time could do in Arabian affairs. He had met some of the men who built and kept intact that imposing structure of world empire. He had chosen for England. Ibn Saʿud, his once eager pupil, was soon to surpass his teacher. Here begins that important chapter in his life story where he first meets, then likes, then understands and uses the omnipresent British, yet all the time retaining an independent judgment of what they meant for Arabia and for the world, assessing their, to him, pleasing and unpleasing characteristics. In later years when he strongly disapproved of some aspects of British policy Ibn Saʿud continued to maintain that Britain was the best-informed and her representatives the most sympathetically disposed of all European nations.

In Kuwait Ibn Saʿud was perhaps the only man unshaken by the defeat. He had seen how tired the tribes and oasis-dwellers were of the Rashidi rule and how gladly they had rallied to him. He felt that the time was ripe for him to strike out for himself. When he tried to convince Mubarak of his chances of success, the Sheikh, fresh from his Rashidi defeat, did not believe him. But possibly to get rid of this restless youth he advanced him some camels, some rifles with ammunition, food and two hundred gold pounds. With that Ibn Saʿud was content. ʿAbd ar-Rahman to whom he now entrusted the care of his small family had no confidence in his success, nor had his mother.[1] The story goes that only his favourite sister, Nura, believed in her brother and in his great destiny. It was not difficult for Ibn Saʿud to get together a handful of friends to join in with him. Invaluable to him was the co-operation of his two cousins Ibn Jiluwi and his brother

---

[1] Ibn Saʿud's first wife, a beduin girl, died within six months of the marriage. He then married two women of whom the first bore him his son and heir, Turki, in 1900. Turki died of influenza shortly after the first World War. His mother bore her second son, Saʿud, at the time when the ancestral capital was wrested from Ibn Rashid. This son lived to succeed his father in November 1953.

Muhammad who were to become his staunchest supporters in the struggle that lay ahead.

Near the end of the summer of the year 1901 Ibn Sa'ud set out with about forty men, including his three sub-commanders, heading southward, equipped in the frugal manner of those who ride on *ghazu*. His training with the Banu Murra now stood him in good stead. He was now just over twenty, and head and shoulders taller than the others. He was stronger and leaner, and without doubt their leader. The desert was before them and a future full of unknown possibilities. Making sharp unexpected attacks they spread fear among the 'Ajman. The Rashids were angry but undisturbed. Too many failures of the Sa'uds had left no cause for enemies to fear or friends to have confidence in their leadership. The beduins had no love for the Rashids but they feared them. Thus it was hard for Ibn Sa'ud and his small band to maintain themselves far inside enemy land and enthusiasm waned, for the desert Arab is not a man of great perseverance. He likes quick results and if booty does not come easily to hand his confidence sags and stealthily he slips away.

Faced with such a situation in the oasis of Yabrin on the borders of the Empty Quarter, Ibn Sa'ud harangued his supporters and succeeded in rallying their failing spirits. But not all, for some of them left. He saw that this was now his last chance and decided to stake all on one last venture. Ar-Riyadh, the home-town of the Sa'uds, was his target! He sent out a spy and got news of the situation within the town. This decided his plan. For fifty long days he and his men, whose numbers by then had sunk to about 200, hid in the empty wastes so as to draw a curtain of silence completely around them. It was not easy to keep his men under control for so long in conditions of such hardship, but he did. A great part of the month of *Ramadhan*—Muslim month of fasting—went by and they observed the Muslim practice of fasting with Wahhabi vigour. But on the twentieth of the month, after breaking of the fast, just after sunset, and after the performance of the ritual prayer prescribed for that time of the day, Ibn Sa'ud gave the order to mount the camels. The days of feasting at the end of Ramadhan were passed unostentatiously near the wells of Abu Jifan, on the way to ar-Riyadh. When they reached the approaches of the Central Plateau, the Jebel Tuwaiq, they had to travel quickly to outpace rumour. They reached the fringe of the date groves that belong to the string of oases in Wadi Hanifa. There Ibn Sa'ud left the camels with men to guard them and on foot he hurried forward with forty men specially selected for this most difficult part of the undertaking until they reached the edge of the gardens facing ar-Riyadh. Here they stopped to cut down a tall date palm whose trunk was carried by six men under the command of 'Abdallah Jiluwi for use as a ladder to climb the town wall.

The rest of the men, with his brother Muhammad, were told to wait there. "If," Ibn Sa'ud said to them, "by tomorrow noon no message has come from me, hurry back to the others and flee together to Kuwait. Tell my father I am dead or prisoner of the Rashids. There is no power nor strength but from Allah the Exalted." In thus repeating to them that familiar Muslim confession of faith Ibn Sa'ud was not only giving voice to his anxiety and making a petition to the Almighty, he was also revealing his true self as the man who placed himself entirely in the hands of Allah.

He and his small band then stole towards the wall. It was dead of night, pitch dark and cold. The young moon had set. It was January 1902. They heard the footsteps of the guard passing overhead on top of the wall. Then quickly putting the palm trunk against the wall where they knew it was in bad repair they swarmed upwards, their arms wrapped in their mantles so as to be less easily seen. Over the wall and down to the other side. Ibn Sa'ud stood on the ground of his native town.

The Rashidi Governor, 'Ajlan, usually passed the night within the fortress Mismak for safety's sake. It was his practice at dawn to appear at the gate which was then opened to let him pass through to his house opposite or for a round of inspection of the town. Both house and fortress stood within the wall. Beside the Governor's house lived Juwaisir, a cowherd and former servant of the

50

Sa'uds. They knocked at his door and found a pretext to obtain admission. Once inside the people in the house recognized Ibn Sa'ud. "It is the master!" and all came to pay him their respects. He was sure of their assistance and discretion. From the flat roof of Juwaisir's house they climbed on to that of the Governor's. The wife of 'Ajlan was found sleeping with her sister in a room on the lower floor. Both were overpowered and locked in. They knew that one scream would mean immediate death for them. Hours of waiting remained. From the women Ibn Sa'ud learned that his information about the Governor's leaving the fortress was correct. A guard then was posted at a window on the street to keep an eye on the gate of the fortress through which the Governor would appear. Another was sent to fetch those who had been left behind in the date grove. When they had all crept in and sat on the floor one of them recited a portion of the *Qur'an*. They then ate a little and sipped coffee for they were too excited to sleep. Before dawn broke they all lined up behind their young leader who acted as *imam* to lead them in prayer. Then they were ready for what they knew to be decisive events.

The sound of hoofs in the street broke at last the silence of the night. It was the horses for the Governor and his bodyguard being brought to Mismak castle. Soon they would ride out. Silently all in the little room stared at the gate. The iron-studded wooden doors scraped open and the Governor slowly stepped into the dim morning light. Ibn Sa'ud jumped through the window and leapt across the court. He had entered the area where the fight for his future and for that of his house was to begin. 'Ajlan stood still in amazement at the sight of the tall young figure that rushed at him shouting a war cry. (Eyewitnesses later said it was the name of Nura that pierced the silence.) 'Ajlan quickly recovered his self-control. He flashed out his sword and attacked Ibn Sa'ud, who parried with his rifle. They then sprang at one another's throats and a moment later they were locked in combat on the ground. Ibn Sa'ud's men held off the Governor's bodyguard with rifle-fire but the firing aroused the garrison. Soldiers began to appear above the door of the fortress, and to return the fire of the

Sa'udis. 'Abdullah ibn Jiluwi who had followed Ibn Sa'ud at his heels struck down a soldier who tried to help his commander.

'Ajlan succeeded in tearing himself loose from his adversary and made a dash back to the gate of the fortress. Ibn Sa'ud snatched up his rifle and shot him in his arm. 'Ajlan dropped his sword and Ibn Sa'ud ran after him and stooping seized the Governor's legs but 'Ajlan clung to the doorpost. Then the men who had been standing by rushed in from all sides. The threshold of the gate became the scene of a confused scuffle. 'Ajlan managed to pull himself a little away from Ibn Sa'ud and to give him a tremendous kick in the loins. Ibn Sa'ud was forced to release his hold and the soldiers seized the opportunity to drag 'Ajlan inside the fortress. They tried to shut the gate but Ibn Jiluwi and three of his men threw themselves against it and kept it open. Ibn Sa'ud who had recovered then pressed through the gate into the fortress. 'Ajlan turned to run towards the mosque on the far side of the inner court and Ibn Sa'ud and Ibn Jiluwi rushed after him with drawn swords. Ibn Jiluwi was the quicker of the two and struck him down on the steps of the mosque.

Two of Ibn Sa'ud's men had now been killed, four were seriously wounded and only about thirty were left. The garrison numbered about eighty. But the attackers still had their leaders and what leaders they were! Ibn Sa'ud and his cousin ran towards the staircase on their way to the men's quarters. All knew that it was a question of win or die.

The garrison panicked and was soon overcome. It was surrounded and made prisoner. The streets of ar-Riyadh awoke to the summons that the fortress having surrendered to young Sa'ud all the males of Ibn Rashid should be seized and brought in as prisoners. The Rashidi posts scattered through the town did not put up any resistance worth mentioning. The inhabitants incredulously stumbled forth from their houses when they saw the men of Ibn Sa'ud and joined them in the pursuit of the rest of Ibn Rashid's men. Soon the task was completed and the citizens of the town could rejoice at the return of the Sa'uds. Allah had granted a great victory and a new and better day had begun.

At ar-Riyadh the mantle of his ancestors fell on the shoulders of Ibn Sa'ud. Yet he knew that the victory of ar-Riyadh was only the beginning of his struggle. Ibn Rashid would not give up easily and behind the Rashids stood the Turks. Around ar-Riyadh stretched an Arabia that had left the path of true belief and drifted to error. Perhaps as early as this Ibn Sa'ud began to realize that his task would not be finished until he had brought his people back to the path on which Muhammad Ibn 'Abd al Wahhab had once taught it to walk. And conversion would be by the sword, in the old Sa'udi way.

5

Consolidation

ALTHOUGH Ibn Sa'ud was back in the town of his fathers and again master of the seat of the once powerful Wahhabi state the area of his conquest was, in comparison with the vast expanse of Arabia or even with Nejd itself, an infinitesimal dot. It would be impossible to retain what had been the reward of courage if the surrounding territory were not conquered as well. The first essential was to prevent Ibn Rashid from sealing off the town and to keep a supply line open with the outside world through which food and arms could be readily obtained. If Ibn Sa'ud appreciated the danger of his position this does not appear to have been true of his enemy. 'Abd al 'Aziz ibn Rashid, although seasoned in warfare, looked on Ibn Sa'ud as an impetuous youth who had made the mistake of setting a trap for himself from which he would be unable to escape. Sure that time would work for him Ibn Rashid was in no hurry. But Ibn Sa'ud realized that it would be his ruin to wait for his much stronger opponent behind the walls of a completely isolated desert town, even if it were a well-protected town. He did not neglect the defences. The wall, the castle and forts within and without ar-Riyadh were quickly repaired and provisioned. Ibn Sa'ud saw that he must himself take the field and that he could only beat his adversary in the open where small groups could manœuvre quickly, make surprise attacks and swift withdrawals. That was how he could best defend his capture and gain time to strengthen and spread his power.

He sent messengers to his father in Kuwait. 'Abd ar-Rahman was only too willing to escape the damp heat of the coast and return to the dry highlands of the interior where, too, he would be spiritually more at ease. He left the town as unostentatiously as he could and, by avoiding caravan routes, was fortunate enough to escape contact with the enemy and eventually reached ar-Riyadh. There he deemed it necessary to abdicate his rights and to transfer them officially to his son in the presence of the assembled population. Ibn Sa'ud accepted the succession but never failed to give publicly to his father the respect that was his due.

Years later, when Ibn Sa'ud had conquered the Hejaz, 'Abd ar-Rahman, then old, came to visit Mecca. The population of the Hejaz still abhorred the rough Wahhabis and disliked, although they feared, their Sa'udi rulers. Ibn Sa'ud, now King, went on foot to meet his father who was riding a horse. He bowed low, knelt near the stirrup, grasped his father's leg and placed the foot on his own shoulder. The father first stepped on his kneeling son and then on to the ground. The King rose to his feet, kissed his father respectfully, took him by the hand to the audience hall, led him to the royal seat and then himself went to the back of the hall and stood there as long as the ceremony of welcome lasted. That was no show-piece, no display of political guile but a demonstration of his true mode of life, and it made a lasting impression upon the Hejazi onlookers. The people of ar-Riyadh had seen the same thing earlier when father and son met for the first time after ar-Riyadh had been regained.

When he was satisfied that the town could withstand attack Ibn Sa'ud left ar-Riyadh with a small mobile force and struck south. His strength lay in the speed of his movements. Success was not always with him and after their many past failures confidence in the Sa'udis was not easily to be won. Power was the only thing to convince the Nejdis. They wanted to see decisive victories. But for Ibn Rashid the progress of his enemy, although slow, was disquieting and when he saw that Ibn Sa'ud did not wait in ar-Riyadh to be trapped but began to raise the standard of revolt among the tribes and the oasis-dwellers Ibn Rashid hurried to put an end to it. On approaching ar-Riyadh he learnt that the town was well provisioned and ready to give him a warm welcome. He had no stomach for a long-drawn-out siege, particularly as it was not 'Abd ar-Rahman but his son who was the enemy. So passing the town he sped south in the tracks of Ibn Saʿud. When the latter heard of the pursuit he at once swung round and after a forced night-march mounted an attack when Ibn Rashid expected him to be far away. Thinking that he had fallen on a small advance guard of beduins, Ibn Rashid straightway rode at them. Too late he discovered that he was confronted by a determined, well-disciplined band under capable command. His troops all unprepared for such opposition wavered and broke their ranks. Ibn Rashid's advance turned into a hasty retreat and ended in disastrous panic. His men did not stop until they were well beyond ar-Riyadh. For the first time after a long series of defeats a Saʿud had again beaten the forces of Ibn Rashid. Southern Nejd heard of it and took confidence in Ibn Saʿud.

The Rashids were good fighters if bad rulers and Ibn Rashid realized that he could not leave matters as they stood. Quick action was imperative if the now growing popularity of the Saʿuds was to be nipped in the bud. Back in his capital of Haʿil he reassembled his army and moved out as if on a punitive expedition against Kuwait. Mubarak immediately sent to ar-Riyadh for help. Ibn Saʿud responded as a friend. He did not forget how much he owed to Mubarak and now that the latter was in need of help he could count on Ibn Saʿud. He left ar-Riyadh at the head of a strong force and marched towards Kuwait. When he was far on his way Ibn Rashid suddenly wheeled round and hurried towards ar-Riyadh. Much to his surprise he found the town alert and ready to resist. For his part Ibn Saʿud realizing that he had been fooled did not lose his head and hurry back but started to attack the settlements on the road along which Ibn Rashid had to return. Reports of his looting their villages made Ibn Rashid's men eager to return home, protect their families and safeguard their possessions. And then as always happens with desert armies when hope of booty fades and their own property is in danger, Ibn Rashid's army began to melt away. Ibn Saʿud took one village after the other and part of northern Nejd now went over to his side. Half of Nejd had returned to the Saʿudi fold. Ibn Rashid had been worsted. With only a dwindled remnant of his army he marched back to his own country, the land of the Shammar tribe. There he was still strong and surrounded by people whose traditions were interwoven with those of his house. What he had lost was Nejd, to which its original rulers had now returned. It was to be expected that they would cling to the Sa'uds so long as they were strong enough to give them protection and to lead them to victory, which meant booty, in their military expeditions.

It could not, as yet, be said that for the Rashids the outlook was black for the Sa'uds had not got back more than what was historically their due. But the situation was not stable. It became more and more evident that the old rivalry between the two leading powers of Central Arabia had revived and that the struggle would end only with the elimination of one of them.

The struggle was between two men rather than between the fighting powers of their respective tribesmen. He who proved to be the better leader, who knew how to inspire his men with confidence and instil the greater fighting spirit in them would be victorious. Ibn Sa'ud's task was to outmanœuvre his opponent. The Qasim—a province north of Nejd with the fertile oases of 'Unaiza and Buraidha—was as yet neutral ground and here was to be the scene of an important action. The province had once been attached to Nejd and the population was still favourably inclined towards the Sa'uds. In 1903 Ibn Sa'ud succeeded in conquering both the towns 'Unaiza and Buraidha and having defeated the Rashidi garrisons in the surrounding country took possession of the Qasim.

So far everything had gone reasonably well for a man who was rebuilding a desert state. But now that power had increased his prestige, a new sort of opposition arose to bar his way. His importance began to outstep the confines of the deserts of Arabia and to impinge on the world outside. Turkey was the first great power involved, for the Rashids were nominally under Turkish suzerainty. The heirs to the world-power of Islam, whose rulers still called themselves *Khalifa*—the name given to the Prophet's successors as leaders of Islam, exercised effective rule as far as the borders of the Arabian Peninsula. In the interior the Turks sought to maintain their influence through balance of power. Support was given to the weak so as to prevent the emergence within Arabia of someone really strong who might be able to oppose Turkey openly.

When Ibn Sa'ud's name began to be heard outside Arabia the Turks were on the alert. Would he upset their method of handling Arabia? If his power grew he might in the end become a near, instead of a distant, neighbour. That would not at all suit the corrupt administration that had its seat in Istanbul. He might become the man who would put an end to their overlordship of Arabia. On balance therefore it seemed better to back the Rashids, and so when they asked for help it was given them. The Governor of Baghdad was ordered to send Turkish troops as reinforcement for Ibn Rashid. Thus in the early spring of 1904 a fresh enemy appeared in the field against Ibn Sa'ud: Turkish troops, trained in Western style and equipped with field guns. Though he was able again to beat the beduins of Ibn Rashid on both flanks, the Turkish troops in the centre withstood all his attacks. Ibn Sa'ud himself was wounded by their artillery fire and was only just able to prevent a panic flight of his men. But the enemy too had suffered heavily and had no thought of pursuit.

Notwithstanding his wound Ibn Sa'ud soon had his men back under control. The Turks with their new weapons were in Western uniforms unsuited for desert use. Choosing a favourable moment, Ibn Sa'ud attacked again, riding himself at the head of his men and again calling on the name of his best-loved sister. This time the Turkish centre was unable to remain intact and Ibn Sa'ud's men broke through. The Turks reformed their ranks and retreated in good order but they lost their transport and their store of water, the bags of goats' skins and the flat metal tanks, both carried by a train of camels, and it was a poor remnant of their force that eventually returned to base in Basra.

Ibn Sa'ud had beaten the *Daula*—the Government—and its European army. His men and even his advisers, the spiritual leaders of Nejd, were elated. They had never thought this possible and now imagined that victory over Turkey was not far ahead. Ibn Sa'ud knew better. He knew how overwhelmingly superior to his own was the real strength of Turkey and that even a united Arabia could not beat Turkey. He did not overrate his powers and never lost sight of reality. He knew that it was advisable to make peace and was willing to do so on mild conditions while he was winning, because fresh menaces were approaching from the side of the Rashids.

It was Mubarak, the ruler of Kuwait, who went to the Governor of Basra as Ibn Sa'ud's peace emissary. The Turks agreed to recognize Ibn Sa'ud as lawful ruler of Nejd, including its former province of Qasim, on condition that a nominal Turkish garrison was accepted for 'Unaiza and Buraidha. In this way they hoped to save their face and Ibn Sa'ud averted the despatch of a punitive expedition that might have been fatal for him. But Ibn Sa'ud saw to it that the Qasim became very unhealthy for the Turkish soldiery. They could only move there in large groups and in military formation and this was soon found to be a heavy drain on available resources. So gradually the troops retired from Central Arabia never to return. Then it was that Ibn Sa'ud knew himself to be the real victor.

But there remained Ibn Rashid. Ibn Sa'ud was not disposed to let him rest and at last he got the occasion for which he was seeking. Once, when Ibn Rashid was returning from a successful *ghazu* and had camped near the village of Muhanna, Ibn Sa'ud swept down on him after a forced night-march. The attack took place at break of day, the ideal moment for desert warfare when men awaking from their sleep cannot distinguish friend from foe. 'Abd al 'Aziz ibn Rashid himself was killed. His successor was a man of lesser calibre, for the Rashid dynasty had disintegrated as a result of jealousy, fratricide and treason. Among peoples with little regard for human life and particularly with persons given to revenge and thirsty for power, disintegration is to be expected. The Sa'uds had at times been very disunited. Fortunately for them they had been able to overcome this source of internal weakness in time to deal with the Rashids.

Ibn Saʿud was now left in peace by the Rashids. He had relaid the foundations of the state of his fathers. But that state, although cemented by the Wahhabi faith, had disintegrated once before. Would it do so again? How could this be prevented? These questions must often have been in Ibn Saʿud's mind during the early morning hours when, after his reading of the *Qurʿan*, he would sit and await daylight and the observance, with his then awakened companions, of the morning *salat*. Who can say how this man grew from a simple guerrilla leader into the strategist who beat the Turks; from a beduin chief to the ruler of a nation? We can best learn from his acts. But here a difficulty arises in the matter of religion. It is virtually impossible for a Westerner, and particularly for a Christian Westerner, to enter fully into the significance of Islam. This is a barrier to a complete understanding of the course that Ibn Saʿud pursued. In current jargon it could be called a Muslim Curtain.

What struck me when I met Ibn Saʿud and his Wahhabis in Jedda was the conspicuous spiritual force behind them. Not lust for power but obedience to divine command seemed to be their driving force. Where did this come from? When had it started? Was Ibn Saʿud the master-psychologist who foresaw what could be done with unruly beduins when religious belief was added to their natural inclination to the *ghazu*? Was he a Wahhabi merely because he had proved faith to be the only way to weld into a durable fighting force undisciplined beduin, whom normally only quick success kept united? Was he, in short, a Wahhabi by materialist calculation rather than by religious conviction? I did not believe it. Yet I think both factors were there and both were strong. I had several opportunities to observe them in mutual competition. His strong convictions as a believer impressed me more than his qualifications as a worldly ruler, or as a man who loved power. It is rare to find in such a man a rock foundation of faith as the guiding principle in life. It is rare too that he shows it to the outside world and openly confesses it to be the background of all his political activity. The faith of the Wahhabis of those days was not superficial. It had sunk deep into their hearts. It was always the opening and the concluding theme of their talk with foreigners or non-Wahhabi Muslims.

When had this creed become such a reality in Ibn Sa'ud's life and when had his followers begun to see in him their *Imam*? I came to the conclusion that his father and his Wahhabi teachers had prepared the ground. Contact with Sheikh Mubarak of Kuwait, his tutor in international diplomacy, doubtless taught him an outlook on life different from that of a simple believer. But having left the coast and its materialism and gone back to his own country he returned to the teaching of his youth. In the unruly desert he soon perceived that his strength would lie in his own steadfast adherence to an austere creed and in imposing it on his followers. Such a creed would discipline his own life in the first place and put an iron girdle round the fighting body that followed him.

Later on I was to see for myself what the strict observance of Allah's command in desert entailed. Travelling with a small group of Wahhabi beduins on the high Nejd plateau in winter, I often woke up in morning-dark to a loud call to prayer. It was not easy to rouse all the sleepers, but eventually all were on their feet and sleepily and crossly starting the ritual washing of hands, fore-arms, faces, genitals and feet. The water-bags had been covered up to prevent their freezing. Then shivering from this chilly contact they lined up behind their *imam*, who led them in prayer. From under my own warm sheepskin I could not help looking at the straggling line that stood unhasting, only half dried, in the cruel night-breeze of the desert highlands. When, after what seemed to me a very long time, one after another dropped away to sit round the rekindled camp fire with its promise of coffee to come, the leader would still be in his place kneeling and prostrating himself in a voluntary extension of the ritual. This is how it was with Ibn Sa'ud, when as the leader of a small group he went off into the desert to conquer a town. They grew accustomed to obeying him because five times a day he was their leader in prayer and he who obeyed God had no difficulty in exacting obedience to himself. In the past Wahhabism had proved itself a weapon ideally suited to desert conditions. It might prove so again. It was Ibn Saʿud's vision that led him to use the impetus of Wahhabism to settle his nomad followers on the land and to create in those settlements the material on which his future state was to be built.

No reference to the resurgence of the state of his fathers, even the briefest, would be complete without this indication of the spiritual foundation on which Ibn Saʿud built. In this he followed the example of the great Saʿud, who put his sword and his all at the disposal not of a political movement but of a religious reformer. It seems that only in this way, even in the Arabia of our era, is state-building beyond tribal limits possible. The founder of Islam, Muhammad, set the first example. He preached a political religion, he built a state of believers. Loyalty to the tribe he replaced by *Islam*—submission to Allah and to His messenger. In this way the watertight compartments of tribal divisions in Arabia were broken down. Loyalty to Allah and therefore to His messenger was to supplant that to family and tribe. The Prophet Muhammad set in motion forces that potentially already existed in Arabia. Thanks to him they got their chance first to change Arabia and then the whole of the surrounding world. Islam became a living force. This miracle had been repeated, on a much smaller scale, by two men, one with the nature of a divine messenger, Muhammad ibn ʿAbd al Wahhab, and the other a temporal leader, the great Saʿud.

Ibn Saʿud at least knew the history of his own house and, having no Muhammad ibn ʿAbd al Wahhab at his side, he realized that he must himself find his path and himself seek divine guidance for the task ahead of him.

The core of his followers consisted of men who above all saw in him their Imam—their spiritual as well as temporal leader. His counsellors and men of confidence were descendants or disciples of the original Sheikh of Wahhabism, Muhammad ibn ʿAbd al Wahhab. They saw that they too could become great with this Saʿud. They offered him whole-hearted support but they were fanatic and narrow-minded. Only a born leader like Ibn Saʿud would be able to make use of them without being used by them.

He, as the head of his house, stood above them in the hierarchy, but after the royal house they formed the highest class in the Wahhabi state. They were the *'ulama*—the learned in theology—the advisers but at the same time the censors of the Amir. Religious instruction given to youth was in their hands. From among them came the *mutawwas*—the missionaries of Wahhabism—whose task it was to teach the tribes the true doctrine, laying upon them Allah's laws, and at the same time fortifying the ascendency of Ibn Sa'ud. And this they did with full conviction believing that he would lead the people into their conception of the way of Allah. As advisers they had little to offer Ibn Sa'ud for his contacts outside Nejd. As censors of his acts, especially of his method of governing, they were as obstacles to be overcome with patience, tact, argument or, on decisive points of policy, with firm determination. But as pillars of support for his authority in the interior and as builders of a unity above rivalries, blood feuds and tribal jealousies he could not have had better helpers.

But this support that made of his state a theocracy of which he was the Imam, was not sufficient for him. He wanted more. He knew from repeated experience that the beduin, the nomad, was a restless, and for that reason an unreliable, element. If they were to continue wandering with their herds it would not be possible to wean them from their native sport, that of the warfare of the *ghazu*. And then the land would always be full of unrest, insecurity and poverty. As the preaching of the *mutawwas* seemed to be unable to change this, Ibn Sa'ud decided to try bending the age-old laws of the desert to his will. He wanted the wandering beduins to settle on fertile plots near wells. From being herdsmen they would become agriculturalists, from free lords of the desert, poor and often lazy but proud of their independence, they would become tillers of the soil, a people living in mud huts instead of the *buyut-ash-sha'r*—houses of goats' hair. And so in their new life they would be men of a kind they had formerly always held in contempt.

Ibn Sa'ud succeeded in doing what no desert ruler before him had done. He approached the problem from a religious angle. He founded colonies of *Ikhwan*—Brothers in faith—the faith preached by Muhammad ibn 'Abd al Wahhab, through which they became new men, ready to undertake new tasks. *Mutawwas* were used as instruments to enforce this policy and the fanaticism bred by Wahhabism served not only to make good soldiers but also to change nomads into settled people.

Ibn Sa'ud showed great personal interest in the *Ikhwan* settlements. He appointed supervisors to instruct the nomads, to teach them how to lay out fields and how to dig trenches for irrigation. Mosques were built with money provided by the Amir, for that is what Ibn Sa'ud was now styled. The prayers, that had to be performed five times a day, united all the men in the mosques and so kept them well under the control and spiritual discipline of the *mutawwas*. This new way of life, the task of making the soil fertile, of producing food in time of peace, and fighting for Allah when their Iman, the Amir, called to them, became part of their creed. All the stress was on devotional obedience and it was imposed on them with all the harshness of religious fanaticism. Youth too came under the control of the *mutawwas*. In order to worship Allah in accordance with His will, young people had to master classical Arabic, the language of the *Qur'an*. This in turn opened up new possibilities: if nomads could be turned into tillers of the soil could not tillers then be made literate, and by study acquire deeper understanding of their unquestioned faith?

I remember at Christmas 1944 being a guest in the extensive *dar adh-dhiafa*—house of hospitality—in ar-Riyadh. How very depressed I felt! The royal servant in charge of me seemed to understand, though he possibly attributed my condition to the chill of a draughty, unheated, mud building in winter. He cannot have known that on Christmas Eve a man from far away Holland could hardly feel happy in the capital of the Wahhabis.

"Why don't you go and see the other *effranji*?"

"Another *effranji*? Is there another *effranji* here?"

I sprang to my feet and followed the servant who had shown such human understanding. He took me to a room, far away in another part of that great building, and there he was, the other foreigner, an Englishman who was nearly as happy as I was when we met so unexpectedly. He was better off than I. He had a brazier in his room piled with red glowing charcoal. He was not alone. Sitting with him round the brazier were his beduin guide with his young son. They had been busy making out the account of the long trip they had made together. The boy had learned to read and write from the *mutawwa* who had been sent to his tribe. And how proud he was to show off his prowess. At his father's dictation he noted down the different items of expenditure and then added it up. Having done that and satisfied the *effranji*, the father decided, after consulting his son, that he would send a letter to his wife, probably the boy's mother, who was with the tribe far away. While I was speaking English with the *Nasrani* —the Christian—the two went quietly on with their work. And difficult work it was for them too. The letter was probably the first they had ever composed. Every sentence was much discussed and changed, often on the advice of the boy, who was the only one who had any idea of expressing thoughts in writing. The simple scene was infinitely touching, an unforgettable revelation of a relationship between a beduin father and his son and a recollection to treasure of the good side of Wahhabism in its heyday.

ıbn Sa'ud was careful to mix the tribes in his *Ikhwan* colonies so as to keep the settlements united in the Wahhabi creed and to exclude any disruptive tribal coteries. The *Ikhwan* looked upon themselves as an élite and soon they acquired a fame that surpassed the fame of the individual tribes of which their poets sang. Theirs was a divine mission. They had no problems. Allah's will and His way lay clear before them. The tribal strife was thus counteracted at its roots and raiding between tribes whose members lived and worked together in *Ikhwan* colonies gradually became inconceivable. This was a positive result of the *Ikhwan* colonies and has up to now proved a lasting one. The *Ikhwan* were allowed to distinguish themselves by wearing a twisted strip of white material round the head-cloth instead of the twisted black wool *iqal* worn by other Arabs.

There were many who were misled by the early successes of Ibn Sa'ud's settlements of beduins to conclude that the experiment would be an enduring success. Some, writing at the time of Ibn Sa'ud's victorious advance in Western Arabia, went so far as to declare that by his settling of the nomads Ibn Sa'ud was entitled to rank as the greatest Arab after the Prophet himself. But their conclusions were premature. Artawiyya, the settlement largely of Harb beduins under their Sheikh Sa'ud ibn Mutib, raised great expectations. This first settlement of the *Ikhwan* had been started in about 1912. It rapidly grew to the dimensions of an Arabian town of more than 10,000 souls. The tribe of Mutair, fired by the example of the Harb, was brought into the *Ikhwan* movement. They too took to agricultural settlements under their Sheikh Faisal ad-Dawwish, after he had surrendered to Ibn Sa'ud and made peace with him. Ibn Sa'ud knew of the qualities of this former rival, and by giving him his confidence he bound him to the new order, making him governor of Artawiyya, through which appointment he also commanded the spearhead of the Wahhabi host. The second *Ikhwan* colony in fame and in success was Ghutghut under its leader, Sultan ibn Bijad. It, too, soon became a small town of more than 10,000 souls.

When the *Ikhwan* movement had reached its peak there were about two hundred settlements of the dimensions of villages. They could put 25,000 soldiers in the field although normally not more than 5,000 were called upon to take part in a military action. The great drive towards the Hejaz probably made the greatest call on them and raised them to their highest peak of military glory, but when that action was over Ibn Sa'ud had little use for them in the Holy Land of Islam and gradually sent them back to their settlements. There, a general feeling of frustration grew up among them for they could not understand why the propagation of the true faith had suddenly to be halted. Should a divine command stop at a frontier line?

This, together with a number of political misunderstandings with adjacent territories, led to the rebellion of 1929-30 which was headed by Faisal ad-Dawwish and Sultan ibn Bijad, leaders of the two greatest *Ikhwan* colonies. They and their *Ikhwan* fought with their habitual courage and Ibn Sa'ud had great difficulty in defeating them. When finally the apparently mortally wounded Faisal ad-Dawwish was made prisoner and brought on a litter into the presence of his King (this happened in the spring of 1929) Ibn Sa'ud forgave him. Then, against all expectations, Faisal ad-Dawwish did not die and as soon as he had recovered his strength he was out in the field again. But his son was killed in battle and he himself fled for refuge to Iraq with King Faisal. Ibn Sa'ud then turned against the other leader, Sultan ibn Bijad, who was defeated and thrown into prison at ar-Riyadh, which usually meant a slow death. His town of Ghut-ghut, the second *Ikhwan* colony in repute, was razed to the ground.

After political discussions with the Iraqi and the British authorities and on Ibn Sa'ud's undertaking not to kill Faisal ad-Dawwish the latter was extradited. He was sent to the same prison ar-Riyadh as his colleague of the Ghut-ghut. Both died some years later, Ibn Bijad in prison and Faisal ad-Dawwish in his tent among his tribe, where his wives on their urgent request had been allowed to bring their dying husband.

When the two leaders of the *Ikhwan* had been beaten and a great many of their men killed in the fighting, the *Ikhwan* were disbanded. The other rebel leaders gave up and were forgiven. The two great original settlements, Artawiyya and Ghut-ghut, ceased to exist, the latter having been demolished and the former abandoned by its inhabitants.

This was the tragic end of a heroic movement. After the rebellion, in 1930, the internal pacification of Sa'udi Arabia was completed. Never again had Ibn Sa'ud to take the field against rebellious tribes and their classical sport, the *ghazu*, did not revive. The instrument he had created to fight his wars had proved its excellence but outlived its purpose. When their task was completed the *Ikhwan* were left without an aim and the King was forced to wipe out the force that served him best.

In Jedda I was a distant observer of the struggle between Ibn Sa'ud and his rebellious and once most faithful, striking force.

When first I met *Ikhwan* they were bedecked with the glory of their heroism and the fanaticism of their sectarian belief. When their proud looks met mine I felt their dislike, not to say contempt, of the *Nasrani*. The local population was worse off, they were not only despised for their laxity as Muslims but were, with harsh command and stick, taught a stricter religious behaviour. So long as there were *Ikhwan* the local population would hate Wahhabism and fear its warriors. In those days we all listened to the stories of their heroism and cruelty.

When in Jedda in 1925 the besieged King 'Ali brought in from overseas aeroplanes and armoured cars and former German and White Russian officers to man them, sorties against the *Ikhwan* were tried. The armoured cars were attacked barehanded by these mad fanatics and in the end were stopped by their mangled bodies. Then the crews were dragged out and cut to pieces. The aeroplanes were better off when they bombed the Wahhabi lines and posts. But if they were brought down their end was the same.

The *Ikhwan* movement demonstrated the extreme to which Wahhabism could lead. If religion is used to encourage self-righteousness and feeling of superiority in primitive souls and if it then teaches the duty of holy war, the result is heroism, cruelty, narrowing of the mind and atrophy of what is humane and what is of true value, in a man and in a people. It was a means to an end. In the hands of a great man it could be used to accomplish what was good but when the purpose it served was no longer good, it had to be destroyed. We who have lived in the days of totalitarianism might have recognized its traits in the inhuman faces of many of the *Ikhwan*. I think without sympathy of what they did because I dislike what they were.

6

First Contacts with Great Britain

THE NEXT STAGE in the annals of the Wahhabi state was its increased contact with the outside world. This first of all meant with Turkey. Turkey, nominally the seat of the Khalifate, and really the heir of the temporal power of the great days of Islam, had for centuries been part of Arabia's history, and therefore could scarcely be considered as the outside world. Now a new influence, that of a power which was not Muslim, or even oriental, slowly came to bear on Ibn Sa'ud. Great Britain had long been on the threshold of Arabia but had hitherto refrained from penetrating into the interior. However, world politics intervened. Arabia lay in England's path as it would lie in the path of any great power if a war of global dimensions were fought. Ibn Sa'ud therefore, and the other leading rulers of the Peninsula, must decide for or against England in any struggle over control of the lines of communication which passed through Arabia, and such control would be a decisive element in winning a war. In the first World War the Grand Sherif of Mecca was won over to the British side thanks to the efforts of Sir Henry MacMahon and the Arab Bureau in Cairo using Lawrence in western Arabia. In eastern Arabia contact with Ibn Sa'ud was left to the Government of India, since it was the Government of India that then administered the British protected territories in the Persian Gulf. With Ibn Sa'ud negotiations took longer and their success was incomplete. In the far off south-west of the Arabian Peninsula was one more Arab ruler of importance, the stubborn Imam Yahya of the Yemen. He was not willing to desert his Sovereign Lord, the Sultan of Istanbul, when the Turks were in the straits of a world war. All through the first World War the Yemen remained a dangerous advance post of the enemy, especially for the British in Aden. The Imam's forces descended on and took Lahej and got as far as Sheikh Othman on the very outskirts of Aden. Their presence was a constant menace to Aden but they played no part in the great campaign waged in the north of the Arabian Peninsula.

The turn of the wheel in the history of Central Arabia can conveniently be presented in the persons of two Arab rulers with two British envoys: the Sherif Husain and Ibn Sa'ud and, respectively attached to them, Lawrence and Philby. The Grand Sherif Husain ibn Ali of Mecca had openly revolted against the Turks in the Hejaz and joined the Allied war effort, lured by the promises made to him by the British. Ibn Sa'ud, being when war broke out already an independent ruler, was far more reluctant to take sides. He could not be won over by promises to take a direct part in the war. He pursued his own line of fighting his own private wars and only helped England in so far as it coincided with his own plans.

When in 1914 war first broke out there was no question then of taking sides, for Turkey had not entered the war. But it soon became evident that she was only awaiting her chance to join Germany and when, after some months of hesitation, she took the plunge, England was forced to take into account the Arabian scene and it fell to the Arab rulers to make up their minds. Already in October 1914 Captain Shakespear, the British Agent in Kuwait, had been instructed to approach Ibn Sa'ud with proposals of official British recognition of his independent rule of Nejd and Al Hasa and of protection against possible Turkish attacks, provided he sided with England and her Allies.

General Townsend had landed an army at Fao at the head of the Persian Gulf in the beginning of the winter 1914. He had at first been successful in driving the unprepared Turkish troops before him, taking Basra and making headway towards Baghdad, but then Turkish resistance stiffened. German-trained officers and reinforcements up-to-date appeared in the field. General Townsend was halted and he had to dig himself in near the village of

Kut. His situation was serious, not to say precarious. England made an urgent appeal to Ibn Saʿud but the Nejdi was not to be won over. Ibn Saʿud knew that a man in distress will give any promise in order to get help, and once the danger is past tends to forget his obligations. His own critical position demanded all his attention, for never had his enemies been so strong as they were now with Turko-German support. So he was again on the move against Ibn Rashid when Captain Shakespear put in his appearance. Ibn Saʿud welcomed him in his camp. He asked of England only official recognition and her guarantee of his independence and bound himself not to deal with other powers without first informing the British. The money and the arms he urgently needed for his fight against Ibn Rashid were given him, as it was known that Ibn Rashid had identified himself with the Turkish cause and had undertaken to keep Ibn Saʿud away from the flank of the Turkish army.

On January 24, 1915, Ibn Saʿud went to meet the Rashidi enemy and Captain Shakespear asked his permission to witness this desert battle in beduin style. Beduins on foot were in the centre, and on the flanks mounted men drawn out in long thin lines: that was the accepted formation for battle in the open desert. It was the task of the cavalry of both armies to charge and gallop through each other's lines, then turn back to attack again. The fight lasted for hours and in the end the Nejdi cavalry were driven back while their infantry pressed forward. When the mounted men of the ʿAjman saw their hope of booty vanishing they turned round and started to loot the camp and train of Ibn Saʿud. The flank of the mounted men now wavered and although Ibn Saʿud himself rushed to them he was unable to rally them and they took flight. According to Philby, it was not clear which of the parties was victorious. He says that the Wahhabi infantry on one wing had the better of things while the Shammar cavalry of Ibn Rashid carried the day on the other. Each of the contending forces claimed victory that day. Armstrong however gives the impression that the Wahhabis suffered defeat but that the *Ikhwan*, taking part for the first time in a fight as an organized military body, held their position to the end and that, together with them, Ibn Sa'ud was able to disengage and withdraw from the battle-field. With these faithful warriors he returned to ar-Riyadh. His unorganized beduin troops had melted down to a small remnant. The treacherous 'Ajmanis had again given proof of their faithlessness.

Captain Shakespear had witnessed a genuine beduin battle. But, alas, it was his last, for, while he was with the field guns directing their fire, conspicuous because he was in British uniform, as he always had refused to dress like an Arab, he was killed. How exactly it happened is not known. Armstrong suggests that he was unprepared for this style of fighting—quick attack followed by still quicker flight, and where the tactics were generally far different from those of Western wars. In the desert one has to be sparing in human blood. Speed, surprise, deftness are of more importance than making a gallant stand. When the British officer was beckoned to come and flee quickly he stuck to his place and paid for it with death. The engagement may have ended in defeat for Ibn Sa'ud but his Rashidi adversary had earned his victory so dearly that he could not think of pursuit.

It was December 1915 before the British authorities were ready to resume the talks inaugurated by Captain Shakespear. Sir Percy Cox, Chief Political Officer of the Expeditionary Force in Iraq, then met Ibn Sa'ud at Qatif, a small village on the coast of the Persian Gulf in the province of Al Hasa and there a treaty was signed by both parties. In addition to the already accorded recognition, Ibn Sa'ud was to receive a monthly subsidy of £5,000. By the time this meeting took place England had already given him a thousand rifles and a total sum of £20,000. His immediate attention was now again directed to the con-solidation of his position, since his adversaries were stronger than ever through Turkish support. He first wanted to punish the tribe of 'Ajman for their treachery which had led to his defeat at the hands of the Rashidis. So he now entered on a long campaign that brought him serious setbacks. The 'Ajman, although un-trustworthy to outsiders, were strong and faithful among themselves. Then again he suffered treason, this time from Mubarak, Sheikh of Kuwait, who in response to a request for help had sent his son Salim with a small force of Kuwaitis.

In one of the engagements with the Rashidi, a brother of Ibn Saʻud was killed and he himself was hit by a bullet but escaped with some bruised ribs. Later Ibn Saʻud fell into an ambush and, being wounded in the thigh, was carried out of the fight by his bodyguard. This was the signal for Salim to desert him and go over to the ʻAjman. So with many adversities the fight dragged on but in the end the ʻAjmani were not able to withstand the unremitting pressure of Ibn Saʻud. Gradually he advanced into their territory and did not rest until the fleeing remnant of the ʻAjman tribe had finally left Al Hasa and sought refuge in Kuwait. That was in September 1915. The years 1916 and 1917 saw much fighting and it was not until near the end of 1917 that Ibn Saʻud could feel he had the whole of Central Arabia well under control.

In the meantime what had become of that other ally of the British, the Grand Sherif of Mecca, whom England was to have rewarded for his revolt against the Turks with the kingship of the Holy Land of Islam and with what else? Those mysterious promises about which Sir Percy Cox and other British officials were so silent, what were they? It was a matter of first importance to Ibn Saʻud that he should know them. At his request, Sir Percy once more came to meet him. This was in November 1916 and the meeting took place at ʻOjair, another small village on the coast of the Persian Gulf. To his questions about the promises given to the now King Husain of Mecca, Ibn Saʻud did not get a straight-forward answer. According to Philby, Sir Percy did not mention that the Grand Sherif presumed that his kingship included rule over all the Arabs.

Although Ibn Saʻud did not know the facts, King Husain made it quite clear to him that he felt strong through British support. Ibn Saʻud was also aware of a change in attitude towards him of the British authorities. Philby quotes in several places Ibn Saʻud's disappointment at the lack of England's understanding and appreciation of his efforts to avoid a collision with his new and potentially dangerous rival, the Grand Sherif, who had become a king. Ibn Sa'ud felt that he was no longer important and that Husain and his sons were. Although Ibn Sa'ud did not know the true extent of the promises given to Husain, his statesman's insight warned him of an imminent, if not clearly visible, danger.

The war against the Turks in Mesopotamia had gone better and when on 11th March 1917 British troops occupied Baghdad there was no longer reason for fear in that part of the Arabian war theatre. From then on full attention could be given to what was happening in the Hejaz, where, towards the end of 1916, Lawrence had reappeared from Cairo, bringing with him much money, war material and his own driving force. He soon succeeded in raising fallen spirits and in getting the Sherifian forces on the move. Northward they went, starting from the small Red Sea port of Rabigh on January 3rd, 1917, marching through the coastal desert and the foothills, blowing up the Hejaz Railway and practically cutting off the garrison in Medina from its base in Palestine. The march ended for the time being in 'Aqaba in August 1917.

Ibn Sa'ud had thus lost much of his importance in the eyes of Britain as compared with King Husain and his sons. The Turks, however, were not yet beaten in Arabia. Ibn Rashid stood firmly at their side and if he could give them support by attacking the Hashimite forces on their east flank, this might be a welcome relief for the Turks. So the British continued to press Ibn Sa'ud into action against his Central Arabian enemy. Several officials were sent to coax him into greater warlike activity, and to direct his thoughts towards the Rashids and away from the Hashimis. Sir Percy Cox kept in contact. Ronald Storrs set out from the Arab Bureau in Cairo to see him but failed to complete the journey. However, Colonel Hamilton (later Lord Belhaven), the Political Agent of Kuwait, succeeded in having discussions with him. But whatever the reason, whether the men concerned were unfamiliar to Ibn Sa'ud, or were restricted in the material help they were authorized to give, or hampered by the commitments already made to the Sherif of Mecca, British-Sa'udi contacts in those days were a disappointment for both parties until the man appeared who was to play such a leading part on the Arabian scene for many years to come.

It was the arrival of Philby at Ibn Sa'ud's side that enabled the Nejdi to follow more closely the trends of British policy. Ibn Sa'ud now no longer had to depend upon rare meetings for short political discussions with British representatives. From the end of November 1917 Philby was permanently with him and Philby appears to have been a man for whom he soon felt a liking. Philby, for his part, reciprocated that liking. Philby had a quick mind and learnt the Arabic of the Nejd and soon they could talk together confidently. Thus their friendship ripened, and Philby had discovered his hero. So began a hero-worship which was to last a lifetime.

In the West Arabian theatre of war another Englishman, Lawrence, had two years earlier undergone a parallel psychological change. He had been sent to the Grand Sherif Husain and there in his sympathy for the Arab cause he was much attracted to one of the Sherif's sons, Amir Faisal, in whom he saw a future leader. With Lawrence, as opposed to Philby, it was not a case of hero-worship but being of a romantic disposition and of a literary turn of mind Lawrence may have seen an epic in the Arab movement with himself in a leading rôle.

Two exceptional Englishmen had thus discovered in the Arabs a great personal opportunity and both played an important part in contemporary Arabian history. Lawrence had the more dominating part because he led his Arab friends to kingly thrones. Philby, on the other hand, was adviser to one who was already a ruler. He sacrificed himself, although doubtless without regarding it as a sacrifice, to Ibn Sa'ud and was content (with the compensations that his own fame brought him) to serve faithfully and devotedly and to bask in the reflected glory of Ibn Sa'ud's throne.

As an insurance against possible encroachments from the West, Ibn Sa'ud sent his *mutawwas* among the 'Utaiba, whose land lay between Nejd and the Hejaz. Their word was so well received by the inhabitants of the hamlet Khurma, who had a dispute with

Husain, that the Hashimite governor was driven away and the people placed themselves under the protection of Ibn Sa'ud. King Husain sent a military force under his second son, Amir 'Abdallah, to teach the town a lesson. The inhabitants defended themselves resolutely and, when Ibn Sa'ud's hurriedly despatched troops arrived, the Sherifian army was defeated. Only a small remnant fled to Mecca, where the Amir and his staff received an angry reception from his father. The battle of Turaba near Khurma was added to the list of victories of Ibn Sa'ud and at the festive gatherings of the Wahhabis at which I, later, was often present, the songs recited by the Nejdi poets never failed to mention the resounding name of Turaba. The annihilation of 'Abdallah's army which rounded off a series of minor battles for the possession of the small but strategically important oasis of Khurma, was the first step towards the conquest of the Hejaz six years later. His *Ikhwan* would have liked to follow up their success but England held Ibn Sa'ud back and Philby advised him to steer clear of overt action against Husain, who so clearly enjoyed British support.

Ibn Sa'ud had to be patient and well understood that he must bide his time, but his Wahhabi followers felt no such restraint. They had been reared in the simple fanaticism of the puritan. If he was to remain their Imam he must lead them in the fight against heresy and loose living. And where was Islam openly more offended than in those very places that ought to be the holiest and best? Was it not the Holy Cities themselves that their fore-fathers, in obedience to the will of Allah, had once before purified?

Ibn Sa'ud saw that his most difficult and immediate task was to keep his fighters under control. They did not understand reasoning. They wanted action. So Ibn Sa'ud planned a diversion where no Great Britain would block his way. First let Central Arabia be cleansed. Ha'il was still in the hands of its Rashidi Amir and so a permanent menace just to the north of Nejd. In that direction they must march first.

The attack that was launched failed although some booty was taken from the herdsmen around the town. Ha'il had been warned in time and had shut its gates. Beduins never were tenacious besiegers but the booty gained was some consolation and Ibn Sa'ud had gained time.

The Spanish influenza that spread across the world at the end of the first World War claimed its victims in Nejd. In the palace in ar-Riyadh the Crown Prince Turki died and Ibn Sa'ud's most beloved wife, Jauhara—Jewel. These two deaths, the one shortly after the other, were perhaps the heaviest personal loss Ibn Sa'ud suffered during his life. Nobody knows just how much he suffered. Ameen Rihani, the Lebanese author who as an Arab and a writer could probably see deeper than most into the heart of Ibn Sa'ud, said how impressed he was at the depth of Ibn Sa'ud's sorrow on the loss of the son who had been his pride and hope.

About women Arabs speak very often but never about their wives. Jauhara, and Nura his sister, may have been the two women who were closest to him. We shall never know what Jauhara meant to Ibn Sa'ud but many years after her death he said to a friend of mine who had then recently lost his wife and was deep in sorrow: "Don't mourn too long. No woman is worth too much lamentation. There are many attractive women left." These words reflected the general valuation of women by him and they are typical of male Arab talk about women. It is only the Arab poets who seem to speak of true love.

From the solitude of mourning Ibn Sa'ud returned to a life of action. There was no rest for him so long as Ha'il was unconquered. In a second attack on this fortress of the Rashids he succeeded in bringing up his *Ikhwan*, followed by the main body of his fighting force, with unexpected speed from the desert. The Shammar were beaten in the field and again Ha'il closed its gates, but the town was taken after a short siege. And so, after long, long years a Sa'ud was again ruler of Ha'il. The people of ar-Riyadh preceded by his old father 'Abd ar-Rahman went out to meet the victor. The surviving Rashids were brought as prisoners to ar-Riyadh where Ibn Sa'ud gave them houses and slaves. He took the leader's widow and made her his wife. The children were adopted as his own.

This was the moment for him to change his style and at a solemn gathering in ar-Riyadh, presided over by his father, he assumed the title of Sultan of Nejd and its dependencies. Up to then he had been called Amir or Imam when he led his men in prayer or when religious matters were discussed. The beduin, and especially the *Ikhwan*, spoke of him as *ash-Shuyukh*—the plural of *ash-Sheikh*—and so they gave expression to their high esteem for the man who was a culmination of sheikhly virtues. But when they expressed to Ibn Sa'ud their complaints or wishes they addressed him in their democratic way: *Ya 'Abd al 'Aziz!*— Oh 'Abd al 'Aziz!

During the political struggle the work of the *mutawwas* had gone on. Ibn Sa'ud was now undisturbed Sultan of a great state in the middle of Arabia but in that state he still regarded himself as Imam, leader of a community of believers in the way of Allah. Meanwhile England in those years of the first World War had penetrated into inner Arabia. It had been a penetration of a much subtler kind than that usually brought about by a war, a penetration by persuasion furthered by two men who were guided by sympathy and personal feelings rather than by diplomacy. Their influence was beginning to show results. Philby was growing in importance at the side of Ibn Sa'ud and they were both coming up against the expanding Hashimite edifice with Lawrence as its architect that had by then won British confidence. Lawrence had had the earlier chances and political success and his ideas were well established when Philby with his hero appeared on the scene claiming that the future of Arabia would only be safe if placed in Sa'udi hands.

We left Lawrence and the Sherifian forces at 'Aqaba. Although they did not succeed in forcing the Turks to surrender Medina, these forces repeatedly blew up the new Hejaz railway that connected the town with what was later Transjordan and Palestine and thus immobilized the Turkish forces in the country. These modernised *ghazus* pleased the Hejazi beduins immensely and Lawrence became popular with them. When General Allenby embarked on his Palestine campaign Lawrence and Amir

Faisal gave him valuable support by covering his flank against Turkish attacks and by harassing the retiring Turkish regiments. The indefatigable band of desert fighters moved north as a spearhead of the victorious Allied force. They were first to reach Damascus and there Lawrence saw his efforts crowned with success, and Husain's son Faisal, in whose qualities Lawrence believed, was made King of Syria. His reign was short as the French drove him out but then Faisal was strongly backed for another throne, that of Iraq to which he succeeded in 1921. A younger brother, Amir 'Abdallah, was content with a smaller gift: the Amirate of a specially created state, that of Transjordan.

Although I never met Lawrence in person I felt that I had met him in spirit when studying Arabic and Islam at Leyden university in the nineteen-twenties. Our professor Snouck Hurgronje had been offered one of the rare copies of the limited first edition of *The Seven Pillars of Wisdom*. This edition was not to appear on the market but was to be placed at the disposal of a carefully selected number of men. Snouck Hurgronje declined the offer because intending purchasers were asked to give an undertaking not to sell the book for a certain number of years. "Very clever and very unattractive publicity," Snouck had said. When some time later I read the book myself I was much impressed by it. There, I felt, was the true Arabia. There were its rugged mountains, its plains and there was Jedda as though silenced by the heat of the sun at noon. I could almost feel the atmosphere. There, too, were the beduins and their hard, materially-minded sheikhs, and, with Lawrence, I seemed to be sharing their life. I felt that I had met a great artist and in spirit I greeted him respectfully, grateful for his gift which I would carefully preserve in my memory. That was one recollection I would never forget.

There was another. It was in Snouck Hurgronje's study, Snouck being then a man in the seventies. He was no longer the eager young man who half a century before had rushed off to Mecca to confirm the conclusions he had arrived at and formulated in his book *The Meccan Feast*. His steel-blue eyes were still as clear as they must then have been but perhaps more penetrating.

They looked straight through one but behind one felt the light of a smile waiting to break through. In his presence I could not help feeling very small and I saw his other former students equally subdued. If Lawrence himself had entered there he would scarcely have been at ease under Snouck's searching scrutiny. It was not Lawrence however who appeared but his publicity agent, the American Lowell Thomas. Lowell Thomas was not awed by the presence of the great Arabist and student of Islam. He seemed to think that Snouck Hurgronje ought to be impressed by him, and so a humorous situation developed which Snouck Hurgronje enjoyed immensely. Lowell Thomas was shocked that the Leyden Arabist had not heard of him or of his book on Lawrence so he at once started to remedy this gap in Snouck's knowledge. He told him how he had made Lawrence famous. He had lectured about him in London and all over Great Britain and then put his story in print saying in the introduction that two million English listeners had been convinced by him, Lowell Thomas, how great a man was living unknown in their midst. Lowell Thomas' book preceded *The Seven Pillars of Wisdom*, and a poor forerunner it was. Lawrence was reduced to the level of a stepping-stone in the career of a publicist.

Lowell Thomas stopped at Leyden on a flying tour round the world paid for by the Ford Motor Company as an advertising stunt and it was Lowell Thomas' visit that occasioned Snouck Hurgronje's reflections on Lawrence and his significance for Arabia. "What," asked Snouck, "had Lawrence done in Arabia? He had not gone there as an explorer although he was a student of archaeology. Lawrence went to Arabia on a political mission. He had to report whether Arabia could be of any use to his country which was then involved in a life-and-death struggle with powerful enemies. There was no war in Arabia. He brought it there using for his purpose a clever tongue, promise of worldly power for the great, and the glittering display of wealth before the greedy eyes of his humbler listeners. He did it by blowing on cinders of passion and proposing *ghazus* for loot and bloodshed. He supplied the Arabs with modern weapons for warfare. He did not plainly tell them that his object in getting them to follow him was that his country might be victorious and go on ruling the world. He told them that he would show them the way to independence, freedom and honour for their people." Snouck continued bitterly: "And what has been the result of all this? The promises given were not kept, could not be kept, by his Government. The man in Mecca who trusted Lawrence and his chiefs in Cairo and who insisted that the British should fulfil the promises they had made, was abandoned and ended his life as Britain's deluded guest in the isle of Cyprus. And what happened to the Arab nations? Great Britain imposed on them rulers for whom they had not asked and whom they did not like. Lawrence was a man who used the Arab people for Great Britain's sake, who had helped to build a political structure which, being based on sand, would be swept away by those who lived in it the moment England was not there to keep it upright. Lawrence's fame was undeserved. What he had done in Arabia was of no real benefit to the country or to its people."

I could not dispute what I felt to be the truth; all I could do was to point to Lawrence's merits as a writer. For the rest I gave the same reply as I later gave to Arab notables: Lawrence believed in what he promised; it was not his fault if his Government let him down. But his critic in Holland and those in Arabia all made the same retort. Snouck said that Lawrence had voluntarily assumed the political responsibilities he took on in Arabia. He should have understood what the promises and methods he used were worth. The Arabs said: he was an English politician and they are clever men and know what they are doing. Snouck Hurgronje committed his views to a series of articles in a leading Dutch newspaper, *De Telegraaf*.

Soon after I arrived in Jedda I invited some of the leading officials of the town to dinner. The meal over, we sat together sipping coffee but it was not easy to keep the conversation alive. It flashed through my mind that I might show them the illustrations in Lawrence's book which I had just received. So I fetched the book and handed it to the old Governor of the town. He knew all the men portrayed and showed the illustrations to the others present. One after the other the pictures were studied and discussed and I began to congratulate myself on a happy inspiration. My guests almost forgot my presence. When they reached the last illustration they all went back to their seats as if unwilling to take their thoughts away from the days thus recalled to them. Carefully, holding it in both hands, the Governor returned the book to me. I had no idea of what they were thinking but expected to find among them some sympathy for the man who had preached the unity of all Arabs in an independent kingdom. So I ventured the question: What do you think of him? In silence all looked at the Governor who spoke and said: "A Muslim could not have done it, I mean written such a book."

"Why not?"

"Because with us a man who has done something that is wrong, will deny it. That is his token of respect for what is good. This man Lawrence not only admits the wrong he did but he even puts it in a book with all these beautiful pictures."

"What wrong do you mean he did?"

"With English gold he bought Arab blood. He told a story that was a lie."

The others nodded. I replied: "Lawrence believed he spoke the truth. His Government let him down and then he was so ashamed that he went away never to return to this country."

Then the answer came: "You underrate the *Ingliz*. He knew and he understood."

I think I understand Lawrence better than they, the Arabs, did. They could not appreciate the artist in him. Lawrence was naïve. He was a very gifted but not a fully mature man. For him Arabia was a road to adventure. Arabia, the beduin, guerrilla warfare in the desert on camel-back was a sport for him, a trial of endurance. He had the inspiration of an artist and the courage of a true leader but behind him there was not the sober conviction of a ripe mind. When the vision faded as it must, it no longer interested him. He shook the dust of Arabia from off his feet for ever. That is to say he intended, he tried, to do so but that Arabian dust clung to him, it clung to his soul. He tried to get rid of it, by forgetting and being forgotten. He gave up his name, renounced his celebrity and disappeared into the anonymity of the ranks of the Royal Air Force as Aircraftsman Shaw. He returned his decorations. He sought the noise of motors and the intoxication of speed and ended by killing himself in a crash on his motor-cycle. Aircraftsman Shaw tried to do penance for what Lawrence in his pursuit of fame and, doubtless, at the prompting of patriotism had done in Arabia and thereafter. He played with Arabia, he had seen it as an episode to be forgotten when it was over. But he could not forget: he became a victim of his own delusion.

And what of the other man who carried British influence deep into the history of Arabia, Philby? He is certainly not an artist and never tried to pose as one although he too has dreamed dreams. I do not know where or when Philby made his pact for life with Arabia. Possibly there was no precise moment of decision but a gradual realization of the boundless and glamorous perspectives that Arabia presented. Once, however, he made up his mind he stuck to the land, or to the man, of his choice. Both seemed to offer him exceptional opportunities. Arabia would satisfy his desire for fame and Ibn Sa'ud was the man who could open for him the roads to it.

It was not, I feel, an urge to serve his country that spurred him on in Arabia, nor was it in the first place his sympathy with the Arab nation. It was his longing to be different from other men, to live a life according to his own tastes and ideas and to make a name for himself. Arabia offered all these possibilities. Once in the heart of the country he met a man who was great because he dared to be himself, to stand alone and to struggle towards his goal believing in his vocation and in divine guidance. Philby was different, he did not go to Arabia because of a vocation and as he did not believe in God how could he believe in His guidance? He put his trust in his own brains and in his own strength of purpose and thought that with them he would make his life a success. Fame was his spur. Having known him for many

years and having had the opportunity of observing him at close
quarters as well as from a distance, having spoken with him and
having heard Arabs and Englishmen speak of him, I could see that
he was burning with ambition and was ready to sacrifice everything to link his name insolubly with that of Arabia. Philby is a
man full of contradictions which make it difficult to understand
him and to be fair in judging him. He had no real friends in the
surroundings in which I met him. He had many enemies, including some among his own countrymen, and there were many both
Arabs and Europeans who did not understand him and therefore
distrusted and disliked him. There were very few who saw that
beneath the surface he was a man not at peace with himself and
with a heart torn by ambition. Those who did, felt sympathy,
not to say compassion, for him. Many have called him a man of
mystery. They did not know him or the land in which he
gathered his laurels. That land, its people and its creed were full
of mystery. Philby tried to belong to them, to be accepted by
them, to assume a garment of mystery and romanticism. The
romantic strain in Philby comes out in his attachment to Arabia,
in his devotion to the heroic figure of Ibn Sa'ud and, a curious
minor manifestation, in the titles of his books. Philby failed to
be accepted because he was too European, too English and Arabia
in the end became restive with him. I think that none the less
Philby will be grateful to the Arabs for their great patience with
him and the generous opportunities they gave him of becoming
famous. It was thanks to them, and especially to the great Arab
who gave him protection, guidance and material help, that at the
summit of his great career as an explorer of unknown Arabia
Philby was able to compose his sadly revealing song of
triumph, dedicated 'to all my predecessors in Arabian exploration':

> *I was the first*
> *that ever burst*
> *upon these teeming lands, etc.*

Philby is the greatest explorer Arabia has yet seen. Exploration was his real work, perhaps his original goal, and the work that will probably fill his life to his dying day. The human heart of Arabia and the profundities of her creed do not seem to have been disclosed to him. His hero was outspoken about that which mattered most for him, his faith. Even Philby must have seen that there was a reality, a source of strength and a means of guidance. But his books about Arabia do not reach beyond what is visible, what is measurable with instruments. He did not speak about that hidden treasure of Arabia, its spiritual wealth. Philby lived in ar-Riyadh among men who claimed that again they had a spiritual message for the world beyond Arabia's deserts. But when Philby said to me in Jedda: "We are not Christians, why should not we become Muslims?" it was clear that he could not become a true Muslim. When eventually he embraced Islam his fellow countrymen and the Christian foreigners did not believe in the sincerity of his conversion for they found the old Philby an unchanged man. The Arabs did not believe in it either. They might have found it easier to accept him had he not become associated with trade and if in conversation and behaviour he had given proof of understanding things of the spirit. So although Philby chose Arabia, Arabia did not choose him.

7

The Dual Monarchy

AFTER the fall of Ha'il and the subjection of the Shammar tribe came the turn of the Ruwalla whose tribal area stretches far northward into the Syrian desert. The *mutawwas* had, as usual, preceded the *Ikhwan* and the doctrine they preached did not pass unheeded by their beduin listeners but it was perhaps the sword that convinced most. Ibn Sa'ud now found it a little difficult to control its use. His followers saw in it a logical, indispensable means of spreading the true faith, and the means they liked best. Why should they not go further on their own? A group of *Ikhwan* attempted a private expedition into Transjordan. They pushed on until they were within some miles of 'Amman, the capital. But they had not reckoned with the British who had a mandate for Transjordan and who came to the aid of the Amir 'Abdallah. With their machines in the air and their motorized transport on the ground they had an easy task. Whoever has seen the empty, undulating landscape of northern Arabia, where the last tree was cut down for fuel ages ago, will easily imagine what befell those rash *Ikhwan*. Spotted from the air and machine-gunned from the ground, they found no cover and they fled with little hope of escape. It is said by Armstrong that only eight out of more than the thousand men who are reputed to have taken part in this private expedition came back alive to Shaqra, whence they had started. These eight were severely punished by Ibn Sa'ud who had long realized that British power in Arabia had to be reckoned with but who, above all, was determined to exact obedience from his own people. He invited Sir Percy Cox to meet him once more in 'Ojair, the village on the coast of the Persian Gulf where they

had met for the first time in 1915. It was now autumn 1922. Much
had happened during the years between these meetings. Ibn
Sa'ud had more than fulfilled Philby's expectations and the British
were having increasing difficulty in handling King Husain.

When now, nearly thirty years after the Husain tragedy, I
think again of the generally anti-Husain attitude of the British and
other foreigners and of the local population in Jedda at the beginning of 1926, when his son 'Ali had given up fighting for his
father's unquestionable rights, I cannot help feeling sympthy for
the old man who, reared in the corruption of pre-war Turkey,
had put his trust in the British. Antonius, in *The Arab Awakening*,
blames the British representative in Jedda for creating in official
circles a climate inimical to Husain. Snouck Hurgronje depicted
his tragedy rightly when in his newspaper articles he spoke of a
disgruntled old man who passed his days as a prisoner in Cyprus,
in front of a box containing British promises.

After Husain's successful revolt against the Turks in 1916 Ibn
Sa'ud had sent him prudent words of congratulation. Husain in
his dealings with Ibn Sa'ud had from the start treated him as one
of the Arab chiefs who would become his subordinate when, after
the victory of the Allies, their promises to him would be fulfilled
and he be made ruler of a great independent Arabian kingdom.
It was quite clear to Ibn Sa'ud that Husain would not dare to
address him in the way he did if he were not convinced of Great
Britain's backing. Ibn Sa'ud wanted to be sure of England's
attitude. He liked Sir Percy and expected him to understand the
difficulty he had in keeping his turbulent *Ikhwan* away from
Iraqi territory. Sir Percy, too, could reassure him about the
danger he feared from the Hashimis.

Ameen Rihani, the Lebanese whom I had met in spirit at
Leyden university when reading his book on the Kings of
Arabia and later in the flesh in the Dutch Legation in Jedda, was a
guest in Ibn Sa'ud's camp in the desert near 'Ojair. In the English
version of his story, *Ibn Sa'ud, His People and His Land*, he gives
a full-flavoured account of what happened. He brings us very near
to Ibn Sa'ud, the fighter who, without the support of Arab

advisers on whom he could fall back, struggled on alone. He was the only one who knew the difficulties within his own territory and who saw the reality of the growing menace from outside. He knew that England still held the balance between the two rivals and that her views were the determining factor. Patiently and with tenacity he tried to win over the Englishman to his side.

For Ibn Saʿud it was his vocation to rule and guide Central Arabia along lines of divine ordinance and every morning he sought to strengthen his soul for the task of the day. At the root of his difficulties was his ever present lack of money and arms. Central Arabia was too poor to produce the means for a government above tribal level and for the time being he could not do without British financial help. If that stopped the age-old law of Inner Arabia would reassert itself, it would be impossible to restrain beduin passions and great *ghazus* would push north to *al Hilal al Akhdar*—the Fertile Crescent. Ibn Saʿud had by then already given proof that he did not wish to submit to the old laws of the desert but to change them and direct beduin energies into new channels. The settlement of his nomadic tribes was one of those channels, but success was precluded for him if the surrounding states did not co-operate. So the question of border conflicts between the Nejdi tribes and those of Iraq had to be discussed. Frontiers as geographical lines were unknown in Arabia. Tribes that live on their herds must be able to seek grazing wherever the rains fall. Besides, there had formerly been no frontiers within the Middle East for it had all been Turkish and spheres of local influence, as in the case of the Rashidi family, varied from one generation to another.

Those taking part in the discussions at ʿOjair were unable to reach a partition satisfactory to both sides and so a compromise was decided on. Neutral border zones were established within which both the Nejdi and the Iraqi tribes had equal grazing rights and free access to the wells. No fortifications were allowed. But the enforcing of this agreement by the Hashimis seemed to Ibn Saʿud to depend on the will of the British and Ibn Saʿud had already seen King Husain attacking the border town of Khurma and Turaba.

A more satisfactory result of the 'Ojair conference was the temporary relief of Ibn Sa'ud's financial difficulties. Reports were already circulating on the possibility of finding oil in Arabia and although Ibn Sa'ud did not credit them and was not yet prepared to look favourably on the prospect of foreigners exploiting oil in his country, his urgent need for money overruled whatever hesitation he may have felt. Ameen Rihani was amused at the haggling that resulted in the grant of a concession to the representative of the British Eastern General Syndicate against a yearly payment of £2,000. Reviewed in the light of the immense royalties that were later to accrue from oil to the Wahhabi state this sum was poor enough but what is more interesting is that after two years of fruitless prospecting by Belgian geologists in the Al Hasa region the Company stopped payment and the concession lapsed.

Shortly after the 'Ojair conference, Ibn Sa'ud contracted a severe type of erysipelas, that spread over his face and ended in an infection of his left eye. Wrong treatment locally and an operation made too late by a specialist called in from Egypt resulted in the loss of the sight of his left eye and some consequent marring of his impressive appearance. For months on end he was unable to do his normal amount of work, but during that time, thanks to King Husain, the situation changed in his favour. Husain's unpopularity with his own people had much increased. He misruled his land, treated its people harshly and tried to squeeze out of them all the money he could. Those who suffered most were the pilgrims to the Holy Places. These he fleeced mercilessly. Their complaints to their Consuls in Jedda resulted in Husain's forfeiting some of the sympathy he might have enjoyed from the foreign governments who had Muslim subjects and were interested in the *hajj*.

In the days of Turkish rule the pilgrims had been robbed by a corrupt administration and by the guild of pilgrim sheikhs, but their caravans were protected from beduin attacks by Turkish troops stationed in forts built on mountain tops near the pilgrim roads and by towers of defence along the roads. Order was maintained in the places where pilgrims foregathered. Under King Husain's rule pilgrims were raided by the 'dogs of the Hejaz'—the beduins—who had always regarded them as their legitimate spoil, and soon found out that King Husain's policing was ineffective. Insecurity increased and on the plains of 'Arafa, Muzdalifa and Muna panic was created among hundreds of thousands of pilgrims by the beduins cutting off the famous Zubaida water conduit. Not only was Husain unable to keep the beduins under control but also his officials were reported as conniving in giving the beduins a free hand in return for money. The King was warned by the complaints of his own people and by representatives of foreign governments in his country but he would not listen. So far as the pilgrims were concerned Husain's only interest seemed to be in the money that he could get out of them and I remember finding in Jedda, as a legacy from my predecessor, lists of pilgrims from the Dutch East Indies who had been killed by beduins and for whom my government demanded financial indemnity.

Such was the deplorable state of the Holy Land of Islam towards the end of King Husain's eight years' reign. Then suddenly fortune seemed to smile on him. Kemal Pasha Attaturk, who was shaping the new Turkey, had determined, in his state, to separate the temporal from the spiritual power. This is a sound idea according to Western democratic political thought and Kemal Pasha was a Muslim in name only. He set out to modernize Turkey on secular lines. He had no place for a *Khalifa* in a political structure in which religion and state were to be kept apart and one doubts whether he really understood what the *Khalifa* of Islam was. Many Muslims had lost sight of its true significance and most Westerners had never understood it. The Turkish Sultan 'Abd al Hamid had made such use of this lack of understanding in the West of his dignity as *Khalifa* that the false idea of its being a clerical dignity comparable to that of the Pope in Roman Catholicism was widespread. In reality, however, the *Khalifa*—the man who comes after or follows—was the successor of the Prophet in *all* his functions except that of being prophet. Like Muhammad the early *Khalifas* were at the same time spiritual and temporal leaders of the community of believers. Thus the true significance of the *Khalifate* was that all Muslims should be united in one spiritual and political unit ruled by the *Khalifa* from which it followed that the *Khalifa* had actually no spiritual authority beyond the limits of his worldly domain.

Turkey had been the heir of the Muslim world-state, that vast empire conquered by the hosts of Islam after the death of the Prophet. Within the space of a century the realm of Islam had stretched from Spain in the West to the shores of India in the East and from the Mediterranean to the Indian Ocean. After three centuries, disintegration of the political structure set in and the community of believers split into several states. Their separate rulers often assumed the title of *Khalifa* but the heirs of the worldly power of the original Muslim state were the Turks and their rulers were generally regarded as the traditional heirs of the original *Khalifate* of Islam.

Ever since the death of the Prophet, Islam had never been without a *Khalifa* and when Kemal Pasha dethroned the last Turkish Sultan he declared that he had destituted him of his temporal not of his spiritual power thus ignoring or showing his ignorance of the fact that as Islam has no clergy there can be no *Khalifa* without temporal power. But having taken this first step, in February 1924 he abolished the *Khalifate* completely. This caused great consternation throughout the world of Islam and many Muslims thought that without a *Khalifa* the disintegration of Islam would increase.

Here it was that King Husain saw his chance. He could point to qualifications that made him one of the most prominent candidates for succession to the *Khalifate*. He could claim relationship with the Prophet because he belonged to the House of Hashim, who was the Prophet's uncle, and he was the ruler of the Holy Land of Islam, protector of the *Haramain*—the two holy places—of Mecca and Medina. He well realized that he was too unpopular in Mecca to try to get himself acclaimed there as *Amir al mu'minin*—Prince of the Believers—so he decided to make a start elsewhere. He chose 'Amman and went there on the pretext of visiting his son 'Abdallah, the Amir of Transjordan. There, in the small town of 'Amman, a quick campaign was sufficient to produce a crowd willing to proclaim King Husain as *Khalifa*. This was followed by a press campaign throughout the astonished world of Islam. (King Husain, as editor of his own newspaper in Mecca, had experience of press propaganda). His official weekly in Mecca, *al Qibla*—the prayer niche in a mosque indicating the direction of Mecca—had published many leading articles on the subject that were, to judge from their tortuous style, written by himself. *Al Qibla* also published telegrams from all over the world of Islam expressing approval and offering congratulations. The new *Khalifa* was in no hurry to return to Mecca. He wanted first to prepare the ground and to be sure that the Holy City of Islam would join in the chorus of acclamation. So he timed his return to take place before reaction could set in there but first he made sure of support in Syria and in the two states ruled by his sons. In the great mosque in Damascus his proclamation as the new *Khalifa*, had preceded by a week his acclamation in 'Amman after the Friday service of 14 March 1924. In the rest of the world of Islam enthusiasm was not great. It was true that he was the ruler of the Holy Cities but who had made him so? A Christian power pushing him to revolt against his lawful Muslim overlord. Could one respect a man Muslims all over the world knew to be an unjust ruler who afforded no protection to pilgrims?

Husain had thrown down a challenge to Muslim opinion and the answer came that he had turned the high status of the *Khalifate* to personal ends. He had sought to have a problem of world importance settled by some beduins in a remote small Arab town. Had not he laid the whole Muslim world open to ridicule?

The excitement caused throughout the Muslim world by the abolition of the *Khalifate* had nowhere been greater than in India where *Khilafate* committees were formed, large meetings were

held and funds collected. Muslims were shocked and grieved by
Kemal Pasha's decision but the question was one in which the
Colonial Powers, although much concerned, could not, out of
respect for Muslim sensibilities, intervene. England and all the
other Western rulers of Muslim nations therefore watched and
waited. Blinded by the outward appearance of success and misled
by flatterers King Husain played his new role to the uttermost.
Al Qibla began to publish his proclamations and continued
printing the text of congratulatory telegrams addressed to the
Khalifa of Muhammad's tribe. Mecca, with the habitual coolness
of the professionally religious, seems to have taken the situation
calmly but not so Nejd. Wahhabi eyes had long been turned
towards the Holy Cities and with increasing distaste at the heresies
and worldliness that flourished there. Mecca and Medina would
clearly have to be purged and the Wahhabis wondered why
their Imam allowed the dotard in Mecca to bring Islam into
contempt.

Ibn Sa'ud saw that a safety valve had to be opened so he called a
meeting where the *'Ulama*, the tribal leaders and the town notables
could give vent to their feelings. His father, 'Abd ar-Rahman,
although advanced in years, was still active and clear of mind and
it was he who took the chair. At his side were seated the *'ulama*,
and, farther off, his son the Sultan. He, Ibn Sa'ud, said little. It
was decided to send a message to the Muslims of all other countries
calling attention to the misdeeds of Husain and to his usurpation
of the *Khalifate*. It was proposed that the people of Nejd, acting
on behalf of all Muslims, should march into the Hejaz after the
pilgrim season and depose Husain. The message was not signed
by Ibn Sa'ud but by his second son Faisal. The Sultan knew full
well the prejudice that existed against himself and his Wahhabi
followers. Setting no great hopes by this proposal he did not want
to be bound by it and in this he judged well. The response was
negligible with one exception: more than 70,000,000 Indian
Muslims rallied to his side. Bad, indeed, must have been the
experience in the Holy Land of Islam of Indian pilgrims, for them
to prefer Wahhabi to King Husain's rule over Mecca the Exalted

and Medina the Enlightened. The effect on the British Government of this Indian support of Ibn Sa'ud must be left to the imagination. It was an embarrassment if they felt bound to continue their support of Husain but an excuse if they decided to drop him.

Ibn Sa'ud clearly judged the support he received sufficient and with the object of disguising his real intentions despatched expeditions in three directions: one to Iraq, one to Transjordan and one to the Hejaz. Once again one of the advance guards got out of control. The men from Khurma and Turaba who had suffered most from King Husain and 'Ali, his eldest son, were eager for revenge. They marched off in the direction of Taif, the mountain resort to which the rich people from Mecca used to escape from the summer heat of the Holy City. Neighbouring beduins joined in, hoping for loot. On learning, when they neared the place, that the Amir 'Ali was in Taif they decided not to wait for orders but to attack the town forthwith. The garrison, taken by complete surprise, fled and 'Ali fled with them. The town was put to sack. Many notables from Mecca and a number of rich pilgrims from overseas were murdered. Rumours exaggerating the already ghastly reality caused a general panic in Mecca and a mass exodus to Jedda. The Hejazis turned against their King and a deputation went to the palace demanding his abdication in favour of his son 'Ali. Husain refused. He determined to defend the town although 'Ali and his troops had by-passed Mecca and taken up positions at Hadda where the *hima*—the forbidden territory—ends and fighting is permissible. But when his soldiers, and even his servants, began to leave Husain realized that Mecca could not be defended and much against his will the old King decided to leave the palace and go to Jedda. Armstrong says that the abdication took place in Mecca, Philby says that it was in Jedda that he yielded to the pressure of public opinion and abdicated in favour of his son 'Ali. The departure from Mecca was made in the few motor-cars he had allowed into the country. Later I heard many stories told by people who saw him go. No one said that he was afraid, all spoke without sympathy and all mentioned his special personal care for his possessions. Many well-soldered petrol tins full of gold were said to have been put on board his private yacht in Jedda: the gold of his British subsidy and the money he had squeezed out of pilgrims and the local merchants. The black, red, green and white flag of the Hashimites was hoisted on 'Al Rahmatain'—the two mercies—and with two other small shabby coasting steamers the ragged little royal squadron set its course northwards to 'Aqaba the furthermost point of his kingdom, the Ezion-Geber of Solomon's days. At 'Aqaba on the Gulf of that name that separates the Sinai Peninsula from the Hejaz, he would be, for the time being, out of reach of the Wahhabis.

The year 1924 neared its end. The reign as King of the Grand Sherif of Mecca had lasted eight brief years; his usurped dignity of *Khalifa* only a few months. He had lasted long enough to show that it takes more than ambition to be a successful ruler. He went filled with rancour against the faithless British whose unfulfilled promises he considered to be the cause of all his ills. He went unregretted by the Hejazis, beduins and townsmen alike, who saw in him a man of the highest local birth who had made life worse for them than the foreigner, the Turk, whom he had replaced. Muslims outside his country knew that as pilgrims they suffered from his mismanagement of the Holy Places. And all knew full well that, after Kemal Attaturk, it was he who dealt the institution of the *Khalifate* its most mortal blow.

His eldest son 'Ali took his place but did not dare to go back to Mecca. So he went to Jedda where he would have the open sea at his back and where he hoped that the presence of the Consuls of Western Powers would preserve him from attack by the Wahhabi troops. King 'Ali was well liked by the local population although the circumstances of his accession were scarcely propitious. The towns of Medina, Yambo and Al Wej sided with him and closed their gates when the Wahhabis approached. The beduins who camped near those towns also kept faith with the Hashimites and so the country waited to see what would happen.

Ar-Riyadh had been much surprised at the news of the capture and sack of the walled and fortified town of Taif by a reconnoitring party with light beduin reinforcement. Ibn Sa'ud issued the strictest orders to the two commanders of his troops in the Hejaz to prevent further murder or looting and he held them personally responsible. With the utmost speed he then prepared to follow with the bulk of his army. The Governor of Khurma, Ibn Luwai, had commanded the advance guard at Taif, the *Ikhwan* were under their leader Sultan Ibn Bijad. The latter had in the meantime gone on to Mecca. He sent into the town four unarmed members of the *Ikhwan* dressed in the ceremonial garb of pilgrims. Mecca looked like a dead place, its shops closed and its inhabitants barricaded within their houses. The four men declared in the name of their commander that security would be afforded to everyone who put himself under the protection of Allah and of Ibn Sa'ud. The following day Ibn Luwai arrived with two thousand men, again dressed in *ihram* but armed. Security in this case seems to have had precedence over divine laws as the wearing of arms was incompatible with the wearing of *ihram*. They marched into the town and occupied the fort and the public buildings. No looting and what in Wahhabi eyes was only very moderate purification took place. The graves of the great men of Islam were levelled to the ground, ornaments on mosques were destroyed and musical instruments and pictures of human beings banished from public places. After what had happened in Taif the first impression made by the Wahhabis on the people of Mecca was not entirely unfavourable.

Fifteen days later Ibn Sa'ud camped with his army before Mecca. He wished to enter the Holy City as a pilgrim, as is the duty of the faithful. So he laid aside his few marks of distinction and, bareheaded, with one piece of white cloth without hem wrapt around his loins and another cloth around his shoulders he rode into the town. Just like every other pilgrim he repeated several times the exclamation: "*labbaik Allahuma, labbaik*"—ready for Thy service O God, I am ready for Thy service. He entered the *Masjid al Haram*—the holy mosque—he drew near to God's House, the Ka'ba—*Bait Ullah*—and performed the seven ritual circumambulations of the Ka'ba, thus completing the *'umra*.

The commanders of his army and the Wahhabi religious leaders all did as he. Ibn Sa'ud laid a heavy discipline on his troops who certainly after waiting so long a time and reaching their real goal Mecca *al Mukarrama*—the exalted Mecca—must well have looked forward to what others might call excesses. And now, after so many years, the centre of the religion of Islam was again in the power of the Wahhabis. From now on the Holy City of Islam would again be pure and holy.

But Medina *al Munawwara*—the enlightened—was still in the hands of the *mushrikin* and they still occupied the three coastal towns. The *Ikhwan* would have liked nothing better than to carry these by storm but Ibn Sa'ud, mindful of his foreign relations, gave no order to storm Jedda. And he stopped the bombardment of Medina when the foreign Consuls through their British colleague protested for, although denied as such by the Wahhabis, the tomb of their Prophet is regarded as sacred by millions of Muslims.

It was December 1925 before Jedda surrendered. 'Ali, realizing that he was without adequate means of continuing the struggle, agreed to abdicate and leave the country. A British warship took him on board and he went off to stay with his brother Faisal, King of Iraq.

Medina had surrendered earlier and so the Hejaz became completely in the power of Ibn Sa'ud. When after his first visit to the last conquered towns of the Hejaz he went back to Mecca the notables of the town came out to meet him. They told him of the wish of the population of the Hejaz that he should be their King. On 8th January 1926 this was confirmed in his official acclamation by all the notables of Mecca, Medina, Jedda and all the other important centres of the country, as King of the Hejaz. He appointed his second son Faisal to be Governor of Mecca and his representative as Viceroy of the Hejaz. After this a public reception was held and the garrison of the fort of Ji'ad was allowed to fire a salute of one hundred guns in honour of the new King, the Lord of the Hejaz and Nejd and Dependencies. The dual monarchy had come into existence. For the time being he retained the title of Sultan of Nejd thus conforming to the sober Wahhabi practice of being sparing in the bestowal of titles.

Ibn Sa'ud now faced a new task in coming into direct contact with the international world of Islam. In Jedda he would also have to deal with the representatives of those Western and Eastern countries who, for the well-being of their Muslim subjects, were interested that law and order should rule in the land of pilgrimage. They would follow closely this new Wahhabi rule of the Holy Places. The first Wahhabi rule had come to an end in 1812, crumbling before the attack of the Egyptian Ibrahim Pasha. Would the second Wahhabi domination of the Holy Land prove more permanent?

On 1st March 1926 the King came for his second official visit to Jedda. A British cruiser had arrived bringing Great Britain's recognition of his rule over the new addition to his state and those foreign representatives who had not been present at His Majesty's first ceremonial entry in Jedda were now given the opportunity to meet him.

I had arrived in Jedda some days earlier and was preparing to take over charge of the Netherlands Consulate there and so went with my predecessor to the patrician dwelling of our learned friend Muhammad Nasif, where Ibn Sa'ud was staying. Apparently he was unwilling to use the building where 'Ali had spent his shortlived reign.

We were introduced by the Foreign Secretary, the Iraqi 'Abdullah al Damluji and with the King was his adviser Sheikh Hafiz Wahba, an Egyptian, a former schoolmaster in Kuwait, educated at Cairo's Al Azhar University and later to become Sa'udi Ambassador in London. 'Abdullah al Damluji made a flattering remark about the Dutch representatives' knowledge of Arabic. The King rose to greet us and gave us a genuinely Arabian welcome. He invited us to sit down, one on each side of him, and then he asked 'Abdullah al Damluji whether it was true that we could converse with him without an interpreter. When the answer was an exaggerated affirmative the King said: "Then let everybody be gone." All disappeared, the beduin guard at the door was given a sign to go, and we were left alone. Even when seated Ibn Sa'ud was much taller than either of us and he looked down upon us. His smile made his face radiate kindness. It was the mobility of his features which were outstanding in Ibn Sa'ud. In repose his face was grim and forbidding but when he smiled it was completely transformed and he became extraordinarily attractive. He pouted as women do and then he began to speak. If I had known Arabic better I could have enjoyed this talk more. But I was like a man too intent on eating to savour the flavour of the food and all my attention was directed to following what he was saying and trying to grasp the full meaning of the long sentences that flowed into the silence of the hall.

"We praise God that you understand us. Now we can be alone without those interpreters, the most dangerous and harmful people in the world. We are here together and we can speak freely. It is important that your Queen should get, through you, correct information about us. We have reserved a liberal space of time for this talk for we want you to understand us well. Now come closer and listen." His hand lightly touched our knees and our shoulders as if to establish quicker and closer contact between man and man. From time to time the smile swept lightly across our eyes, inviting us to feel at ease, as true guests in his warm-hearted beduin hospitality. A spate of words flooded over us, unusual words many of them and heavy with the deep guttural sounds of beduin speech.

"We want you to know who we are, what we are doing and how and why," he said. "You, like all the others from the West, think of us as wild, rough fanatics, backward and narrow-minded people. Up to now that has been the trend of your reports to your government." We protested in polite denial. "No, do not deny, we know exactly what people are thinking of us, but now we want them to know the truth. Your Queen has the right to know the truth. We have often acted severely, even mercilessly and with Allah's help we have beaten a wicked enemy.

This country shall now at last have security, peace and order, and will know justice. Robbers and other evil-doers have had to be dealt with in a way understood by beduins for we ourselves know how to rule beduins as you and other critics do not. Beduins have to be treated in a very hard way for only then do they learn their lesson and, *in sha'a Allah*—if Allah wills—once they have learnt it they will never forget it. We teach them the hard way, not to be cruel, but out of mercy. And once we have punished them we shall not in the mercy of Allah have to do it again as long as we live.

"The distances in our country are great. We can often only make justice effective in the remoteness of our deserts by the reports spread of the justice we dealt out to the dogs of the Hejaz, those robbers of the Banu Malik (a tribe in whose midst a caravan had been robbed and some people murdered) of whom we killed several hundreds. Far away in the deserts this news will be applauded because it will mean that caravans can at last travel in peace and security where till now they were kept away by fear. We have heard that your government favours light punishment. Did not you build large houses where you keep your evil-doers? Have you many of these houses? And are they not full? Well, that, to our mind, is what is cruel. You punish year in year out and yet it does not seem to be effective. I punish in such a way that it has not to be repeated. We know the beduin and we know how he has to be ruled. Is it not safe now in this country, where the robbing of pilgrims flourished for centuries? By Allah, people have only begun to know us here, but we assure you that there will be no more stealing or waylaying.

"You have doubtless also heard many stories about the fanaticism of the Wahhabis. It is good that you should know the truth about our creed and that of our brothers. We believe that Allah the Exalted One uses us as His instrument. As long as we serve Him we will succeed, no power can check us and no enemy will be able to kill us. Should we become a useless weapon in His hands then He will throw us aside, *wa sanahmiduhu*—and we shall praise Him."

His long sentences, full of ideas, were periodically broken off with "*Na'am?*"—Yes?—meaning 'Do you follow me?' He spoke as a man of great conviction and concluded in a credo of short, terse remarks each of which was preceded by the words "We believe".

Ibn Sa'ud impressed on us that whatever he was and whatever he did could be reduced to what he believed. His confession of faith was that of the Wahhabi. He seemed a quite different person from that of the fantastic tales that had come to us in Jedda from Nejd. His creed was that of a Wahhabi who looked beyond the frontiers of his desert land, who had now come into contact with international Islam and who understood that he could only rule the Holy Land of Islam as the trustee of the world-embracing community of Muhammad. He thought himself competent to do this and he felt the urge to formulate his task for himself and for others because by doing so his ideas became crystallized. I had to admit to being most impressed. Ibn Sa'ud was the first Muslim who gave me a feeling of closeness to my own innermost convictions. Perhaps that was caused by his simple respect of and belief in divine guidance in his life, perhaps it was his inner urge to share what was deepest of himself. He had the courage to bare before strangers the very foundation of his life. He was proud of his uncomplicated creed, sure that he held the truth and convinced that his hearers would at least respect him for it. And that we did.

This meeting was more than an official audience. For me it was like being admitted into another's sanctum sanctorum. My heart warmed to Ibn Sa'ud and I could not help being moved. I knew that I had met a man who aroused expectations in me. This man would be a blessing to his land and to its tens of thousands of yearly visitors. I even cherished the hope that this would be the man to find for Islam the solution to its growing spiritual crisis. Whoever could have expected that from a Wahhabi from Nejd!

8

First Wahhabi Impacts

THE WAHHABIS were burdened with the record of their first conquest of the country, more than a century ago. Their purifying of the Holy Cities had at that time been so rigorous and the reaction of orthodox, that is to say non-Wahhabi, Islam so violent that the Turkish government had been forced to intervene. As her centre of power was too far away and too weak to act she was happy to pass on the task to Egypt, her vassal. Two Egyptian military expeditions had driven the Wahhabis from the Holy Places back to the interior, to the deserts whence they had come and where they could do no more harm to the pilgrimage.

Fear and anxiety had followed the rise of the second Wahhabi tide and its movement towards the holy territory. Taif had confirmed the worst fears and although the behaviour of the Wahhabis in Mecca and, later, in Medina was much less open to objection, the world of Islam was by no means generally reassured. Had not those who marched on Medina, the very town of the Prophet, wantonly directed their primitive artillery at the golden dome built over the tomb of the most blessed of men? What was to be expected from nomad followers of the doctrine of 'Abd al Wahhab for whom the Prophet had been no more than a man not free from sin? Orthodox Islam, impressed by the sinlessness of the Founder of Christianity, had long since virtually adopted the same dogma for Muhammad. Not so the Wahhabis. They insisted that not even the Prophet of Islam was entitled to a dome over his tomb, a place to be venerated. Had not the Wahhabi artillery been so poorly directed and above all, had not the foreign representatives in Jedda, the non-Muslims, rushed in and prevented such an outrage, the sanctuary in Medina might

A STREET IN OLD JEDDA

THE KING AND HIS SON, THEN CROWN PRINCE

have crumbled into dust. The foreigners had once kept them in check. A second time they might not be so successful.

Ibn Sa'ud well knew that the Holy Land could not be ordered on simple Wahhabi lines. But could he succeed in making himself acceptable to the world of Islam as the new protector of *al Haramain*—the two sanctuaries—Mecca and Medina, and at the same time not lose the confidence of his own people and particularly of his *Ikhwan*?

Owing to the pilgrimage he would meet the most devout of the faithful from abroad. To them he would have to prove that at long last the Holy Land was again a land of peace and security where pilgrims were treated as welcome and honoured guests and no longer as objects for plunder as had been the case during the reign of King Husain. So far as peace and security were concerned he felt reassured. But he was not nearly so happy at the prospect of the meeting of his Wahhabis with Muslims from abroad whom they mostly looked upon as heretics if not complete unbelievers. And the Wahhabis who had been cut off from the pilgrimage during the Hashimite reign made themselves ready in tens of thousands to visit the now cleansed Holy Places.

Ibn Sa'ud did his utmost to prevent conflicts. He kept his fanatical troops away from Mecca and Medina and at the places of the great assemblies of the *hajj* he kept them apart, camped in military order. With his sons he rode ahead of them to the plains of 'Arafa, Muzdalifa and Muna. He gave them strict orders to treat the pilgrims as foreign guests and to bear with their shortcomings. The pilgrims were requested to refrain from the sinful habit of smoking and in any case never to smoke in public. Visits to tombs and praying there were forbidden. In actual fact little of the tombs remained. The dome-shaped structures over those graves, the *qubbas*, had, with the single exception of the gilded copper dome over the tomb of the Prophet in Medina, been destroyed. The pilgrims going to pray near that tomb and wishing to prostrate themselves in front of it, found Wahhabi soldiers who prevented their kneeling, forbade prostrations and allowed only the reciting of the prayer specially prepared for this occasion by royal command. The text of that prayer had been published in the Meccan weekly, no longer called *al Qibla* but now *'Umm al Qura*—the Mother of Cities—that is Mecca. The *ziyara*—the visiting of the tomb of the Prophet—thus lost its attraction for many of the pilgrims as did the visit to the grave of *'Ummina Hawa*—our Mother Eve—half a mile north-east of the town wall of Jedda. A small domed structure had been built over the place of the navel of this giant of a woman, giant because her grave was nearly two hundred yards long: a curious conceit for the only woman, presumably, to have come into this world without a navel. But the dome was demolished and when pilgrims, and especially women, continued to visit the place the government ordered every stone to be carried away. Minor frictions of this sort arising between pilgrims and Wahhabi Government gave rise to no political trouble but caused loss of sympathy for the new rulers. A pilgrim who comes from afar, some taking years on the journey, is perhaps easily disappointed. Such disappointments in the Hejaz helped to perpetuate the antipathy towards Wahhabism which had remained from the time the Wahhabis first conquered the Holy Land. Antipathy such as this was prejudicial to a just appreciation of this second period of Wahhabi rule in the country.

With the Egyptians it was a case of something much more serious than disappointment. From the early days of Islam it had been the custom for Muslim governments to send a *Mahmal*—a profusely decorated litter heading the caravan of their pilgrims—to the *hajj*. The Egyptian government was the only one that still followed that custom. With her *Mahmal* she used to send each year the new *kiswa*—the black carpet to cover the Ka'ba—with a gift of money, wheat and flour for the poor of the *Haramain*. The *Mahmal*, borne by an exceptionally big camel, the cases with money and the sacks with foodstuffs following in a long caravan, were escorted by Egyptian troops and preceded by a band. This now presented a difficult problem. Music in general was abhorred by the Wahhabis because it easily led to sin. All modern music belonged to the category of sinful inventions of the days after the

Prophet, and foreign soldiers carrying arms in their country were nearly as repugnant to the Wahhabis.

Ibn Sa'ud had no wish to offend Egypt by refusing the customary gift and in order not to lose the gift he decided to accept the escort on condition that the instruments of the band were left in Jedda. The *Ikhwan* looked suspiciously at the Egyptian escort, marching and camping in modern style. They sniffed idolatry of some kind behind it. In the plain of Muna there was trouble. Towards evening a bugle call was heard in camp. It echoed against the walls of rock that enclose the long, narrow plain. What was that? Music? In that holy place? Those impious Egyptian dogs! The *Ikhwan* rushed out to the Egyptian camp demanding that the music should cease. They began to throw stones. The Egyptians in alarm hurriedly took up their arms and drew up their ranks. This incensed the already infuriated Nejdis. They closed in upon the soldiers, whose officer gave the order to fire. The shooting was heard by young Amir Faisal and his brothers. He jumped on his horse and threw himself between the zealots who were crowding in front of the Egyptian troops, causing a panic among the pilgrims who camped near-by. *Ikhwan* and pilgrims began to fall under the bullets of the Egyptian machine-guns. By his bravery the Sa'udi Prince put a stop to further casualties and loss of life and avoided a general panic among the pilgrims.

As a result of this incident diplomatic relations were severed with Egypt and not resumed until ten years later. During those years the *kiswa* was woven in Mecca by Indian craftsmen. It is said to have been of inferior quality and the poor of the *Haramain* had to go without the Egyptian gifts in kind.

Although Indian Muslims had been very outspoken critics of the Hashimite régime and had supported Nejdi rejection of King Husain's claim to the Khalifate, they were no friends of the Wahhabis. These 70,000,000 Indian Muslims had outstanding leaders like Muhammad and Shauqat 'Ali who had acquired their training in anti-British and anti-Hindu activities. Indian Muslims were either of the Sunni or the Shi'a persuasion (the two great divisions of Islam) but in either case they were anti-Wahhabi.

The criticism of these Indians was very frank and caused Ibn Saʿud to draw on all his patience and wisdom to keep his followers in check. The Indians asked for pan-Islamic control of the Holy Places and that Ibn Saʿud should accept the position of a mandatory power. How would it be possible to reconcile a mandatory position over the Holy Places and still govern the remainder of the country? Ibn Saʿud had the courage to face up to these problems and proposed they should be discussed by a pan-Islamic congress held in Mecca.

He knew that he was a convincing talker and had repeatedly proved his ability to sway his Arabian subjects. Why should not he succeed in swaying the representatives of Muslim nations? They would see that Mecca had been purged and that he had made the pilgrimage safe for them; they would taste of his Arab hospitality. Then he would address them and win their sympathy by his tolerance and mildness and the power of his word.

The Congress met in the summer of 1926 with the eyes of the whole world, and particularly those of the Muslims, fixed on it. It was not the first nor the last congress of Islam. More than one Muslim effort had been made to restore the moral damage caused by Kemal Attaturk's abrupt abolition of the Khalifate. Husain's solution with himself as Khalifa had been generally inacceptable. Pan-Islam congresses had met in Cairo and Jerusalem but no unanimous conclusion was reached. Possibly an Islamic Congress in Mecca, the real centre of Islam, would stand the best chance of success. Seventy delegates represented nearly all the Muslim peoples, Iraq and Transjordan where sons of ex-King Husain were reigning being among the exceptions, as were the Muslims of Persia who are Shiʿas. Between the Shiʿas and the Wahhabi no common accord was then possible, they did not recognize each other as 'brethren in the faith'.

Al Muʿtammar al Islam al aʿla—the Highest Congress of Islam— as it was called, opened with the King's speech. He invited the delegates to investigate every path that might lead to moral and religious improvement of the Hejaz and be pleasing to both God and man. He did not allow his kingship to be questioned nor the administrative problems of the country. Efforts to do so and bold criticism of his policy, most of which came from Indians, were disregarded. Even so the congress led to no practical solution. It merely turned out to be a demonstration of the disunity within Islam and of the incompetence of the Muslim world in general to grapple with new problems.

Indonesia had been represented by the old leader of the *Sarikat Islam*—the union of Islam—Tjokro Aminoto. The language difficulty, classical Arabic being the language of the congress, had been brushed aside by the Indians who used English, but this was of no help to those who knew neither Arabic nor English. Hajji Agus Salim, who represented Indonesia in the congress of the following year, could speak fluently both Arabic and English and if he had been present at that first meeting, perhaps a way might have been found of bridging the gulf that separated Ibn Sa'ud and the Indians. As it was, the great Muslim communities of India and Indonesia turned away from the Wahhabi leader and denied him their confidence.

The Congress of 1927 was much less important but equally ineffective. Thus pan-Islamic congresses failed in the three classical cities of Islam: in Mecca its spiritual centre, in Cairo its intellectual centre and in Jerusalem the town held second in holiness. And the leader of a movement that claimed to know the only right way for the whole of Islam had also failed.

But Ibn Sa'ud had gained valuable experience. He now knew that his work could not extend beyond the limits of Arabia proper. He had also seen that no help from the outside Muslim world was to be expected for their Holy Land. And since he had to shoulder the burden alone he determined not to suffer interference from outside. The Hejaz had to be ruled in a non-sectarian way. Wahhabism of course would come first but there must be place for all the other sects of Islam, and freedom of opinion. Even so he would not permit proselytizing of doctrines other than that of the great Sheikh. No political activity by pilgrims would he allow, not even the anti-colonial activities for which Mecca had often been so safe a centre.

The Hejaz and the pilgrimage claimed so much of his attention that he stayed away from Nejd longer than proved to be wise. Two years on end had he spent in the Holy Land meeting the world of Islam. The Foreign representatives in Jedda remained deeply interested onlookers of the activities of the King. They soon saw that Ibn Saʿud was great enough to understand where his limits lay and to stay inside them. He stated clearly that he did not want to follow a pan-Islamic policy nor yet a pan-Arabic one and he stuck to this principle. The efforts made by a large Soviet representation in Jedda to start an anti-Western campaign with Muslim subjects of what were called the Colonial Powers, failed completely. Nationalist leaders from India, Indonesia and French North Africa who tried from Mecca to rebuild their organizations, when these had been uprooted by the Western governments, soon learnt that Ibn Saʿud kept the promises he had given to the Western governments. Thus there arose between him and those governments a confidence that for long years had not been thought possible between the ruler of the Holy Land of Islam and the rulers of the Christian West. He was the first Ruler in Mecca who ever thought of sending his son to Europe in order to convey the thanks of his father to the governments who had officially recognized him. Several times he sent on missions abroad the Amir Faisal, whom he had made Viceroy of the Hejaz and his Foreign Secretary. Later on even his eldest son, the Crown Prince Saʿud, whom he made Governor of Nejd, went abroad. In this way he succeeded in establishing personal relations with Western governments and rulers by which he and his country benefited.

There remained one other weighty matter that demanded the attention of the informed foreign observer, and that was whether this second Wahhabi wave would contribute to the solution of the spiritual crisis in which Islam was involved. Islam had been stagnant after its initial great period of world domination. It was as if that outpouring of energy had been too great and so there followed a long reaction. Efforts at expansion in the Christian-ized West had long ceased. East and south where Islam met polytheistic creeds the propaganda went on successfully and when Islam hit up against Christian Missions she more than held her ground. Africa proved to be a promising field for Islam and what was then British India and the Dutch East Indies contained the future Muslim Republics of Pakistan and Indonesia. The indisputable fact remained, however, that the world was dominated by the Christian West and the defection of Turkey from the Muslim ranks served to underline Western supremacy. The Muslim nations thus realized how far they had lagged behind, materially and spiritually, and began to look for an answer to the challenge of the West. It was then that the East realized that its religious code, made to suit the entirely different conditions of hundreds of years ago, was unsuited to the changed world of today and unable to provide the desired answer.

Some radical reform was necessary and several were tried. An earlier reform that had once made some impression had been undertaken by the Sheikh Muhammad Ibn 'Abd al Wahhab in combination with the Sa'uds more than a hundred years ago. It had failed as soon as in Mecca it came in contact with the international world of Islam, for in those days Islam was not ready for such a radical attempt at reformation. Cairo which considers itself the intellectual centre of Islam had made its contribution to the problem in the modernist movement started by Jamal ad-Din al Afghani, and deepened and expanded by Muhammad 'Abduh, but this movement is in decline in spite of Rashid Ridha's activity.

I used to take particular note of the *fatwas* issued by the *'Ulama* —the scholars of religion—now established in Mecca, but formerly in ar-Riyadh, in which they gave authoritative pronouncements on the problems of Islam. In tone they sounded curiously remote from modern times yet it was just this archaism that prevailed in Mecca. The International University of Islam as orientalists once had called the gathering of teachers and students of theology in the *Masjid al Haram* in Mecca, seemed to be withering under the desert breath of Wahhabism.

Thus expectations of a spiritual rebirth of Islam aroused by first contacts with Ibn Sa'ud gradually faded. Not the least of his difficulties in giving a spiritual lead was Ibn Sa'ud's need to soften the asperities of his Wahhabi mentors. In those early days he had no alternative but to acquiesce in the introduction of Nejdi puritanism in the Hejaz. Smoking, music-making, the consumption of alcohol and the wearing of gold and jewellery and silk garments were strictly forbidden and performance of the five daily ritual prayers in the mosque was made obligatory. When the *azan*—the call to prayer—sounded police patrols with long canes would stride through the streets shouting: *as-salat! as-salat!*— to prayer! to prayer!—and beat upon the closed shutters and doors of the shops in the markets to frighten any who might be hiding there. Those who did not walk in the direction of the mosque were helped on their way. Five times a day the town was like a town of the dead. No sound was to be heard other than the shouts of the patrols followed by the murmur of prayers punctuated with the massive "*amins*" of the gathered crowds. Often on leaving the mosques the names of the faithful were checked. Thus much of the day-time was taken up with the outward performance of religious duties, enforced and police-controlled. Soon it proved to be impossible to force this rhythm of life on the towns of pilgrimage of Jedda, Mecca and Medina, but in the rest of the Wahhabi state it was carried out. The result was that spontaneous devotions gave place to organized religion and the basis of worship changed from love to fear.

The hard, set faces of those who practised Wahhabi doctrine, the harsh voices that used to echo through the streets when the call of prayer sounded, and the blows rained on doors and shutters, seemed to suggest a sinister side to these earnest attempts at reformation. Qur'anic punishments were reintroduced: amputation of a hand or foot for theft, beating with a stick for drunkenness, hanging and stoning to death for worse offences. Punishments were carried out in the principal squares, preferably, for maximum effect, on Fridays when the men came from the *salat*. But how primitive they seemed to onlookers with a background other than that of a desert *ghazu*! Where only Sa'udi subjects, beduins and slaves were concerned such practices could not be questioned but it is noteworthy that no general attempt was made to apply qur'anic punishments to non-Sa'udis.

Then little by little Ibn Sa'ud withdrew his Nejdis from the towns of the Hejaz and in their place put more mundane persons to ensure obedience to the rules of public worship and to watch over public morals. The committees he had established throughout the Wahhabi state 'to encourage that which is good and to shun that which is evil' were now, in the Hejaz, chosen from the local population although central control remained in Nejd.

I myself noted how difficult the position often became for Ibn Sa'ud during his popular public audiences. Dozens of local notables, some of the Nejdi *'ulama* and guests of different nationalities were usually to be found there. On one occasion I had the good fortune to meet there the then well-known Shekib Arslan, a Syrian nationalist who used to live in Geneva, then the seat of the League of Nations.

Shekib had come hoping to pursuade Ibn Sa'ud not to go to war with his southern neighbour, the Imam Yahya of the Yemen, when war seemed imminent. Shekib was an orator and thought his arguments convincing, and with much feeling he tried to dissuade his fellow Arab from embarking on a fratricidal war. The Nejdis listened first in amazement and then with growing vexation. The Hejazis enjoyed a discussion such as they imagined to be common in political circles in the outside world. The King listened with a tolerant smile and only occasionally interposed a remark. Shekib, much encouraged, grew bold. He produced his final, conclusive argument: "Oh Your Majesty the King, just think of all the trouble, the never-ending anxiety and work this war would bring on you!"

Ibn Sa'ud laughed amusedly. "Oh my dear honoured friend Shekib," he said, "how much you are mistaken! Troubles, you say, if there is war? Not at all; quiet, I tell you, a wonderful time of repose! Wartime is always my best time. When there is no war the sheikhs of the tribes sit in my palace, as do the religious leaders. They all come and bother me with their many complaints and requests. They stay as long as possible knowing that in the palace kitchen there is good and plentiful fare. One thousand you say? I tell you that every day there are three or four thousand who enjoy my hospitality in ar-Riyadh. But when the word is given for war, they all jump to their feet, take their camels and go to the storehouses where each one receives his bag of flour and dates and his supply of munitions and off they go to war! What quiet for me! It is my best time, I assure you, when I am at war!" The King laughed, the Nejdis roared aloud, everyone enjoyed the joke and Shekib, too, smiled. He understood that he had been outwitted.

Another time it was Philby whom the King, in his ignorance, silenced. It was after Philby had become a Muslim, and a Wahhabi, and so had the rights of a brother. *Al akh* (brother) 'Abdallah Philby dared to take part in the public conversation more freely. The subject on this occasion was natural phenomena and Philby had said that the earth was round like a very big ball.

"I tell you, Philby, that it is flat," the King retorted.

"Your Majesty, it is really round and you will soon see this proved. We all heard that some days ago the airship *Graf Zeppelin* left Lake Constance in South Germany on a tour round the world. The airship is sailing straight ahead, crossing the Atlantic to North America and then on and on and *in sha'a Allah*— if God wills—she will pass over Siberia and eventually come down again at Lake Constance. She does not sail away from this flat disc to disappear into the unending space. You will see her return to her starting point."

"Philby," said the King, "Allah's word says that the earth is flat, and thus it is," and that was the end of the discussion. But what light did it throw on Ibn Sa'ud's fitness to deal with the problem of reconciling Islam to the needs of the modern world?

'Brother' Philby was often a thorn in the King's side, so much so that Arabs connected with the court told me that at times the King asked Philby to go away for some months. These absences Philby most profitably spent in exploration of the interior to his own refreshment and to the advancement of the common fund of knowledge. It is likely too that reports spread about Philby were more likely to be actuated by jealous than by friendly feelings towards him. But sometimes there were facts even more annoying than a Philby. What the King had denied to Philby appeared some days later printed and illustrated in new books that had been ordered from Egypt for the schools of the Hejaz. Possibly to Ibn Sa'ud Western geographical knowledge was simple modernism but in print at least he was to let it pass as long as it did not upset his Wahhabi advisers and censors. He knew full well that Wahhabism had no answer to many modern problems. His great forefather had had a spiritual guide at his side, 'Abd al Wahhab, but Ibn Sa'ud had to answer all his own problems himself, and this made him a lonely man. He was a great desert warrior, he could understand and lead men, he was even a statesman with understanding of world politics, but he was no real spiritual leader, and he failed to guide his people in the present day problems of Islam. But it is only fair to add that where he failed no one else throughout the whole world of Islam has yet succeeded. The spiritual rebirth of Islam is yet to come.

9

The Pilgrimage

IN the Hejaz Ibn Saʿud's chief problem was that of the pilgrimage. Pilgrims, coming as they did from all over the Muslim world could make or mar him. The pilgrimage, too, had in those days to provide his government with its major source of income. It was the Hejaz and not Nejd that now ran his kingdom for him. Wahhabi criticism of King Husain's exploitation and ill-treatment of pilgrims had been loud and long. Now it was for the Wahhabi to show what he could do.

The first benefit Ibn Saʿud brought to the pilgrims was complete security. Pilgrim memories, however, are short and this greatest gift was soon taken for granted. In King Husain's days the foreign Consuls at the end of each *hajj* season used to present to the King their bills of indemnities claimed in respect of pilgrims killed by beduins. The object of these claims was to spur the authorities into protecting the pilgrim caravans. No claims were made once Ibn Saʿud had taken over control of the country, for pilgrims were no longer killed or robbed.

But the pilgrim was exposed to other, if lesser, ills and had also to be protected against them. One of these had been the shortage of water in Jedda and in the meeting-places of the *hajj*. Jedda depended a great deal on condensed sea-water. A second condenser for the town was ordered from Scotland and a capable British mechanic was put in charge of the water-condensing units of the town. In my ten years of residence in Jedda I never experienced any serious shortage of drinking water but the poorer classes could not afford to buy the expensive *moya kindasa*—condensed water—that was sold by Negro women carrying tins on their heads and loudly praising its qualities as they walked through the back streets. The poor lived on brackish water from the wells in the desert or on rain-water from the *zagharij*—underground reservoirs—that dated from pre-condenser days. In the pilgrims' meeting-places in the desert the water supply was largely a question of distribution and in the hands of a strong government no shortages were to be feared. Pilgrims suffered too from manipulation of the rates of exchange, so Ibn Sa'ud kept the money-changers under sharp control. He also admitted a foreign bank, the Netherlands Trading Society, into the country and even used it as a kind of State bank.

Hygiene was another important problem. Western governments had long been obliged to protect pilgrims against the danger of their contracting infections during the *hajj*, and spreading epidemics on return to their own countries.

Internationally the Hejaz had a bad reputation for health and the pilgrims had to suffer for it in quarantine stations established to prevent the contamination of the outside world. From the beginning Ibn Sa'ud gave much attention to this problem. He sought foreign advice and soon realized that a bacteriological laboratory was essential. The Netherlands Government sent him a good bacteriologist and, together with his own medical service headed by a capable Syrian, they worked well so that from the third year of his accession onwards no major epidemic marred the pilgrimage. This does not mean that performing the *hajj* at once became a healthy undertaking. By no means. There were no more raging epidemics but a good many pilgrims still paid for their obedience to the 'fifth pillar' of the Muslim creed, the *hajj*, with death. I myself have seen sick and dying pilgrims in the crowded streets and squares of Jedda where they were camping in the open. They could have been taken to the town hospital, but that was then a place of despair and feared by every pilgrim who was not on the point of death. I shall never forget those hospital wards full of dying patients who had been picked up in the streets for I used to go there with our Javanese doctor to make sure that there were no Jawi patients among them. These poor creatures, covered with flies, for whom there was but little care and less treatment, had no better hope than early death for they all knew that they had reached the end of their earthly pilgrimage. One could smell the different diseases and one could tell from the corridors which wards were for cases of dysentery as the faeces would flow under the doors. Here I saw diseases known to me by name only and long since banished from the lands of Western hygiene. I remember a dying black man from south of Lake Tsad who kept me by his bedside by his imploring eyes. In vain his wife tried to keep the flies away from his face. She helped him utter his appeal to me.

"Do get him away from here! If only we reach the deck of one of your ships he will be saved." He followed my reactions with his eyes and made a great effort pointing to his mattress:

"There is money, a lot. I can pay. I have kept it from their clutches. For God's sake, help me!" And then to know I could do nothing.

The Hejaz at that time was a long way from having a clean hospital with a good staff of doctors, with nurses trained for their task and, above all, with food suitable for their starved patients and medicines to treat them. All that would take time and money. It would also mean employing a new type of men, not the scum of nearby nations but men of professional competence who were willing to serve the suffering and the dying on Allah's road. The number who fell on that road, in the desert and in the streets of Jedda was still great but the Sa'udi administration brought about many improvements and the horrifying tales of Jedda stricken with epidemics and quarantine stations that were places of despair, belonged to the past.

It must also not be forgotten that the sojourn in the Hejaz is only part of the pilgrimage. Before they arrive at the gates of their Holy Land many pilgrims have already gone through their greatest trials. I met some along the desert tracks of Arabia who told me astonishing stories of wanderings on their road to salvation. Some were African pilgrims who had walked across the whole breadth of the Dark Continent and had been years on the way. I had a black servant who, as a child, travelled four years with his parents to reach Mecca. There both parents died and he went the way of all black children left without protection in this land: he was sold as a slave. A predecessor of mine had bought him and set him free. I met straggling groups of Indians, men and women, who had come in sailing boats to some East Arabian harbour. There they started to walk inland across the Peninsula. I remember a group I had once met at night walking from the south coast of Arabia in the direction of Mecca. It was long since they had left their villages, setting out without money. Life before them could scarcely be harder than it had been at home. They had no luggage and for food and water they depended on the tribes through whose territory they passed. Next year they hoped to be in Mecca if God willed.

Even the pilgrims travelling by ship often had to go through many hardships. Here it was their governments or the governments of the nationality of the ships concerned who were to be blamed when pilgrims suffered on board and not the Wahhabi administration. I saw many cases of sufferings that ought never to have happened. In the case of the burning of the French ship *Asia* both sides were to be blamed.

The *Asia* rode at anchor in the outer harbour of Jedda with a full complement of pilgrims on board, ready to sail before day-break the following morning. Before taking her North African pilgrims back to the Mediterranean the *Asia* proposed to make a short trip to harbours on the other side of the Red Sea. There was not much in the way of control of live cargo in those days and a dangerously large number of passengers had been taken on board. It was a sticky, hot night on which only coloured passengers could survive in the holds of a ship lying at anchor in the outer harbour of Jedda in summer-time. The wind-sails had been hoisted to catch every bit of breeze. And then the tragedy happened. Fire broke out. Breaking open the sealed wireless cabin the ship signalled for assistance to the shore when the crew failed to get the fire under control. The shore did not answer as the men of the wireless station were not on duty. Then rockets were fired from the bridge. The people on shore seeing the many-coloured fireworks said:

"They are having a *fantasia*—a show—to divert their pilgrims as all is ready now for sailing to-morrow."

The captain of the *Asia* then let the ship's syren roar its SOS to inform the ships in the inner harbour because their wireless cabins were still sealed. Only then did they become aware of what was going on. Immediately the other ships lowered and manned their life-boats and rowed in the dark to the French ship where flames now began to appear and were soon roaring upwards. On board the *Asia* the crew had given up the struggle and tried to get the boats lowered. The eighteen hundred odd pilgrims were seized with panic and stormed the boats, some of which turned over while still hanging in the davits, others were not properly lowered and were hanging upside down having shot their occupants into the water, with others the ropes had snapped and the boats were dangling idly against the side of the ship. Hell had broken loose. The captain gave the word "sauve qui peut" and pilgrims who had the courage to jump overboard or who had climbed down ropes fastened to the rails were picked up by boats from the other ships. When I, having been roused by my launch driver in the middle of the night, arrived on the scene the *Asia* was ablaze from stem to stern and the roar of the flames drowned the cries of despair of the victims of the disaster. Many days later I saw *sambuks* piled with the dead bodies of drowned pilgrims who had been washed ashore to the south on coral reefs and islands. Jedda had proved to be unequal to deal with such emergencies; the crew of the *Asia* too. International regulations for the sea transport of the pilgrims had to be improved and control tightened.

Ibn Sa'ud, with very restricted means, did whatever he could. This problem of human masses, nearly all coming from underdeveloped parts of the world, travelling without experience and often with insufficient means, was absolutely new to him. In those first two years of his rule of the Holy Land of Islam he was confronted with many difficulties. The men from Syria, Egypt,

PILGRIMS LANDING AT JEDDA

JAVANESE PILGRIMS

PILGRIMS LEAVING THE SHIP AT JEDDA

Iraq and other Arab countries who offered their services were as little experienced as he and their standards were very low. Ibn Sa'ud was badly hampered by lack of money, and here we touch upon Ibn Sa'ud's abiding problem. This pageant of humanity that yearly moved towards his country had to be protected and helped but at the same time it brought to his country its means of existence. The first World War had been followed by years of misrule and then of internal war; so it is not to be wondered at that the economic situation was very weak. The King could not afford to lower the pilgrim's taxes, all he could do was to make sure that the pilgrim got service for what he paid so dearly.

The first pilgrimage after the conquest of Jedda had, in the Hejaz, been awaited with small hopes. The outside world neither trusted nor liked Wahhabi doctrine and methods. They were feared, those fanatics from the desert. In that first year of Wahhabi triumph only the brave came to see whether the Holy Land under its new order was safe for pilgrims. The impressions which they took home with them must have been good indeed for the following season of 1926-7 was to bring in a record number of pilgrims. The Dutch Consulate, for instance, had never before registered such a number: more than sixty-five thousand pilgrims came from the Dutch East Indies alone. A sigh of relief went up from the people of the Hejaz and also, no doubt, from the man at the helm. The blessings for which so many prayers had been said, were so sudden and abundant that the country could scarcely cope with them. Transport by primitive motor-buses had made its appearance and began to compete with the camel which had been sanctioned for the performance of the *hajj* by the Prophet himself. When it was seen how great were the profits made in motor transport the government decided to monopolize that trade for itself. But its organization soon broke down much to the satisfaction of the bus companies. Gradually the regulations concerned with the *hajj* improved.

We, the foreign representatives, all of us interested in the well-being of our nationals, saw how vain it was to expect rapid progress in a country as backward as was the Hejaz after centuries of Turkish misrule and ten years of Hashimi administration. Corruption could not be eradicated by fear only. It soon re-appeared and became firmly seated, first in the high places and then in the lower ranks. This evil was beyond Ibn Sa'ud's power to control and possibly he was not very interested in it. To him money and property had never been more than a means to an end. He wanted money, but not for himself to live in luxury. He preferred the beduin way of living, the simple food of the desert, eaten with the fingers, life in tents with the breeze and the smell of the desert around him. That is what he told me and my col-leagues on several occasions when he, after a polite struggle with cutlery, reverted to eating with his hands and praising the best of all food: camel's milk, dates, rice and a whole-cooked sheep. He wanted money to distribute among the poor of the towns, villages and tribes he passed on his way. He wanted to give royal presents to his visitors and to the men who served him. The financial part of the administration he completely left to the untrained hands of his naturally gifted Minister of Finance, his most faithful servant 'Abdullah as-Sulaiman al Hamdan. This man of unimpressive appearance was never prominent in public, but in reality, after the King, he was the most influential person during the whole of the latter's reign. 'Abdullah as-Sulaiman had his own ideas about state finances. He never admitted that such a thing existed, nor did the King. For him it was the King's private money and he as a trusted servant could make free use of it so long as the King's financial demands were met.

In the years of financial straits time-honoured oriental weak-nesses began to appear: lavish gifts to friends and immediate associates and neglect of the under-dog who was often left long in arrears of pay. I saw again around me the seemingly illogical fact that in a very poor country there is always a chance for unscrupulous officials to make money out of the utter poverty of the mass. Here, too, I saw how frugally this semi-desert society could live and how it could tighten its belt round an empty stomach. For, after the years of pilgrim abundance lean years followed. The cost of the administration had to be reduced and owing to the diminishing number of pilgrims those that came had to be taxed more heavily to meet the needs of the state. By acting thus Ibn Sa'ud quickly lost the good reputation he had sought to establish in Muslim countries. The income from the pilgrimage proved to be unstable and was dependent more on uncontrollable circumstances in the outside world than on conditions in Arabia itself. However receipts from the pilgrimage were his main pillar of support and morally a very weak pillar, for whoever depends for his income on other people's obedience to divine laws is in danger of commercializing religion. It is the danger to which all inhabitants of holy places or centres of pilgrimage and devotional ceremonies are exposed. There is much truth in the saying: 'The nearer to Rome the worse the Roman Catholic.' No one was more aware of the demoralization of the Hejazis by their commercialized religion than Ibn Sa'ud and his Wahhabis. They had come to purify the temple and now they felt the contamination attacking themselves. The double task of making the Hejaz a holy land, a place where pilgrims would be able to enter into the presence of Allah and the collection of their money as a means of sustenance for the land was too difficult even for Ibn Sa'ud. He at least saw the danger and wanted to be free of it but in those early years of his rule over the Holy Land he could find no other way of paying for his government.

The income from the *hajj* had now not only to provide for the needs of the Holy Land but also to meet the yearly deficit on the rest of the Wahhabi state. The Hejaz now had to provide for itself and for Nejd as well. Thus to put it crudely the disintegration of Wahhabism set in when the Wahhabis cashed in on the Hejaz. We in Jedda in those years did not know that a remedy was near at hand. All our attention was concentrated on the pilgrimage and most of the local conversation turned on that problem. Would the *hajj* increase in importance in the world of Islam or would obedience to the fifth pillar of the faith decrease? Would the amelioration of conditions in the Holy Land draw more pilgrims to Mecca or would it make this road to salvation ɪose its value? The better hygienic conditions, a modernized transport system, security, in short a stream-lining of the *hajj* in conformity with the rest of the world—would it attract greater numbers of believers? I did not think so.

I spent many hours watching the pilgrim caravans pressing through the narrow Mecca gate of Jedda and then fanning out into the desert when the setting sun lit up the sand and wreathed the distant hills. The pilgrim believes that in going to Mecca he obeys a divine command. At the holy places he will earn manifold blessings. His heart is longing for peace, for happiness, and being a Muslim he yearns to deserve them. That is why Mecca is such an ideal goal for the pilgrim. Mecca, the town of which the *Quʿran* says that 'Allah placed it in a wadi without vegetation', where dark-coloured rocks close in from all sides on the narrow sandy valley. Mecca has no scenery to refresh the eye and its climate is one of the worst imaginable. The night breeze refreshes a town like Jedda, but the walls of rock around Mecca radiate the heat absorbed during the day and the breeze becomes dry and burning hot. Thus the people in Mecca have no respite even at night. No one goes to Mecca to enjoy the scenery or the climate but only in obedience to the will of God, accepting suffering and even seeking hardships in the simple conviction that the promised blessing will then be merited. It is the same with the long, trying journey to reach this land of promise. This journey offers plenty of time for meditation, for prayer and devout living. It provides an opportunity to acquire merit and to reap the blessings reserved for the soul at peace with itself. The attendant circumstances of the pilgrimage should approximate as nearly as possible those of the days of the Prophet. The Holy Land of Islam should not offer material comfort nor resemble the rest of the world. It should remain unchanged, a hard country, so that he who goes there must suffer and sacrifice at least some of the comforts he enjoys in his normal life.

Ibn Saʿud never spoke to me about this but he referred several times to a danger that threatened other Muslim countries. This was that the independence of Muslim nations who were formerly under Western domination led to neglect of the *hajj* by their governments and peoples. Where politics and economics become a national preoccupation religion is pushed into the background. The Holy Land of Islam in the past profited by the fact that Western rulers of Muslim nations never interfered with the freedom of the subjects to perform the *hajj* and this not merely for political reasons but out of respect for religion. Under their rule these countries prospered and the number of pilgrims increased yearly. But other governments have interfered with and restricted the number of pilgrims for various reasons. Russia and Persia, for instance, Afghanistan and modern Turkey. Newly independent Muslim governments have followed the same line and proved that Ibn Sa'ud was right in being apprehensive about the future of the *hajj*.

In our days the *hajj* is rapidly losing its importance. The profits have sunk and other, far more important, sources of income have taken their place in the Sa'udi budget. Pilgrims and pilgrim sheikhs are no longer the chief topic of conversation in Jedda. Pilgrims now walk ashore from ships that tie up alongside a modern pier. They then go straight through concrete customs buildings to 'pilgrim town', a practical, ugly, modern kind of pilgrim barracks and in motor-buses they are carried over an asphalt road to Mecca. An ever-growing number of pilgrims arrive by air and touch the sacred soil of the Hejaz when they climb down to the concrete runway of an American-built aerodrome. If they arrive at night-time they are greeted by the neon lights and advertisements telling them that Coca-Cola will do them good.

I was very fortunate to have been in the Hejaz before the *hajj* was modernized, although I paid for sharing in its picturesque and romantic side by also sharing in the risks to one's health. In those days the presence of pilgrims gave a festive air to the crowded bazaars and lanes of Jedda. The crowds were representatives of all the lands of Islam. They came in their national costumes, often more fitted for snow and hail than the sweltering heat of Jedda. Some put up tents in the open squares of the town or in the desert outside the town wall but the majority waited in houses in Jedda for camel transport. Those camels with cumbersome litters, the so-called *shuqdufs*—which were slung in pairs, one on each side of the animal and protected against the sun by a hood of palm-matting—would choke the streets of the town. How diverting it was to see them being loaded with pilgrims who had never seen a camel before and who were obviously scared by the curious animal. Fear and laughter often go together and so it was when pilgrims from Java took their first ride on a camel. If one had the ear one could also learn much of the Arab art of swearing on those occasions. Then one after the other the caravans would wind out of the gate, men and animals happy to regain the wide open spaces with their silence and fresh desert air. The pilgrims, all dressed in *ihram*, the head of the men shaved, much resembled one another. Yet it was easy to tell which pilgrims were coming. One had only to listen. A caravan of Javanese would resound with the merry gossip and laughter of these grown-up children from Java who had never before seen either desert or camel and enjoyed the excitement of this last part of their long journey. There would be shouts from one *shuqduf* to another until an older traveller would recall the holy purpose of their journey and start reciting some verses of the Qu'ran. A sudden silence would fall on the caravan as the younger members waited for the 'ameen' in which they would join with fervour. Then the whispering would soon begin again, their hearts being too uplifted for them to be silent in those hours of approaching fulfilment. As the music of happiness slowly faded with the passing of that caravan, the sound of the following one would draw nearer. Here instead of laughter there would be whining, short prayers as lamentations; a procession of poor, sorrowful people was drawing near. They must be Indian pilgrims. There were only few *shuqdufs* in their caravan and those who could afford to ride had no money to pay for a protecting hood overhead. Many of their company could not even afford to ride but stumbled painfully through the sand trying to keep up with the long strides of the camels. In true hardship they struggled on the last stretch of their journey. I remember an old, bent, little woman, who, dimly aware of my motor-car parked beside the track, came tottering my way. She evidently hoped for a lift and in a plaintive voice started telling Allah how ill and tired she was and how much she feared to fail so near the goal. Then she came close enough to discover that it was a *nasrani* who was standing there. I saw the expression of her face change to one of horror. Allah! O God! and, starting her complaint anew, she tried to catch up with the caravan that had moved on.

The Indians were followed by the poorest of all the pilgrims to Allah's House: the black men and women from Africa. They had no camels and usually all of them walked. The desert was not new to them, it was no enemy. Their *ihram* was of the cheapest material, a thin yellowish cotton with their black bodies shining through. There was a father, tall and upright with a bundle of spears for self-defence on his shoulder and two or three kettles dangling from it. Then a mother with a cumbrous bundle on her head, some calabashes peeping out of it, a child holding on to her loin-cloth and another being carried on her hip. There followed similar families, quietly and happily walking on with their trust in Allah. They answered with a broad smile when I called out a word of greeting. The black man was a humble man and liked to talk with the *nasrani* who paid attention to him and was kind. I had long talks with some of these men from the Dark Continent and all had a story to tell of their years of travel. They did not walk all the time. "When we got tired and thin, we would stop and work till we were rested and fed and sometimes we had a ride on a railway, sitting together on top of the goods in open vans, in the heat and the dust, but going at speed in the good direction towards Mecca." Simple but moving were the stories I heard. Can one forget a man seen further inland, resting with his lean, naked, little son? I asked him why he took this child with him, exposing him to all the dangers of such a hard journey. Did he not love the child? He stared at me.

"Not love my boy, you said?"

"Why then did you take him with you?"

Then he told me his story. He was well-to-do for a black man, he was happy and he had not thought of going to Mecca. Then he had a dream and on waking up he knew what he had to do. He left his cows and wife and children and started on his way to Mecca. But after some months he got so homesick that he turned round and walked back.

"When I saw that all was right," he continued, "I took this boy with me, I had to have with me someone from home. He was still very small and used to ride on my shoulder as I went. and now, look how tall he is! He walked all the way to Medina and back and now I shall go once more to Mecca to say goodbye to '*Bait Ullah*'.

"How long," I asked, "did it take you to walk to Medina?"

"We did it in forty nights, and back in the same time," and while he said it his eyes caressed the lean black little body beside him.

These are glimpses at the human drama of the *hajj*. They touched me deeply as I have no doubt they would touch any onlooker. One does not associate the tenderer feelings much with Philby but in the early days many is the time that I have seen Philby take some ill or exhausted pilgrim into his car and bring him safely in. I saw this great human striving after salvation while it was still at its peak. Islam is nearing its crisis and so is the *hajj*. Ibn Saʿud's rule of the land of pilgrimage sped the process. He made the *hajj* a safe, healthy and easy undertaking. At the very end of his life, when his land was no longer dependent on the income of the *hajj*, he even made it cheap. In doing all this he made the *hajj* spiritually cheap too. An impressive institution of Islam seems thus to be in rapid decline in the world of Islam today.

10

The Arrival of the Americans

MY FIRST period of service in Arabia came to an end in August 1931. It had been an unusually hot summer. The pilgrimage was over and Jedda had sunk back into her months of rest and into her private self now that all her visitors had left with their small remnant of luggage, their exhausted bodies and their longing to be away from the land where they were no longer welcome. Jedda had entered upon her half year of being left alone, a friendly, dreamy little town where the streets were empty and the *suqs* silenced. Inside the houses one tried to sleep away the heavy hours of the heat waiting for the sunset, when the little breeze of the night would make life supportable for a while. With my head wrapped in a towel and arms leaking on to blotting-paper I sweated through the days finishing my last reports, my farewell to the work I had done in Ibn Sa'ud's country.

My activities had recently extended beyond the borders of the Wahhabi land, for my Government had ordered me to undertake some diplomatic missions. The first was to the other side of the Red Sea to report on conditions in Eritrea where Mussolini no longer made a secret of his imperialistic plans of expansion. For me, with my background of the Civil Service in the Dutch East Indies, it was very interesting to see what Fascism with its young energy and its ruthless short-cut to power did and said. The second journey, a reconnaissance in the Yemen, was a very different task and one I liked much better. The Yemen was a world by itself and an antiquated one. Travelling into this forbidden country where behind the ranges of high, rocky mountains an old, grey-bearded, thick-set patriarch ruled, was for me a

second venture into Arabia. It was a country of inspiring mountain scenery, a museum of antiquity, a land where the friendly
picturesqueness of its people was infinitely attractive to the
traveller from the West. The Yemeni officials were oppressive
but Arabs and Jews alike, and of the latter there were many
living, as always in the Yemen, in segregation, seemed to believe
in a just, fatherly ruler far-away in San'a.

After the Yemeni journey I had set out for what later proved
to be my greatest Arabian adventure and the one that caused me
to be dubbed 'The Dutchman who added a province to the
British Empire.' Our Foreign Department sent me to the Hadhramaut, the native land of the nearly one hundred thousand
Arabs who lived in the Dutch East Indies and who, although
small in number in that great country had for centuries taken an
important place in its religious and economic life. The Hadhramaut had had its Western travellers in the second half of the nineteenth century but since the eighteen-nineties visits had stopped
and I was, much to my astonishment, to inaugurate a new period
of exploration of that unique land of which the world then knew
so little but many of whose inhabitants knew so much of the
world. Some indeed had made great fortunes abroad and returned
home to enjoy them. They had made their wadi into a series of
oases where a notable architecture flourished in the pure Arabian
tradition but where, unhappily, internal wars and blood feuds
banished security. My friend Dr. Von Wissmann accompanied
me and so turned the journey into a scientific mission.

Tired, but much enriched, and more enamoured than ever with
Arabia and Arabs, I returned to Jedda in July 1931. There I
prepared to leave the place where I had seen a great man making
history. There I had been permitted a glimpse of Arabia's mystery,
the greatness of its past and the potentialities of its future. But I
felt that my farewell to Jedda was not to be a goodbye to Arabia.
There was more work there for Von Wissmann and myself. We
had promised each other that one day we would go back to South
West Arabia and try to complete what we had left unfinished.

So the early part of 1939 saw us back in the Aden hinterland

and the Hadhramaut and that seemed to be the end of it so far as I was concerned. Again I went back to the Civil Service in the Dutch East Indies as I had done after leaving Jedda in 1931. Then the second World War came, Holland was overrun and the Netherlands Government transferred itself to London.

There it was decided to send me back to Jedda rather than keep the post vacant because the official nominally in charge had happened to be in Holland when the Germans invaded the country. So from Macassar in Celebes, where I was then an Assistant Resident, my wife and I set out in January 1941 on what proved to be a long and eventful journey. But it ended well when our small party landed safely in Jedda on the first of April 1941. I found a country in much difficulty.

The flow of pilgrims, which up to then had been the principal source of revenue, had practically stopped with the outbreak of the war. Sea transport was seriously imperilled by German submarines and there was a great demand for ships for war purposes. Those employed on regular services were diverted to other uses and the Red Sea remained a danger zone until the Italians in Ethiopia and Eritrea surrendered. As a port Jedda was unvisited. An unusually long period of drought had caused the harvest of *dukhn* and *dhurra*—millet—to fail in nearly the whole of the Arabian Peninsula. Even in good years the harvests of Arabia were never sufficient to satisfy the needs of the population and now famine knocked at the door. Had not Great Britain, hard pressed though she herself was, come to the rescue the consequences might have been much more serious than they were. But in addition to supplying her own territories of Aden with its hinterland and the Hadhramaut for which she had a direct responsibility, England brought relief to Ibn Sa'ud. This was less a question of sympathy than of policy. The British government realized that there was no more effective means of ensuring the goodwill of the Muslim world than in keeping the Holy Land of Islam viable. Thus not only was it necessary for foodstuffs to be sent to Ibn Sa'ud, although he was unable to pay for them, but also money was required to pay his police, army and administrative staff on whom order, security and the organization of government, such as it was, depended.

At regular intervals therefore ships arrived with Canadian flour, Egyptian wheat and Indian rice. From time to time small British patrol boats and larger naval vessels arrived bringing cases of newly minted Sa'udi riyals and English gold pounds, the standard coin of the country. Only those who lived through those anxious days can fully understand what this meant to England at a time when she was fighting alone against a much stronger enemy. Throughout the whole of that period there was never any shortage of food in the centres of Muslim pilgrimage and no great rise in the cost of living. Great Britain gave effective help to Ibn Sa'ud from the dark beginning till the victorious end of the struggle. For his part Ibn Sa'ud had contacts with the Germans but was quite outspoken in front of us, Representatives from the West, even in public audience, in declaring that Winston Churchill was the outstanding leader of the war and that he, with Allah's help, would lead the Allies to victory. Seldom could his word have carried so much useful weight in the Muslim world.

Yet the situation in Arabia did not make this attitude easy for him at all. Sa'udi government officials were, without exception, markedly pro-German. Philby himself did not seem to believe that England could once more be victorious in a war against Germany. He decided to go to the United States on a lecturing tour and propagate his rather defeatist ideas dressed in the garments of love of world peace. Philby seemed not to understand the real danger of Hitlerism, the imperative need to protect the world from it and the inescapable fact that immunity could only be achieved by force. For Ibn Sa'ud it must have been a relief when Philby left Arabia on his way to America via India. The French Minister in Jedda, who later was to desert the ranks of the Allies, vehemently insisted on Philby's being put under arrest before he could do any further harm. In Bombay Philby was arrested and sent to England where he was under supervision until the course of events rendered his defeatist views innocuous.

The English are said to be bad starters and so indeed it seemed again in the first two years of the war when everything went wrong for them. The Germans on the other hand made excellent propaganda use of their initial victories. They had with them in Berlin an Iraqi journalist-adventurer, Yunus al Bahri, whom I had met in Jedda in autumn 1930 and in the Yemen when we both were travelling there in the beginning of 1931. At that time he called himself 'as-Sa'ih al Iraqi'—the Iraqi traveller—and he could scarcely then have foreseen how high his star was to rise when Hitler provided him with a rostrum from which to address the whole Arab world. Yunus al Bahri was an immense success. His mordant tones were perfectly attuned to Arab ears and he quickly became the darling of coffee-shops throughout the Middle East. His heroes were the conquering Nazis and his butts the weakling English and their feeble allies. Germany was the real friend of the Arabs. In the Jews, did she not share the same enemy? The mercurial Yunus was soon to be joined in Berlin by another dangerous opponent of English policy in Arabia, the former Grand Mufti of Jerusalem, Al Hajj Amin al Husaini.

Although the number of wireless sets was small in these poor countries they attracted large, attentive audiences. The great success of Mussolini's Bari broadcasting station followed by the even more dangerous Berlin one convinced the B.B.C. that it was not sufficient to broadcast in one language, even though it was the world language of English. Events in the Arab world showed the B.B.C. that her previous attitude was wrong and so the first foreign language broadcast was made from London and was in classical Arabic, a world language too.

During this period of Allied reverses my Government sent me on a mission to the Ruler of the Yemen, the Imam Yahya. I arrived at San'a, the capital, in August 1942. Those who comprised the Imam's government were well informed of the German viewpoint, for they of course listened to Yunus al Bahri, the Grand Mufti and other Arab speakers of the Berlin Radio. When I asked the Imam's Secretary of Foreign Affairs, Qadhi Muhammad Raghib, whether they ever listened to the B.B.C. he pretended to be offended. "Of course we do! Did not I tell you my government is neutral? We listen to all the voices in the air." Early next morning after this conversation Qadhi Raghib sent me a letter with the text of what the B.B.C. had broadcast the previous night and throughout my stay in San'a the B.B.C. news bulletin in Arabic was handed to me every morning.

Later I had a talk with the Qadhi about broadcasting.

"Do you believe everything you hear on the German radio or do you think that the B.B.C. may possibly be correct?"

"We know, dear friend, that the air is full of lies. We don't give our confidence to either of them."

"What do you think of this B.B.C.?"

"Dull, hopelessly dull, I tell you. That man speaks just like the fellow of the weather forecast. Dull facts given in a monotonous voice. Then take the Berlin speakers! It is sheer delight to listen to them. Sparks seem to spring from the wireless set when they are speaking. Do you like that dull English way?"

"Your Excellency, that is exactly what I like about the British and what gives me confidence in their broadcasts. This man of the B.B.C. cannot be funny and he ought not try. There is no reason for us to joke. All the news is sad news for us and that man speaks like the weather forecaster because he tells the truth. That is why I like him."

I hoped that I spoilt some of Qadhi Raghib's enjoyment of the Berlin radio in Arabic.

But to go back to Jedda where I had arrived on 1st April 1941. During the night of our crossing from Port Sudan to Jedda the sea battle for Massawa was fought. We only saw the flashes of the salvoes of the warships and heard the rumble of the guns. Next day towards sunset the first group of escaping Italian seamen approached Jedda walking along the shore from the south. They were dead tired and straggled along showing every sign of hunger and thirst. They were stark naked, sunburnt and very dirty. The population came pouring out of the gates to witness this unheard-of spectacle and followed them as they were guided to the barracks.

"These are no men. They must be monkeys," I heard some

Arabs say. Word went round through the town asking owners of motor vehicles to go out with water and bread to meet the men who came from ships that were sunk farther to the south.

The local credit of Vichy France was at that time far from high. The Vichy Minister in Jedda had lost all influence and sympathy but he stayed on and tried to make the views of Pétain acceptable to the King. The Italians in the town were soon fortified by two thousand of their compatriots, the crews of those brand-new Italian torpedo-boats that had escaped from Massawa when the English attacked it. The ships had not succeeded in reaching the neutral harbour of Jedda and ran ashore south of the town. The crews were interned and sent to the quarantine islands south of Jedda. The Italians were hated by the Arabs because of their conquest of Ethiopia and despised because they did not put up a better fight against the British. After the battle of Matapan in 1942 the Allies no longer objected to the repatriation of the Italian naval crews and with them our Italian colleague, who had become very lonely in Jedda, disappeared from the Arabian scene. The Vichy colleague followed when his money ran out and he received no further supplies from his government. But Vichy treason opened the door to a bold German attack on Arabia. With Vichy-governed Syria as a base and refuelling station for German planes Rashid 'Ali raised the standard of revolt in Iraq. The 'Golden Square', so called because the four leaders were bought with German gold, nearly succeeded in throwing the country open to the Germans. They failed and Rashid 'Ali Gulaini took refuge in ar-Riyadh where he was personally safe and politically no longer a danger.

Another, more spectacular, German effort that commanded the attention of the Arab world over a much longer period was Rommel's campaign in the Western desert. He too failed in his effort to force a way for Germany into Arabia. When his army stood at al 'Alamain where at night the lights of Alexandria could be seen reflected in the sky, Rommel in Berlin spoke these proud words: "I have my foot between the doors of the gate to Egypt and I shall enter through them." Rommel did not enter those doors but his victories in the Western desert caused a panic in Egypt and Palestine and again it was not easy for an Arab ruler to remain faithful to the Allies.

When the fortunes of war began to turn the Arabs gradually turned with them and began to believe what Ibn Sa'ud re-iterated that justice was on the side of the Allies and that therefore Allah would give them victory. When America had taken her place in the ranks of the Allies Ibn Sa'ud's entourage grudgingly admitted that the King had been right and that Germany would be defeated again.

It now became urgent for England to be relieved of a part of her responsibilities in Arabia, and America began to help finan-cially, in the food supply and in a scheme for military training. Sa'udi Arabia welcomed this fresh source of assistance. America was big and rich and had long aroused great expectations in the Arabs. Her motor-cars had conquered the desert tracks of Sa'udi Arabia and the people that built the strongest, most durable, and shiniest motor-cars could be sure of the admiration of Middle East countries. They had great expectations of America, as a rich, new nation with vast technical resources.

Ibn Sa'ud did not let his sympathies be guided by motor-cars or riches but his increasing financial difficulties pressed him in their direction. Before America took a share in the second World War and before she took over the greater part of British relief work in Sa'udi Arabia Ibn Sa'ud had already met a vanguard of American technicians. He had met them at a time when the rapidly falling revenues from the *hajj* forced him to see that the pilgrimage was too uncertain and too feeble a source of income for a modernized Arabia. Although the acquisition of wealth had never been a preoccupation of Ibn Sa'ud it was clear to him that he must have a large and regular income to ensure the healthy growth of his kingdom. Where could he find that wealth? He had first sought the advice of those who administered the land from which came the pilgrims that brought most money into his country, that is the people of Java and neighbouring islands. Under the Dutch those islands had become prosperous and the

Dutch themselves had the reputation of being very rich. Skilled in money matters, they were a nation too small ever to become a danger to the Sa'ud. So when Ibn Sa'ud wanted a bank he gave the monopoly for his country to a Dutch bank. This had been done immediately after his occupation of Jedda in 1926 when the Netherlands Trading Society started an agency. And for prospective sources of wealth within his own borders he asked the Dutch government to send him specialists to prospect for minerals. That minerals existed he was sure. Every Arab of education knew that ancient authors and even the holy books of Jews and Christians mentioned Arabia as a land of gold, incense and myrrh. Western science should be able to trace the veins of gold and to exploit them on modern lines. And who knew what other minerals, including such as had become valuable only in modern times, might not come to light?

The Dutch geologists produced an extensive plan for a geological survey of the whole country which would take time and cost much money but would at least ensure that nothing would be overlooked. But the stipulation that funds to cover the cost should, before the work started, be lodged in the Dutch Bank in Jedda was inacceptable to the Sa'udi government and caused the plan to be rejected. This happened in 1928. Other small nations were invited and produced less elaborate and so less expensive projects. But before anything could be undertaken two remarkable Americans appeared in Sa'udi Arabia: the multi-millionaire Charles Crane and the man who carried out his Arabian plans, Karl S. Twitchell.

Mr. Crane's hobby was to make the acquaintance of outstanding men in the East. Already in the autumn of 1926 he had appeared in Jedda where he fulfilled a wish to shake hands with the man who had proved stronger than King-Khalifa Husain, the Ruler at the time of Mr. Crane's earlier visit to Jedda. Mr. Crane, whose father had made a fortune out of sanitary fittings, was out for no personal advantage: on the contrary he wanted these lands and peoples of his fancy to benefit from his wealth. He had paid for the Western education of promising but poor sons of outstanding Arabs. He had supported youth organizations and Boy Scout work in Iraq and Syria but he wanted to do some more, something on a greater scale and of more lasting effect.

The Yemen as the most backward, and at the same time potentially one of the richest, of the Arab countries had been first chosen for his munificence after his visit to the Imam in Sanʿa in the winter of 1926-7, and many were the opportunities Twitchell and his helpers saw in the Yemen. The strong winds that blow unceasingly along the coastal strip of the Tihama gave them the idea of importing American windmills to raise water for irrigation purposes and also to generate electric power for lighting plants. The plan worked and on my visit to the Yemen in the beginning of 1931 I saw some of the windmills still in working order and electric bulbs burning in the palace of Saif al Islam Muhammad, one of Imam Yahya's sons, who was then Governor of Hodeida. The title means Sword of Islam, and is given to all the sons of the Imam.

Twitchell and his men believed it possible to change the sandy wastes of the Tihama into date-groves with the water raised by their windmills and being good Americans they did not believe in the use of the backs of donkeys and camels for carrying purposes but imported big-wheeled wagons from America to be drawn by those animals. They made greater plans for transport and wanted to build a road for motor traffic between the port of Hodeida and the mountain capital, Sanʿa, nearly 7,000 feet above sea-level. And so they started to bridge a *wadi* through which periodically great floods rushed towards the sea. On my way from the capital back to Hodeida, I insisted on travelling along the Crane-Twitchell motor road. It was a real adventure and only a skilled driver could bring one safely down from the mountains to the Tihama. Many more years of work and much money would still have had to be spent on this road to make it a safe motor road. In the foothills I met Twitchell's assistant trying to rebuild an iron bridge that had been severely damaged by the floods. Alas, the bridge was never completed, the existing southern route was preferred by the Imam and the American road languished.

Poor indeed were the results of all Twitchell's efforts in the

Yemen. His ideas were sound and his practical methods would have led to good results in any normal country but the Yemen was by no means normal. Its population was backward and the rulers of the land more backward still. They were full of suspicion and fear that once the outside world were let in there would be an end to their independence. So after five years of frustration Twitchell advised his patron to withdraw and turn north where a man of a very different calibre was the ruler.

Ibn Sa'ud welcomed Twitchell. He, and even more his Minister of Finance, 'Abdullah as-Sulaiman, saw in him a most providential arrival and Twitchell gradually came to realize that he had found the chance of a lifetime. The King first asked him to prospect for water. The results were not encouraging in the Hejaz but proved to be better in Al Hasa. The King was appreciative of Twitchell's activities and of his reports and he asked him to continue prospecting. 'Abdullah as-Sulaiman in search of fresh sources of income thought of gold and possibly oil. Twitchell was convinced that there must be gold in Arabia for he knew his Bible and believed what was written in it. Beduin sheikhs had told 'Abdullah as-Sulaiman of ancient workings of gold-mines they had seen in the interior and Twitchell went to investigate them. Was it the name that drew him first to al Mahad adh-Dhahab (the Cradle of the Gold), an ancient mine some fifty miles south of Medina? Beduin information had been right, for here in olden days people had dug and cut into the mountains. And so it was that at Mahad adh-Dhahab, two hundred and forty-six miles inland from Jedda, Twitchell made the first effort to extract gold in Arabia since Biblical times.

Great technical difficulties had to be overcome, a road had to be built and water had to be made available in virtually unlimited quantities. Expert labour had to be imported and it was not easy to get American miners to work so far away in the heat of the Arabian desert. Alcohol was strictly forbidden them and the way of life of this vanguard of Western Christians so near the holy, and to them forbidden, precincts of Medina was subject to severe constraint. But the lessons learnt there were not restricted to mining. The Saʿudi government learnt how to handle foreigners working in their midst and the Americans learnt to behave in such a way as not to offend Wahhabi sensibilities. The gold-mine was no great financial success. It could not stand up to the competition of the richer veins of South African gold and had not the second World War caused the price of gold to soar this pioneer mining activity in Saʿudi Arabia would probably have soon come to an end. As it was, it managed to survive and only now, in 1955, is it reported that the 'Cradle of the Gold' is about to close down.

In 1940 Ibn Saʿud, whose confidence in Twitchell had steadily grown, asked him if he could find anyone interested in making a thorough examination of the water resources and agricultural possibilities of Nejd. Twitchell tried privately in the United States but did not succeed and then the State Department stepped in and offered to send a government mission. This was to be the first official mission of goodwill sent by the United States to Ibn Saʿud. Twitchell himself was made Head of the Mission and J. G. Hamilton of the Soil Conservation Service and A. L. Wathen, Chief Engineer of the Bureau of Indian Affairs, were its members. Both the latter men had years of experience in the desert parts of the south-western states of America. In Cairo the mission was joined by the United States Minister to Egypt, Alexander Kirk, his staff and some military advisers who were going to use this excellent opportunity to establish the first American Legation in Saʿudi Arabia. The party travelled by air via Bahrain to the camp of Ibn Saʿud which was pitched some fifty miles south of Ruma Wells. The plane made a good landing on a strip of desert and then and there Mr. Alexander Kirk handed his credentials to the King of Saʿudi Arabia. A few moments later he introduced the first American Agricultural Mission to His Majesty. With the King were his sons, the Amir al Ahd—Crown Prince—Saʿud, who was Governor of Nejd and the Amir Faisal, Viceroy of the Hejaz and, of course, the Finance Minister, Sheikh ʿAbdullah as-Sulaiman al Hamdan to whom, with Twitchell, the presence of the mission was due.

The Americans, from the Minister down to the lowest member

of his staff, could have had no finer introduction to Arabia's great beduin King than at this audience in the desert. It appealed to their romantically naïve idea of Arabia. They were completely captivated next day when the whole party was invited to ar-Riyadh (that stronghold of Wahhabism into which no Western Christian could enter unless invited by Ibn Sa'ud himself) as guests in the King's Murabba'a palace. The Crown Prince had given them a lunch in Western style. The King fed his guests in the beduin way. Mr. Kirk described to me how they had sat round a wide table, and how in a long line in the middle of the table were placed eight huge copper platters heaped with pyramids of rice. On the top of each pyramid of rice rested a whole sheep. Around the platters the rest of the menu, from start to finish, was arranged in a colourful disorder. Then the Amir Sa'ud had regaled his guests with the newest and most un-Wahhabi entertainment of the town of those days: sound films sent to him as a present from the British Legation in Jedda. And so on news-reels the Americans and the younger Sa'udi generation saw the meeting of President Roosevelt and Prime Minister Churchill on the Atlantic Ocean. England and America together in the very heart of Sa'udi Arabia.

America's advent was not looked upon by England as that of an intruder, rather were the Americans welcomed as helpers in a task that was weighing too heavily on England alone.

In 1943 another, chiefly military, mission was sent under General Royce and this was followed in the same year by a third under Lieutenant-Colonel Hoskins. But the real guide of America in her first steps into that difficult and completely unfamiliar land was Colonel William A. Eddy, her first, and for a long time to be, the foremost diplomat in Ibn Sa'ud's country. He arrived in Jedda in the beginning of 1944. The son of a missionary, he grew up in the little town of Sa'ida (Sidon). There he learnt to speak Arabic with the local Arab boys as one of them and to understand the Arab way of life as we his colleagues in Jedda could never hope to do. Although he was the last of the small body of foreign representatives to arrive in Jedda during the years of the second World War, he and his wife were soon looked upon as old friends and were given a central place in our foreign colony.

As I have said, before America had put in her official appearance in Arabia there had been forerunners announcing her approach. Crane and Twitchell had shown a philanthropical influence combined with a practical and technical appreciation of possible openings. Not only had Twitchell started the exploitation of gold but had also revived prospecting for oil. Whilst at Ruma Wells there were representatives of the two activities by which America was to be chiefly identified with Saʿudi Arabia: water and oil. For water there was Twitchell and the Agricultural Mission; and for oil Floyd Ohliger and Max Steineke who had joined the Ministerial party at Bahrain.

The question of the country's water I will reserve for a later chapter. Here I shall deal only with the question of oil. As far back as December 1931 ʿAbdullah as-Sulaiman had asked Twitchell to investigate the possibilities of oil along Al Hasa coast of the Persian Gulf. Seeing the geological connexion between the Bahrain Isles and the adjacent Al Hasa coast, Twitchell advised waiting to see what progress was made in prospecting for oil in Bahrain. When the results proved to be favourable Twitchell was asked to find people in America interested in the oil of Saʿudi Arabia. The former British concession had lapsed and so the road was clear. America of those years was in the throes of an economical crisis and it was hard to find listening ears. But Twitchell is a tough American who tenaciously pursues his object and he finally succeeded in convincing the heads of the Standard Oil of California that the Saʿudi proposition was a promising one. Twitchell in his *Saʿudi Arabia* commends these men for the foresight that gave America control of what was to prove to be possibly the greatest oil reserve in the world.

Negotiations with the Saʿudi Government came to a successful conclusion in Jedda in May 1933 and a special company was formed for the production of oil in Arabia and called the California Arabian Standard Oil Company, later to change its name to the Arabian American Oil Company, known to the world of our day as 'Aramco'. An advance to the Sa'udi Government of thirty thousand gold pounds was paid by the Americans to the Netherlands Trading Society in Jedda and then the work could begin. The new oil company was fortunate in being able to profit by the services of a man like Twitchell, who was so well-informed on matters of local knowledge in Sa'udi Arabia and was so experienced in dealing with the local authorities. In the autumn 1933, the Jabal Dhahran, a conspicuous dome formation, was chosen for the first probe in Arabia's desert soil. The probe had to be a very deep one but once oil had been struck it was not long before the Americans could proudly assert that "the deserts of this land are floating on oil".

It was England who had done the preliminary work for the penetration of the West into Arabia and now the moment was drawing near in which the age-long barriers were to be lowered. Ibn Sa'ud became convinced that Central Arabia must become a modernized state and that it had fallen to him to lead his people out of their traditional seclusion. There was no question now of admitting only a few individuals. Whole armies of foreigners with their infernal machines must be granted admission if a new Arabia was to be built in the place of the old that could provide no future for its inhabitants.

Although they might be said to have an acquired right to the task and the necessary political experience it was not the British who were to transform Arabia into this new Land of Promise, but the newcomers whose qualifications were technical rather than historical or political and for whom the lack of past contacts was an advantage rather than a drawback. When Turkey disappeared from the Arabian scene, England took over and cleared the path along which America was to reap rewards that no one had ever expected to find waiting in desert Arabia. I could not help feeling sad at this turn in the wheel of fortune and of fate. Sad, too, for the Englishmen in Arabia who saw the reins slipping from their worn hands.

America however was not entirely new in the Arabian field.

American missionary effort had begun there at the turn of the century but had been confined to the periphery of the peninsula. At that time some American missionary leaders had decided that the heart of Islam could not be approached by the traditional missionary method of preaching the gospel. That is the method of direct attack, and it was felt better to try an indirect method. They felt that by the spread of Western education in Arab countries closed doors could be opened and a common meeting-ground prepared on which East and West could listen to each other. Other American Christians were not satisfied with this proposal but wished to combine the indirect with the direct methods. The supporters of the indirect method founded the three American Universities along the Western border of Arabia: Robert College in Istanbul, and the American Universities in Beirut and Cairo. Those in favour of the compromise method began operations along the eastern borders of Arabia where British political influence was strong enough to protect them. Education and medical aid were prominent in their work, but preaching of the Gospel never failed, and in Bahrain they have more than half a century to their credit. For their Arab staffs the Legation, and even more Aramco, drew largely on former pupils of these American Universities.

The arrival of the Americans in Jedda made a great change in the life of the foreign colony there. As soon as it was decided that a Legation was to be established in Jedda American technicians were sent from Cairo to supervise the equipment of offices and living quarters. Both were screened against mosquitoes and flies, air-conditioned and equipped with electric light and refrigerators. Up to then (it was the end of 1942) all of us had gone without these expensive innovations and had paid for it with frequent illnesses. The British Minister was the only one who had an air-cooler in his room and in that one room he worked and slept. The Americans provided material comfort for every member of their staff and were rewarded in the quality of the work done and the absence of sickness and sick leave. Their example was gradually followed by the other foreigners, and, after some hesitation, by the leading Arabs too.

When the equipment of the American military mission was brought ashore I looked at it in amazement. Such vehicles I had never seen. There were large, all-steel cars big enough to work, eat and sleep in. With my experience of travel in Arabia it seemed incredible that one could go into the desert, cool, free from flies and mosquitoes and with iced drinks. I said to the sergeants in charge: "Do you people realize that no asphalt roads exist in this country? How do you propose to transport those huge wagons and all your other machinery, your sleeping- and dining-cars, your cinema, your kitchen wagons, ice plants and so on across roadless desert?"

"We have powerful tractors," they replied.

"So I see, but they will not work in soft sand."

"We are going to take all this up to the mountains of Taif. If one tractor is not enough to move our machinery we will put on others until it does move. If need be we can add jeeps."

They did arrive in Taif with all their equipment and were warmly welcomed by the young Sa'udi officers. The American instructors soon outshone the British with their free cigarettes, chewing-gum and iced water—in the liberal use they made of films for purposes of instruction, and in the nightly talkie shows they gave. America showed how a completely new way of life could be introduced into desert Arabia if one had the money.

Although American oil activity in Arabia had begun under the guidance of Twitchell in 1933, the war had hindered development because American financers were reluctant to spend money on distant projects. But when America joined the Allied war effort the position changed completely. The nearest source of oil supply for the Japanese front, which was America's particular responsibility, was the Middle East and so Aramco suddenly came in to the limelight. Development became a war priority and for this none was happier than the Sa'udi Government. The oil town of Dhahran sprang up in the desert almost overnight. More crude oil was produced than could be handled, so a small refinery in Dhahran was soon got going while a big one was under construction at Ras Tanura, some thirty miles to the north on the

Persian Gulf, and crude oil was carried by pipe-line over the bottom of the shallow sea to the existing refinery in the Bahrain islands. Now, at last, Ibn Sa'ud was getting the money he wanted for the growing needs of his state. He no longer had to ask for loans that he could never pay back, nor for subsidies of money, food supplies, and arms.

For Sa'udi Arabia a new chapter in her struggle had begun. From now on Ibn Sa'ud's attention was concentrated on the Americans. America in those happy first days of courtship with her romantic Arabia-bride was so enamoured of the people of her fantasy and so impressed by the great ruler she met in Arabia that she saw the future in nothing but the rosiest colours. The Arabs, for their part, were much impressed by the technical wonders the Americans brought to their deserts. Oil-money and oil-equipment and, particularly, as we shall see, the water the Americans produced meant a revolution in desert life. All this was a revelation to the Arabs who up till then had justifiably believed in their supremacy in the desert. So now the attitude of the desert Arab towards foreigners, the white *nasranis* from the West, began to change. Never had they appeared before him in such numbers nor had reports of them spread so far. For almost the first time these were encouraging reports. The Americans brought about the first meeting of many Westerners with many desert Arabs. Up till then the contact of the desert Arab with the Westerner had been sporadic and limited to the Consul or Political Officer or occasional traveller. The Westerners in Arabia, for their part, had hitherto mostly restricted themselves to those Arabs who lived in similar conditions to themselves, that is to the higher classes of Arab society. The workings for gold had brought no change to this situation. The mine was only a small one and the profits made were so low that the Americans employed were forced to live as soberly as the little foreign colony in Jedda.

But on the eastern side of the country something very different now appeared. Towards the end of 1944 I went to Dhahran to see for myself what was happening. My Government, then in exile in London, was anxious to learn about the Americans in Arabia.

The King had given me permission to pay him a courtesy visit in his capital and then to proceed to the Persian Gulf coast. On this journey I came to grief five times—the last time between the capital and the coast when the last of the five spare axles I had brought with me from Jedda broke. We had a hundred miles still to go when a rescue party found us and brought us to the haven of Dhahran where we were soon at the end of our troubles. And a haven indeed it proved to be for us. The oil camp had been built at great speed not by Americans but by Italians flown in from Ethiopia and Eritrea where they had been made prisoners of war. Italians can stand heat and hard conditions. Thousands of workmen were also imported from India and Iraq and it was only after they had built these air-conditioned, fly-proof living and working quarters that the permanent staff of the oil personnel moved in.

On the eastern side of Ibn Sa'ud's kingdom not only had an oil town come into being but oil camps were scattered around in the desert where the gulf between the Americans and the local desert population was wide and deep. Spiritually the Americans were as dangerous as they were unfamiliar to the Wahhabis who had never before had such contacts. Not only the beduins and the people living in the nearby oasis towns of Al Qatif and Al Hasa but even the Governors of the King were confronted with problems they were unable to solve. I remember my accompanying the first American Consul in Dhahran, whom I had known in Jedda, on visits to the local Sa'udi Governors. Good Wahhabis they were, members of the Sudairi and the Jiluwi families and their problem was always the same: they were the true servants of Allah and strove day after day to do His will, the Americans on the other hand gave no sign of belief in God at all; they, the Wahhabis, were poor and constrained, the Americans were wealthy and unrepressed. How was that possible, God being righteous? Something was wrong somewhere, but where and what was it? Yet Allah did not make mistakes!

Ibn Sa'ud realized that he had to give a lead to his Wahhabis. When Mecca was conquered by his troops he had then been faced with a problem. There the Wahhabis had met Muslims, orientals with the same spiritual background as their own. They had met them with a positive message. The Wahhabis were convinced that they had found again the path of true belief and that their mission to purify Islam did not stop in Mecca but in fact only began there. The international Islam they met in Mecca, however, turned away from them and the spiritual leaders of Wahhabism did not learn from this setback. Wahhabism did not modify its doctrine and its failure in Mecca brought with it no spiritual crisis. Conflicting points of view met and parted without fertilization but also without mutual damage. The Wahhabi did not lose his convictions or his self-confidence. All he lost in Mecca was his expectation of the revival of a purified Islam.

What the Wahhabis met on the other side of Sa'udi Arabia was very different: they met the American way of life. Just that. Neither its basis nor its spiritual background was visible but only its outward appearance in a technical setting, scientific knowledge and highly developed skill, a mechanized culture and a very high standard of living. Here Wahhabism had nothing to offer and no hope of convincing these Americans who seemed to be utterly remote even from a primitive recognition of Allah as the First, the One from whom all things derived. Ibn Sa'ud seemed to have no better solution than that of preventing, as far as possible, contact between Americans and his subjects. Americans were a spiritual danger to his Arabs and so to prevent spiritual infection they had to be kept at a distance. That was the Muslim side of the encounter. There was another, the American side, and that, in my view, was even more deplorable than the Sa'udi.

The Americans decided to enter the religious Arabia of the Wahhabis without introducing their own religion. I do not know whether this was a condition Ibn Sa'ud imposed on them, or if they themselves suggested it, or whether, by mutual consent, it was left unmentioned. If so, it was little to the credit of either party. The early Ibn Sa'ud was a man of faith and a respecter of other people's. It is not to be imagined that he would himself suggest the introduction of open evidence of Christian worship in his dominions but he would certainly have responded to any advance made by the other side. The early Ibn Sa'ud abhorred the atheist and materialist. Had then he himself changed? Had the relations of God to man and man to God lost their value in his eyes? It seems so. The earlier Ibn Sa'ud would not have been content with thinking that the Americans were not interested in religion but only in oil and money.

In their timorousness the Americans had taken refuge in believing that the problem of the open profession of the Christian faith was not ripe for discussion. Let us, they said, wait ten years. By that time the Arabs will have become accustomed to our presence, we shall have established ourselves in the country and can then bring up the matter.

If the Americans had, from the start, insisted on entering the country as confessed Christians with open freedom for their belief, such an attitude would have commanded Ibn Sa'ud's respect. As it was, America came to this land of religion without the right to build churches, to have ministers of religion living among them, and that equivalent of the Muslim *mu'ezzin* the tolling of bells to announce services. She should have insisted upon these rights which would have put the relations of Christian Westerners with ultra-religious Muslims on a sound foundation. These first Americans discarded one essential element in any real contact, for the Arab who believes will only trust the Christian if he shows that he too believes in the One God. They made a profound initial mistake, and even if it is not irreparable the harm it has done will last long.

Ibn Sa'ud decided on strict measures to ward off the danger of moral and spiritual infection from the American camps. When I visited Dhahran and other oil centres towards the end of 1944 Americans were not allowed to leave their camps and go to the villages or to the beduin tribes. Once a week, on Fridays, outings were arranged for parties going by bus to the oases and towns like Hufhuf, to the coast at Al Khobar, Dammam or to Al Qatif and its date-groves. These excursions were well supervised. Arabs were not allowed in places where the Americans lived if their work did not oblige them to go there. The film-shows, often given in the

open, were strictly barred to the Arabs. Wahhabism was originally strongly opposed to pictures of living beings and 'Abd al
Wahhab had been a stern enemy of our music because it came
after the Prophet and so had not been sanctioned by him. So
far as films are concerned one can sympathize with Arab authorities in their aversion to some of the products of Hollywood.

Even football and other games played by the Americans at first
gave rise to difficulties with the Wahhabi authorities. To appear
in public in shorts was deemed indecent for a man and they had
no words for a woman who dared appear in public as she should
only appear to her husband.

Much of this original severity was relaxed and many a ban was
lifted when Sa'udi Arabia got used to the increasing number of
Americans living on her borders and gradually moving inland
with their complicated train of machinery. It proved impossible to
keep young Wahhabi Arabia away from the openly-shown films
and their music and from American sports. Those stern Wahhabi
'ulama fought a losing battle, human nature being stronger than
doctrine. And in this respect it was the individual American whose
democratic, direct and unprejudiced attitude towards the Arab
helped most.

The Wahhabi attitude to the problem was at the start negative:
it sought to avoid difficulty by prohibition. This attitude of fear
was bound to fail. I expected this to happen when I first saw the
situation with my own eyes and subsequent visits confirmed my
anticipation. Although Ibn Sa'ud was still in full command of his
faculties and still had his people completely in hand, it was
becoming clear that in his country something had begun to move.
When the rain comes down the barren wadis of Arabia it takes the
form of a *sail*—a water-flood—that sweeps everything before it.
Some such catastrophe was now bearing down on Arabia as a
result of this clash of two so widely different people of such diverse
spiritual composition. Mercilessly this *sail* was to tear at Wahhabi
doctrine, at the proud self-satisfied life of the desert, and at the
composed, if not tranquil, life of the country. America had set the
sail in motion and who knows what the end will be?

The Palestine Problem

ALTHOUGH in principle Ibn Saʻud set his limits on the borders of Saʻudi Arabia yet he could not remain aloof from two problems of wider geographical range: the Arab League and Palestine, problems that for Arabs were inseparable. The Balfour declaration of November 1917 had had for them alarming consequences. In January 1918 D. G. Hogarth went expressly to Jedda to give King Husain an explicit assurance on behalf of the British Government that the Jewish settlement in Palestine would only be allowed in so far as it was compatible with 'the political and economic freedom' of the Arab population. King Husain was to learn later into what an entanglement of conflicting promises and declarations the British Government had tied itself and to realize that he had been leaning on a reed that was to pierce his hand, before it broke under him. As time went on the Arab nations grew increasingly alarmed at the turn of events in Palestine and Ibn Saʻud naturally followed the situation very closely. As, however, England was responsible for the administration of Palestine he did not openly criticize the Zionist experiment started under her protection.

During my first visit to Palestine in December 1941 I had the good fortune to meet in Jerusalem the President of the Hebrew University, Professor Judah Magnes. I questioned him on the possibility of a peaceful solution of the problem. Dr. Magnes believed it possible and, to my astonishment, even saw in the Arabs a readiness to come to terms with the Jews. I asked him whether he had sound reasons for his optimism and found that they were better than I expected. King Faisal's attitude at the Peace Conference in Paris and his draft agreement with Dr. Chaim

Weizmann were mentioned. This agreement was Chaim Weizmann's effort to get Faisal's co-operation (he was referred to as representing and acting on behalf of the Arab Kingdom of the Hejaz) in furthering the national aspirations of both parties through the closest possible collaboration in the development of the Arab State and Palestine. Its nine articles deal amongst other minor matters with the proper execution of the Balfour declaration, the encouragment of large-scale Jewish immigration, the protection of the rights of Arab peasants and the free exercise of religion. The full text is to be found in Appendix F of George Antonius' book. Although this agreement was not well received in the Arab world and in any case became of no effect because Faisal's condition that it should be dependent upon the Arabs obtaining their independence was not fulfilled, it seemed to give proof of Arab readiness to accept the idea of a Jewish State in Palestine. Faisal was at the time no doubt anxious to gain every possible bit of support he could obtain in British and even Jewish quarters.

More impressive, to me at least, was an exchange of letters between Magnes and Philby in which the latter spoke of Arab willingness to come to terms and in which he mentioned a feasible plan. I could not help being less optimistic than Philby. If the majority of the Zionist leaders had been of Magnes' mentality I might have believed in peace between Jew and Arab in Palestine. But I had heard too much already of bitter Jewish opposition to Magnes and his small following in Palestine to think that Magnes could sway his co-religionists. Was Philby for his part more representative of the Arab view than Magnes proved to be of the Zionist one? I doubted it. Philby was a stout supporter of the Arabs but he was a man used to speaking for himself. He could not be considered the official mouthpiece of ar-Riyadh.

Details of the Philby plan for a Jewish State in Palestine appeared in his book, *Arabian Jubilee*, where he proposes 'to aim at an obtainable quid pro quo at the expense of an undeniable right'. In that book at least twice and in the same wording he declares: 'I have always held and still hold that the Jews have not a shadow of

A PART OF THE ROYAL PALACE, AL-MURABBA‘A, AR-RIYADH, 1944

FROM A WINDOW IN AR-RIYADH, LOOKING OVER THE MARKET PLACE
TOWARDS THE CENTRAL MOSQUE

KING IBN SAʿUDʾS PALACE, AL-MURABBAʿA, AT A MILEʾS DISTANCE FROM
AR-RIYADH, 1952

legal or historical right to Palestine.' But he proposed (a) that the whole of Palestine should be left to the Jews, (b) that all displaced Arabs should be resettled elsewhere at the expense of the Jews (a sum of £20 million being placed by them at the disposal of King Ibn Sa'ud for this purpose) and (c) that all the other Asiatic Arab countries, except Aden, should be formally recognized as completely independent. These arrangements were to be guaranteed by Great Britain and America jointly with King Ibn Sa'ud as the principal Arab ruler.

What Ibn Sa'ud thought of all this Philby does not say but he wrote: 'Is it not at least possible that a statesman of Ibn Sa'ud's calibre might have thought it in the interest of the Arab cause to compromise on the Palestine issue in favour of the very solid advantages offered by the (that is his, Philby's) Plan?' Professor Magnes and a number of Jewish leaders in the Jerusalem of 1942 fervently hoped that Philby might be voicing the ideas of the great man who was behind him and who, for them, was of course the person who really mattered.

More important than Philby's ideas on the Palestine Problem were those of Ibn Sa'ud and these I got to know of two years later. It was in December 1944 and the second World War was drawing to its end. Then the political truce in Palestine, too, would come to an end, and the tension between the Jews and the original inhabitants of the country be resumed with increased bitterness. The British as rulers of the country knew full well that the Palestine Arabs were virtually unorganized, were largely illiterate and lived in constant fear. Better than anyone else the Jews knew it. The political Zionists who had built their National Home in what they called 'the Land of their Fathers' were determined to increase their numbers so as to attain a majority in the country. They were preparing for a life and death struggle. Ibn Sa'ud was well informed of the position and he neither underrated their strength nor was he blind to the inadequacy of the Arab League. Ibn Sa'ud had no confidence in the Arab League as an effective force and must have been disturbed when he saw the storm-clouds gather over Palestine.

Philby does not say much about Ibn Saʿud's attitude towards the Jewish experiment, although at least twice he submitted his 'plan' to the King shortly after its conception. Ibn Saʿud seems to have been working on a plan of his own which matured while Philby was away in England between 1940 and 1945. He must have felt that his opportunity had come when he learnt that the two great leaders who had it in their power to save the Palestinians were due to arrive in Egypt. At least one of them, Winston Churchill, thought he had that power for Dr. Chaim Weizmann in his autobiography, *Trial and Error*, tells of an interview he had with Winston Churchill on 11th March 1942 when he, Dr. Weizmann, was about to leave for America. Churchill told him that he had a plan to settle the Palestine problem and ended by saying: "There is nothing he [President Roosevelt] and I cannot do if we set our minds on it."

President Roosevelt and Winston Churchill would be in Egypt on their way back to their own countries after the talks with Stalin at Yalta. Ibn Saʿud knew the value of both of them and he had confidence in their word and when Roosevelt invited him to a meeting in the Suez Canal Ibn Saʿud was more than ready to accept. His decision and travel arrangements were kept secret and the engagements he had already made were not cancelled. For that reason I myself was on my way eastwards from Jedda to ar-Riyadh to visit Ibn Saʿud on the very same day that he was travelling westwards from ar-Riyadh to Jedda to embark for Suez. My colleagues in Jedda knowing that I had been invited to meet him in ar-Riyadh were convinced that the King was in his capital.

For the first time in nearly ten years I had got this much desired permission to visit the Wahhabi capital and have an audience there with the King and the Crown Prince. It was in the middle of December 1944 and travel on the high Arabian plateau was cold and exhausting. It rained continuously and I ended by becoming marooned with my small party on a dry eminence in the midst of flooded depressions. The King had sent out a party to find me and as at night we saw them approaching the headlights of their cars were reflected in the water around us. Slowly one after the other they failed and became stuck in water and mud. We saw them signalling with their lamps and deduced that they were military personnel. That night none succeeded in reaching us and as we could not help them there was nothing to be done except wait for daylight. In the morning an officer waded over to us. He told me that his was the first of a group of jeeps on their way to report to the King. They had been trained in Taif. While in the fort of Dawademi they had received a wireless message from the King asking whether they had seen the Dutch Minister on his way to ar-Riyadh. When they said no they were ordered out to meet me. They got my station-wagon through the water and mud and soon we were in the extensive fort of the Governor of Dawademi.

I had no idea that at the very same time a royal caravan of two hundred motor vehicles was vainly trying to advance in our direction heading for Jedda. We were the more successful and after a nine-day struggle were at a distance of a day and a half by car from ar-Riyadh. The royal caravan had meanwhile got stuck in soft ground some eighty miles from ar-Riyadh and had been camping for a whole week waiting for the rains to stop. I had reached the small oasis of Marat and the lonely old mud fort that had once protected the oasis of Marat was now a welcome refuge for us against the merciless rain, this *rahmat Allah*—blessing of Allah—turned as a scourge against us. The fort was half in ruins and seemed to have changed its military function for that of a public latrine for those using the oasis. We had no choice of lodging and at least the fort kept out the wind and rain. As diversion we had a view of the desert and to our astonishment we saw a heavily laden truck coming towards us. Others followed and trucks continued to come long after nightfall. It was the royal caravan that had arrived and a great camp of tents grew up in the desert quite near us. At the corners were red lorries with machine-guns manned by the bodyguard of the King. Two radio units soon had their masts in the air and started working. A long tent for public audiences, connected with the King's tent, was put up in the centre of the camp. The kitchen lay not far from where we were sitting. Sheep and goats filled the air with their cries and firewood was piled near the huge cooking-pots that stood in rows in the open. At some distance from the main camp a smaller one was erected. We were told that this was the women's camp in which the seventy odd female members of the royal caravan were accommodated. The caravan had set out from ar-Riyadh without women but when the rain forced a halt for a whole week the King decided to have the women brought out. The camp was still not ready when His Majesty arrived with his suite. The women travelled in cars with darkened windows with black window-curtains, driven by Javanese, who had a reputation for politeness and careful driving.

I sent word to the King informing him of my presence and recalling his invitation to me to visit him in his capital. After some time I was invited to the small audience tent to meet His Majesty. I hurriedly put on the best clothes I had with me and, shivering in the cold night breeze, walked over to the royal lines. Passing the guard of tired and sleepy men, I entered the carpet-covered tent. His Majesty's welcome was as cordial as ever and I found myself alone with him, this being no hour for public audience. Our talks were interrupted by telegrams brought in to the King from time to time by secretaries and answered on the spot. I cautiously asked where the caravan was going. The answer "We are travelling to the west" was no news to me as it was clear for everyone to see but it meant I had asked too much. I tried again saying that I had hoped to be His Majesty's guest in ar-Riyadh. The King answered: "We left orders with our son the Crown Prince and are sure that you will find him a good host." With his kind smile he added: "And don't go back at once. Do stay as long as you like."

Our conversation was interrupted by more secretaries with more telegrams and to my great regret I realized that His Majesty was preoccupied. While I was searching for some topic of conversation that might interest the King a further secretary entered with a pile of papers, and, kneeling at His Majesty's feet, presented one paper after the other. The King dictated some words in answer to each and seemed to forget my presence. I asked permission to leave and walked back to the cold, dirty room in the mud fort. I gloomily put aside my western dress that was so unsuited to the place and tried to find some comfort under the sheepskin cover on my camp bed. It was sad to think that this spiritless talk might have been my last personal contact with this man with whom I had had so many unforgettable conversations!

The high, central plateau of Arabia on a winter's night when rain is pouring down and a biting wind sweeps over the endless waste can be very disheartening, but sleep came to me at last and made me forget my surroundings.

In the middle of the night I suddenly woke and saw my secretary standing over me with a lantern in his hand trying to recall me to the reality of the desert fort of Marat. "*Ya Sidi*—Oh, sir—wake up and be quick. *Wallahi*—By Allah!—a messenger of the King wants to see you: he is the chief of the King's slaves, a man of high rank, a chamberlain!" I hurried to the outer room and found there a whole procession of black men.

"His Majesty sends you his greetings and ordered me to bring some gifts to you and to your men."

He beckoned the first of the tall black men who carried a big bundle on top of his head. He knelt and put his load in front of me. The man behind him knelt and put his bundle in front of my secretary and so on till every one of us had received a present. We opened the outer covering and each found inside a complete outfit of beduin clothes. Mine were the most valuable but I was no happier than was the humble driver's mate with his simple, royal gift.

"His Majesty heard that you were travelling without a tent as you did not expect the rains to come so I have brought you one and my men are putting it up in front of the fort. As it is too heavy and too big to go in your station-wagon, a truck of His Majesty will go with you and carry the tent. As there is no time to invite you to a meal His Majesty sends you a fat sheep to slaughter and eat with your men." Here he stopped to look at our now beaming faces. He then asked permission to leave and as we shook hands he added: "Tomorrow morning the big audience tent will be ready, if you would like to come, His Majesty will take pleasure in having one more talk with you. Do come if you like; you are free to choose."

Then followed by the bearers he walked off leaving us behind as happy as children with a Dutch Santa Claus. I no longer felt depressed by the dirty surroundings and by the fear that I had had my last contact with the great King. Tomorrow I should see the real Ibn Sa'ud surrounded by his desert Sheikhs, his Wahhabi scholars and his *Ikhwan*. He had not forgotten my presence, he had thought of the tent I lacked, and he was a great host! With one warm embrace he had taken me into his hospitality, showering his generosity on me and on every one of my men.

Next morning I discarded my western dress and donned the wide royal mantle over a warm Kashmir woollen undergown and I put the golden dagger in my waist-belt. I felt comfortable, properly dressed, a beduin among the beduins in the desert.

As I walked towards the great audience imitating, I hope successfully, the long, careless stride of the beduin I passed a double row of the colourful guard of honour who gave a reluctant Wahhabi salute to the *nasrani*. When I entered the tent a crowd of Nejdi *'Ulama*, of *Ikhwan* with the twisted white strips round their head-cloths, of notables from the Marat oasis and the Sheikhs of the tribes, had arranged themselves alongside the walls. In the middle of the shorter side His Majesty was seated. On my arrival he rose and offered me the place at his right hand. I sat down. With his customary ease the King started the conversation with some brief words of welcome and enquired about the journey, my health and my Queen. Gradually the range of topics widened. He still seemed to speak to me yet what he said was intended for his wider audience. A little later he no longer turned his face to me but directly addressed the leaders of his people. Most of those present had, in beduin fashion, blacked the lids of their eyes with *kohl* for this ceremonial occasion, thus giving their dark eyes a still darker, an almost sinister, expression.

Ibn Sa'ud spoke about the World War, about the Allies who had justice on their side and who were approaching victory. What would the world then be like? Would there be a place in it for the Arabs? Were they of any significance in the world or had their time gone for ever? He spoke with conviction of its central geographical situation in the world, and of its spiritual message for the world in times past and present. Here was a great beduin orator speaking to the heart of his people, comforting them and inspiring them with hope for the future which there would yet be for Arabs. How they listened, how they stared at him! And how grateful I was to be a witness. But what I heard was only an introduction. What was he aiming at? The King paused a moment and then went on speaking of the dangers that confronted this small, yet to the world, important people. From which side did the menace come? From the side of the enemies of the Prophet, from the people who had withstood him in Medina, from the *Yahud*—the Jews. He reminded his listeners of their history, full as it was of rebellion against Allah. He pointed to the role they had played in world history where they had been harmful to nearly every nation in whose midst they had lived. The *Yahud* are our arch-enemies, he said. This they have been from the time they stood at the cradle of our creed when their dispute with the Prophet ended in Muhammad's cursing them and when he beat them and drove them away. Yet he did not advocate a Hitlerite attitude. Even the *Yahudis* would be treated like guests in Arab countries but on one condition: that they should behave like guests. Not like the Zionists in Palestine who were driving a small, weak Arab people away from the soil of their fathers and who dared to refer to that land as the land of THEIR fathers, may they be cursed! We, the Arabs, will not stand idle and look on. Our Muslim brothers in other lands will rally to our side. These Jews who violated Arab hospitality—what more was there to be said about them? Why should we try to say more? Better that we should listen to Allah's word as it was written in the Holy Book. Then the texts resounded through the tent in which the bitterness of Muhammad's conflict with the Jews in Medina was recounted for the benefit of all later generations of Muslims. In that great tent no other sound was heard. He who recited the words from the *Qur'an* was no longer the kind host and King, he was the Arab, the Muslim, the Wahhabi, their Imam and he was preparing to get their assent to the steps he intended to take. When his speech had reached its culminating point and the sound of his mighty voice filled the tent he suddenly stopped. The men along the sides of the tent stared fascinated at their King with eyes glowing with hatred. For a long moment there was silence.

"*Na'am, wallahi*—yes, by Allah—so it was."

The King seemed to remember my presence. The strain of passion faded from his face, his voice which for a moment ago had roared, was now soft and kind. He put his hand on my knee and smiled:

"And you, my Dutch friend, what do you think of the Jews? Speak. You are among friends."

I felt the ground sinking from under me. With growing uneasiness I had listened to this indictment of a party that could not defend itself. I felt it a little unfair. The origin of the dispute between Jews and Arabs, which went back to the early days of Islam, had been sketched in with great mastery. But then, how tendentiously the further development in history had been presented to an uncritical audience. With a master's hand the primitive instinct of simple souls had been played upon. And how spontaneously it had responded. Not for one moment had I expected to see myself drawn into these discussions. My eyes wandered round the sides of the tent and met the baleful looks of the Wahhabis. They could not understand why their King pushed this honouring of a guest so far as to ask his opinion in that moment, the opinion of a *nasrani*! What need had they of it? Would he dare to utter one good word about those despicable Jews? As I made no answer the King looked at me and probably saw how I was gauging his audience. He seemed to have understood my thoughts and said:

"I did not ask you to speak as the representative of the

Netherlands but just as a friend, as a man among his friends".

For him, the King, this was easy enough to say; for me the case was different. Everyone of my words would be considered by these desert Sheikhs as the official Netherlands' opinion. They would probably not understand them, still less appreciate them and would not want to do so. I was not free to follow the prompting of my heart and say a few words in favour of the absent party that had no other defender here. But as I could not remain silent I ventured some hesitating remarks about the conflict going back into history much farther than had been mentioned, that it had also other sides that required consideration, and that it should therefore be taken away from the two parties most concerned and brought into the openness of a United Nations tribunal.

"What did he say, that stuttering *nasrani*?"

They looked at me in disgust. Their own idea of settling the dispute was to fight it out. How little they guessed that their King was on his way to discuss this very question with the Western war leaders. The King shook his head and interrupted me. Fortunately for me the discussion was abruptly brought to an end by a secretary entering with a pile of telegrams. The King began to read and his attention was soon carried away far from all of us. He was preparing his first appearance on the stage of world history outside his own country. Silence no longer reigned in the tent broken by the King's peremptory demands of "*Na'am*?" made, orator-like, to induce general murmurs of agreement. The listeners relaxed and started to break up their ranks, speaking softly among themselves.

There was a move towards the opening of the tent and with relief I too grasped my chance to get away. I begged leave of His Majesty who, still absent in spirit from this place, mechanically stretched out his hand and said goodbye. Profoundly disappointed with myself I followed out after this unsympathetic crowd. Even the guards seemed to look at me disdainfully and no longer thought of giving a salute to the foreigner. Within me I felt that although the crisis had passed tension remained.

That meeting would for me be unforgettable but there was some bitterness in the taste it left behind in me.

Once outside the tent I wanted to get away from these self-righteous sectarians who had no wish to ponder on the great issues that had been raised and who, in fact, had long since lost the capacity of doing so. I longed to be far from this crowd, to be alone and reflect on what I had done wrong and how I could have done better. To have succeeded in what I attempted I should have required a mastery of the colloquial language of the nomad, a deep understanding of his soul and a masterly skill in oratory. All the qualities, in fact, that Ibn Sa'ud possessed. And even then! Speaking after such a man, how could I hope to win them against their King, their Imam!

Straight in front of me rose the solitary rocky hill that is the landmark of Marat and I soon found myself climbing it, away from what seemed to me the hostile spirit of the camp. Nobody paid any attention to me as I climbed higher and higher over the boulders. The emptiness and silence soothed me. I recalled the whole audience, that simple, magnetic, majestic speech of the King, the moment when the King turned from his *Ikhwan*, the silence that followed and the chance I then had to say a word, in favour of a people that at that very moment was going through untold suffering. I was no supporter of political Zionism and had not the slightest sympathy for a Jewish National Home built on injustice. My dilemma had been made more difficult by the King's invitation to speak on my own behalf and not as Dutch representative. He, the King, could make such a distinction but not his followers. Whilst I was thinking I became conscious that something unusual was happening. The silence had been broken as if something had occurred in the camp below. A confused noise, with much shouting, mounted, rose towards me. Looking round and below me I realized that I was the cause of the commotion. A crowd had gathered at the foot of the hill gesticulating and screaming in my direction. What could I have done to cause this? Then a man broke out the crowd and came climbing towards me. It was my guide, the man sent by His

Majesty to be responsible for me during this journey to the capital. As soon as he was within ear-shot he began abusively referring to my practice of continually running away by myself, at a speed at which it was impossible for him to keep up with me. Never before had a foreigner behaved as I behaved. Never before had any man tried to climb a hill so as to look down into the women's quarters! I swung round as he said this and was petrified to realize that I was looking down straight into the camp of the seventy women! I could say nothing in my defence or by way of explanation. I swallowed the man's abuse and meekly followed him realizing that I had done the one thing that is unpardonable in Arab eyes. A fine way to round off my performance at the public audience!

At the foot of the hill the crowd reluctantly obeyed the orders of my guide to let me pass and then, to my great relief, I saw the King's private secretary who, hearing the noise, had come to see what it was about. He took me by the arm and quickly led me to his tent while reproaching me for what I had done.

"But you don't really believe that I meant to look into the women's camp, do you?"

"I do not understand, *wallahi*, why you went there. But first come away from this crowd; you need a cup of coffee to restore your nerves."

I felt that I did and soon we were seated on a rug in front of the secretary's tent. Rushdi Bey al Mulhas, for that was his name, now smiled again: he was my host.

"Let us praise Allah that all ended well but be more prudent in future and never lose sight of the fact that you are in Wahhabi country."

The clever Palestinian soon put me at ease. It was said that in nationalistic activities in Palestine he had come in conflict with the Mandatory Power and so had sought protection with Ibn Sa'ud. He had become a devoted servant of the King who took a liking to this discreet and trustworthy man.

All around us there was the bustle of men breaking camp. That day the King wanted to reach the border of the Nufud, a twenty-mile stretch of high sand-dunes, a river of pure sand, that was difficult to cross with motor vehicles. The Nufud can best be passed in the early morning when the sand is still cool and as the Arabs say 'heavy' so that the wheels of the cars sink in it less easily. Next morning the procession of two hundred cars would 'take' the Nufud on its way to Jedda where an American gunboat would be waiting to carry the King and a small following.

Nobody paid any attention to us as we sat sipping our tiny cups of bitter coffee mixed with cardamom. I felt that this was an opportunity to make good my failure in the audience tent. It was true that the secretary was himself a Palestinian, a political enemy of the British rulers of his country and an arch-enemy of the invading Zionists, but he was also a man who had the King's confidence. Whenever I had met him before he had been kind to me. So I would ask him to convey to the King what was his Dutch guest's personal view of the *Yahud*.

"You realize," I said, "that it was impossible for me to do what His Majesty asked and give my personal opinion about the Jews in front of that audience? It was not fair."

"His Majesty is always fair and you can always do whatever he asks you."

"I was the loser, ya Rushdi. I started off on the wrong foot and could not say there what I hope to say here. Will you promise to tell His Majesty as soon as you have an opportunity what I am going to say now?"

Rushdi promised and his sharp features showed he was listening attentively.

"His Majesty based his exposition of the Palestinian problem on the axiom that Palestine is an Arab-Muslim land and that no nation or government has any say over it but, exclusively and only, the Arab people living there, supported if need be by their brother Arabs. I am sure that one cannot dispose of the problem so simply. Palestine is not like any other country to which such an axiom might apply. In the whole world there is only one Palestine. It does not belong exclusively to the Palestinian Arabs any more than it belongs to all the Arabs, or all the Muslims because they have particular interests in it and call it a Holy Country with sanctuaries that are dear to them. The same is true of the Jews, even more true because for them it is not only Holy Land, the land of their fathers, the land to which they were divinely led and the cradle of their great traditions. For them it is the land where their prophets lived and had the words of God revealed to them. You yourselves know these prophets for they are your prophets too and many of their words are to be found in your Holy Book. Then again for Christians Palestine is the Holy Land and the land of their Holy Book, the land that saw the ministry of Jesus and the birth of the Christian religion. Palestine belongs to the whole world, and whoever governs that country must do so as mandatory of the whole world. It is not only the Arabs in Palestine, nor yet the Zionist who, thanks to the British, were able to settle there and who now with ruse and terrorism try to establish themselves as sole rulers that have the right to decide the destiny of Palestine. The whole world represented by a true League of Nations should determine the affairs of this unique land. The Palestine problem has a profounder historical background and significance to many more peoples than was mentioned by His Majesty."

The Palestinian followed my talk with close attention but not I think with approval. How was approval to be expected from one who himself was a victim of the course of events in Palestine? I expected none but I wonder if he ever told the King what I said to him that morning sitting in front of his tent until it was carried away to the luggage van? Such words could not have been spoken in the audience tent but I could have said them to His Majesty alone talking as man to man. For I myself knew from previous experience that Ibn Sa'ud was always willing to listen to opinions contrary to his own. His staff knew that and, choosing their opportunities well, turned it to their own advantage. It must also have given Philby many opportunities to advance unpalatable views.

Even if Rushdi Bey did give a report of our conversation to the King it is not to be imagined that it would have changed his opinion about the Jews and Palestine. He approached the problem from a political angle and made use of the spiritual background as it appeared to Muslims to win support for the policy he intended to follow. And most probably Rushdi Bey never spoke.

From Marat the King went westward to his meeting in Egypt with Roosevelt and Churchill. In the audience tent at Marat, Ibn Saʿud had explained to his people why the Jews, the enemies of Allah and His Messenger, had to be opposed. It was for this reason he was going to ask help in preventing a great injustice from falling on a small, weak, Arab, Muslim people. He was going in answer to a call of duty. After listening to his arguments the *ʿUlama* would certainly agree to his abandoning the rule he had established of never leaving his own country. In the audience tent at Marat he had prepared them for it and he now continued on his way to see the two great *nasranis*, sure of their approval.

The meeting with President Roosevelt took place on February 14, 1945 in the Great Bitter Lake on board the American cruiser *Quincy*. After five hours' talk the President continued his voyage home and Ibn Saʿud went to Wadi Faiyum near Cairo to meet Winston Churchill. The oral assurances the President gave were set down on paper a week before his death in a letter to Ibn Saʿud dated April 5, 1945 when Roosevelt confirmed that:

(1) He personally, as President, would never do anything that might prove hostile to the Arabs; and

(2) the United States government would make no change in its basic policy in Palestine without full and prior consultation with both Jews and Arabs."

Ibn Saʿud returned to Jedda visibly relieved of the forebodings he had had over Palestine. The population of the town went out to meet him and a great reception took place near the harbour. The representatives of Foreign Governments were invited and had seats near the King. There was a ceaseless flow of speeches and poems to which the King sat happily listening. This was the accepted manner of official Arab receptions. But here was also something in addition: genuine rejoicing. These people of Jedda, the last-conquered port of the kingdom, had never got to like the

Nejdis or their Wahhabism but they seemed to realize that Ibn Sa'ud was a blessing to them and to the country. The King spoke publicly of his experiences with the President who had become his friend and of the promise he had given for the Arabs of Palestine.

Shortly after this public reception I had a private meeting with the King where he told me of his encounters in Egypt. Roosevelt had captured both the confidence and the personal friendship of the Arab ruler and the words he was reported to have spoken had surely been dictated by personal conviction and by the wish to help this new friend in need. But the man who gave this word, which was accepted by the Arab as a solemn promise, died some months later and as Colonel Eddy[1] wrote: 'The King never seemed to distinguish between F.D.R. as a person and as a President of the U.S.A. To an absolute, as well as benevolent, monarch the Chief and the State are the same.' Had the President been prudent enough in what he said and in the way he spoke? Listening to Ibn Sa'ud's words of fervent gratitude I had my misgivings.

Compared with the complete success of President Roosevelt Winston Churchill made a poor showing. It was evident that Churchill had been a disappointment to Ibn Sa'ud. Churchill had refrained from giving any promise. What else could he have done? He knew only too well how weak was England's position in the Palestine affair. His country had given promises before to both sides and conflicting promises can lead to no good end. The Head of the British Government had nothing more to promise and was at least sincere in making no pretence and in letting Ibn Sa'ud go without any assurance from the British side.

But the high expectations staked on America were to prove a bitter deception. When the Palestine crisis reached its peak there was no longer a President Roosevelt to honour the promise given: another President had taken his place. And if Colonel Eddy had not stated the facts about President Truman's abrupt change in America's Palestine policy, I would not have believed

[1] *F.D.R. meets Ibn Sa'ud*, by W. A. Eddy, published 1954.

them. But here is what Colonel Eddy wrote: 'Finally Mr. Truman summed up his position with the utmost candor: I'm sorry, gentlemen, but I have to answer to hundreds of thousands who are anxious for the success of Zionism; I do not have hundreds of thousands of Arabs among my constituents.'

Ibn Saʿud's effort to secure foreign help for his Muslim brothers in Palestine ended in a complete failure. When fighting broke out the Arab armies tried in vain to stem the Jewish advance. Ibn Saʿud himself could have made a decisive gesture for the Arab cause. He could have cut off the Trans-Arabian Pipeline transporting the bulk of the American oil production in his country to the Mediterranean coast. That would have been the worthy reaction of a man who trusted the word of America's President and who was let down by his successor. Had such been his answer to Truman's swinging over to the Zionists, then the outside world would have understood what the injustice done to the Palestinians meant to an Arab brother nation. It would have roused an uninformed American nation to the dangers of a Middle East policy based on yielding to the pressure of a Jewish minority. Was Ibn Saʿud too old to understand how powerful a weapon was in his hands? Had his Wahhabi faith left him? Or was he too firmly bound with golden ties to the American oil production in his land to be able to act in the way expected by the other Arab nations and certainly by those Westerners who had known him as a Wahhabi and had listened to his words about Jews and Zionism. Ibn Saʿud's contribution to the war effort of the Arab League was limited to sending a token detachment and a small amount of money. His geographical borders were indeed the limit of his range.

ARCHITECTURAL STYLE IN SAN'A, CAPITAL OF THE YEMEN

THE SUMMER PALACE OF THE IMAM OF THE YEMEN IN WADI ADH-DHAI

12

The Arab League

WITHOUT the menace of a Zionist attack the Arab League would not have come into being, at least not when it did. It has been said that the League owed much to British planning and encouragement: that would not have been a recommendation for a man like Ibn Sa'ud who was by nature and experience averse to foreign interference in the policies of the Arab countries. In her Palestine policy Great Britain gave him more reason for distrust than for confidence but he himself had taken one of the first steps towards an alliance of Arab nations when he expanded his territory and absorbed the Hejaz and 'Asir within his kingdom. He did more when he established a relationship with his neighbours which was new in Arabia's history, original and wise. Political developments outside the Peninsula later intervened and deprived him of the initiative which was then taken over by Egypt.

A union of Arab peoples was no new thing in history, every Arab with a little education knew that. He knew that Arabs who had accepted Islam in the first century of its existence had raised armies that conquered the world. The Arabs know they are descendants of the men who once built that world-wide empire, the last remnant of which—Turkey ruled by its Sultan and *Khalifa*—only disappeared as a great power at the end of the first World War. Ibn Sa'ud and his fellow Wahhabis held that this had been a divine punishment for their straying from the path of true belief. Arab, even Muslim, unity, religious and political, would return when Allah willed it: that was part of their creed.

I never heard Ibn Sa'ud expand on this conviction nor on how their hopes were to be realized. He did not claim that his own political activities helped towards that end. The first time I heard him mention the idea of a relationship, friendship and even brotherhood between Arab-Muslim peoples was after his war with the Yemen. He had probably realized that conquest of that formidable mountainous country would be impossible for him and that he would do well to stop his armies when they had reached the mountains. In his audiences Ibn Sa'ud had explained that the war with the Imam was inevitable. I had been present when Shekib Arslan had tried in Jedda to dissuade him from this war between brothers. We who were near to him knew of Ibn Sa'ud's patience and of his conclusion that the Imam could only be convinced by force.

On the southern border of the Hejaz the buffer state of 'Asir had already been a bone of contention between King Husain and the Imam Yahya. Its ruler, Sayyid Hasan al Idrisi, sought to maintain some semblance of independence leaning now to the one, now to the other, neighbour. In 1926 after the conquest of Jedda Ibn Sa'ud had agreed with Sayyid Hasan that 'Asir would have the status of a Sa'udi protectorate.

In the interior the fertile Wadi Nejran, nominally part of 'Asir, had, already in Husain's days, also given rise to frontier disputes between the Hejaz and the Yemen. The undemarcated frontier was a constant source of trouble and in the winter of 1931-2 a Yemeni force occupied the Wadi. Ibn Sa'ud could not accept this violation of the status quo and Khalid ibn Luwai, the *Ikhwan* chief who had found fame in the fighting around Khurma between 1918 and 1925, was despatched to the Nejran in the spring of 1932. The Iman Yahya's troops were not able to withstand him and retired to the Yemen. Then a Sa'udi deputation was sent to San'a to start negotiating a settlement with an unwilling Imam. The talks dragged on until the spring of 1934 when the patience of Ibn Sa'ud became exhausted. He sent an ultimatum but had already assembled troops for eventual action. When no satisfactory reply came from Imam Yahya the Crown Prince Sa'ud on 5th April 1934 marched into the Yemen's eastern mountains, coming from the Nejd plateau, while his brother, the

Amir Faisal began moving through the Tihama along the Red
Sea Coast. Both armies used motor transport but the going
was much easier on the sandy coastal plain than in the rocky
mountain country through which the Amir Sa'ud had to advance.
The decisive action fell to the Amir Faisal who had embarked
part of his troops on dhows which he sailed along the coast. His
double attack from sea and land together took the Imam's forces
by complete surprise. When the small coastal town of Lohaiya
fell the motorized column went on to Hodeida, the chief port of
the Yemen.

The speed with which these operations were conducted and the
success that attended them not only caused the government in
San'a to panic but also impressed those foreign powers who were
most interested in a balance of power in Arabia. British, French
and Italian warships hastened to Hodeida. A truce was arranged
much to the comfort of the Imam and to the satisfaction of the
Crown Prince who could now reorganize his broken-down
transport in the rough mountain approaches to the East Yemen.
The truce was followed by negotiations in Taif and there the
unusual happened. No foreign power kept a supervising eye on
the proceedings but a conciliation committee sent by other Arab
states was present with counsels of moderation and peace among
brother nations. The political scene in Arabia was clearly changing
and Ibn Sa'ud was quick to profit by it. As a victor he had always
been magnanimous. Now he came before the assembled Arab
representatives with proposals of peace based on 'Muslim friendship and Arab brotherhood'. He shunned any annexation of
territory and only insisted on an official demarcation of the
frontier and payment of the cost of his military expedition.
Both rulers declared in the peace treaty that their two peoples
were of one single Arab nation.

When in July 1942 I made my way for the second time to the
capital of the Yemen, I took the overland route because the war
had made sea transport in the Red Sea very scarce. With the
help of Sa'udi guides I followed with two cars the tracks left by
Faisal in the spring of 1934. Sandstorms had obliterated much of

the traces but in some of the more treacherous stretches rusted parts of lorries were left to show where Faisal's men had struggled fruitlessly to get their vehicles out of the mud. I saw the fort of Lohaiya that had been built in the days of the Turks and had surrendered so easily to the Sa'udis. Hodeida was an open town with an antiquated mud wall that could give no protection against the light modern artillery brought up by Faisal. In the Tihama the Yemenis clearly could not have withstood the Wahhabis but when I headed for the mountains beyond Hodeida and entered the real Yemen it seemed to me that Ibn Sa'ud had given proof of more than love for moderation when he made peace with the Imam for the precipitous, but by no means barren, mountains of the Yemen might well have put a stop to his victorious advance. There the Imam's soldiers might have proved superior to the bravest Wahhabi warrior unaccustomed as he was to fighting in mountains and in climatic conditions with which he, unlike the Yemeni, was quite unfamiliar. For the high Yemen is like any mountainous region in Europe and Nejd is largely composed of barren sandy plateaux. As it was, Ibn Sa'ud's last war was practically bloodless and it was his quick political vision that enabled him to turn it into the first step on the path of Arab unity.

In official speeches and in his Mecca newspaper Ibn Sa'ud set up this type of peace treaty as an example for the outside world to follow. With his other rival, the Hashimite on the north of the Arabian Peninsula, King Faisal of Iraq, Ibn Sa'ud concluded a treaty on the same lines of Muslim friendship and Arab brotherhood. This was the treaty of Baghdad of 2nd April 1936. Therein both Kings declared their willingness to see the Yemen associated with it and 'every independent Arab state that would ask for it'. Here was the real beginning of the Arab League of which Ibn Sa'ud is entitled to be called the spiritual father. To call Great Britain 'the sponsor' seems to me exaggerated but certainly British representatives in Arab territory did much to foster the idea.

In April 1937 the Yemen joined in this embryo Arab alliance, as foreshadowed in the treaty of Baghdad. For her part Egypt had, in May 1936, concluded a treaty of friendship with Sa'udi Arabia thus putting an end to ten years of estrangement between the two countries. The idea of co-operation was growing among the Arab peoples but having initiated the movement Ibn Sa'ud seems to have left its development to other hands. It was Zionist activities in Palestine that quickened it, although not immediately, for with the outbreak of the second World War England succeeded in establishing a truce in Palestine between Jew and Arab for the duration of the war.

On 24th February 1943 Mr. Eden, in the British House of Commons, made a cordial reference to Arab steps towards political harmony. Great Britain was still in need of the sympathy of the Arab nations although her most anxious period of the war was by then over. But certainly it was not political interest alone that moved England to this declaration, part of her motive was the long-standing mutual attraction between her and the Arabs.

In Cairo in that same year the Egyptian Premier Nahhas Pasha supported by the Iraqi Premier Nuri as-Sa'id invited representatives of the other Arab states to discuss the possibility of forming a federation of the seven Arab nations. The British Government repeated her promise of sympathy and support and in the autumn of 1944 the preliminary conference for creating a League was held in Alexandria, again under the chairmanship of Nahhas Pasha. On 22nd March 1945, the General Arab Congress met where six Arab states were represented and only the Yemen was absent. This Congress formulated the charter of the Arab League which was signed by all parties present. On 10th May 1945 the Yemen joined and signed the charter. In the third appendix to the charter the signatories declared themselves unanimous in appointing 'Abd ar-Rahman 'Azam Bey as Secretary-General of the League. He seemed to be a happy choice and full of enthusiasm started on his task. Thanks to his great activity the voice of the League was heard on the international forum whenever Arab interests were at stake. In the two world-centres of importance for the Arab countries, London and Washington, bureaux were established for information and propaganda and were very active. Under 'Azam Bey the Arab League began to make progress. Then fate intervened in the form of Great Britain's announcement of her decision to give up her mandate for Palestine. Outside criticism was unable to shake Great Britain's determination to free herself of her responsibility for Palestine. As America refused to step into the vacant place Arabs and Zionists were directedly confronted with one another and war seemed inevitable. Both Jews and Arabs knew that if the world left them to their own devices war must follow.

It did follow. On the one side were the Zionists many of whom had succeeded in escaping from the Nazi mass-slaughter or from concentration camps in Europe. Nearly all of them had suffered irreplaceable personal losses and had been robbed of their possessions and Palestine had been for them their last hope. On the other side was another people, claiming a common descent from the same forebear, Abraham, members of a brother nation that far from doing them harm had accepted them as guests only to find themselves driven away from their native soil by these newcomers and thrown upon the brother Arab nations for support.

And so it happened that the Arab League, after barely three years of existence, found itself in a war for which it was quite unready. With the exception of Transjordan none of the Arab states had an effective modernized army. The Jews on the other hand had learnt modern fighting in the ranks of the Allies during World War Two. The Arab armies fought at the end of long lines of communication, the Jews on interior lines. The Beduin Legion, the creation of Glubb Pasha, bore the brunt of the fighting and was the only Arab army that emerged from the fight with credit, not to say glory. The Iraqi army played no effective part, the Syrian, Lebanese and Saʿudi armies scarcely existed. The Egyptian army, from which much might have been expected, was crippled by corruption in its higher ranks. More, perhaps, than anything else the failure of the Egyptian army precipitated the revolution that swept King Faruk off his throne. With the Arab failure in Palestine 'Azam Pasha's noisy organization (he had meanwhile been promoted in rank by King Faruk) nearly dissolved. He himself had to disappear from it.

The rickety skeleton of the Arab League was thus exposed to view. From the beginning Egypt had used the League as a means of strengthening her cultural and political ascendancy over the other Arab nations. With the Hashimites fostering the idea of a 'Greater Syria' to embrace Syria and Iraq Sa'udi distrust of the family they had supplanted in the rule of the Holy Places was revived—not that it was ever very far dead—and the Sa'udis used the League merely as a stick with which to beat their Hashimi 'enemies' and to keep them at bay. Thus the League was divided into two factions with Egypt and Sa'udi Arabia on one side, Iraq and Jordan on the other and Syria uneasily torn between them. This rift prevented the creation of a High Arab Command during the Palestine war and the implementation of a concerted plan of campaign to cover all fronts.

The Zionists had brought the League into being and they were responsible for its virtual collapse. Musa al Alami, a former secretary to the High Commissioner in Jerusalem, had the courage to tell the Arabs that they themselves were to blame for losing the Palestine war. His '*Ibrat Falastin*—The Warning Example of Palestine—exposed their weaknesses, their dissensions, their backwardness and the corruption of many of their rulers. Ibn Sa'ud on whose statesmanlike foundation the League was based himself undermined it when he allowed himself to be ruled by his old enmity with the Hashimites.

How far all this was from the glowing talk about '*al Aruba*' —the Arab Nation—I had once heard in the audience tent at Marat. And yet the Arabs are a nation. They share a common language and a common faith and with vision they might be an effective force for good in the world.

13

Interlude and Return to Arabia

THE KING had come back from his visit to Egypt, from his first absence abroad. The outbreak of joy among the people of Jedda was proof of their gratitude for the years of peace and prosperity he had brought them. I do not think that the fate of Palestine weighed very heavily with them but the rumour that the King had been successful in his talks with the great ones of the earth added to their feeling of security under his rule. The festivities lasted three days. There had again been dances accompanied by singing, hand-clapping and the beating of drums. Wahhabis had not interfered. Of course not! Where were they, those nearly-forgotten invaders of 1925? Some days later we read in the *Umm al Qura* that even the stern capital of Wahhabism had for once abandoned its principles and had been beside itself with joy when the greatest of the Sa'uds returned in its midst after what had been deemed a dangerous expedition into the sinful world outside.

On his return I had one more contact with the King in the extensive palace compound of Nuzla, built under the supervision of Sheikh Abdullah as-Sulaiman in the desert to the east of Jedda. These new palaces were so large that one had difficulty in recalling that in the first years of Ibn Sa'ud's rule of the Hejaz the house of our friend Muhammad Nasif had been sufficient for him. Muhammad Nasif's house had been superseded by *al Qasr al Akhdar*—the green palace—which Philby later made the headquarters of his import business of Sharqiya Ltd. The palace of Nuzla succeeded *al Qasr al Akhdar* and additions had recently been built on to Nuzla. As the King was no longer able to climb

174

stairs, because an old wound in his left knee caused him much pain, and as lifts could not be installed in mud houses, ramps were built to the first storey along which a car could drive the King directly to his apartments.

It was in the summer of 1945 that I had a parting meeting with Ibn Sa'ud. He had always disliked the Jedda climate, a distaste I cordially shared, and now that he was physically on the decline, he tried to make his visits on the Red Sea coast as short as possible. So my talk with him was short and was followed by a dinner, and left little impression. The King seemed to be tired; life was becoming a burden to him. Now that his task was fulfilled he seemed to have lost his sparkle. When I shook hands with him he did not rise as was his practice in days gone by and this little change of habit left me feeling depressed. The glory of manhood of the Sultan I had met in Muhammad Nasif's house was passing. It was not so much the thought that most probably we should not meet again that made me melancholy, as fear that the great work he had been permitted to perform, of which I had been witness, might now begin to wither in his weakening hands. For a man like him, who as a boy knew that he was born to rule it would be difficult to realize that with the years his wisdom and strength must weaken, and eventually a stronger hand would be needed at the head of the affairs.

When in 1945 the war with Germany was over and the Dutch government could find time to give attention to her Jedda Legation I was relieved of my post and with difficulty worked my way home. Ibn Sa'ud's country had been an island of peace and security in the midst of an agonized world. This cruel reality was brought home to me when on board a crowded British troopship we sailed into Malta in the beginning of August 1945 and eventually approached the wreck-littered coast of England. From Liverpool we were carried to London in long military trains. Halfway we stopped in the middle of the fields. We waited and waited but nothing happened. What was the reason for the delay? We left the carriages and as all of us had come back from the Far and Near East we sat down on the grass along the railroad and were happy to look at the simple wayside flowers. Then word was passed along: "Japan had surrendered. The war is over." And then? Was there a wild outburst of relief, shouts and rejoicing in the fields? No, only an amazed silence and then a murmur of subdued excitement. For these homecoming soldiers who found part of their country in ruin, the news seemed too great: there was not yet room for joy in their longing hearts. We climbed on to the train again and arrived at night in an unreal, dark, empty London. How it had suffered!

The nearer I came to Holland the more difficult the question of transport became. The landing-grounds were ruined, unmapped mine-fields blocked the sea-route and the Dutch sea approaches and harbours had been left by the retiring enemy in a tragic state. I saw my country again after an absence of more than six years. Three months after the armistice dwellers along the North Sea canal that links Amsterdam with the North Sea were still unaccustomed to seeing ships come in from abroad. They stared at our little steamer as a harbinger of good: the days of old were coming back. My countrymen, poorly dressed, with hollow cheeks and riding bicycles without tires, cheered us. I stood and gazed on my ill-treated country and I too found it hard to rejoice at her new-found freedom. I had first to get beyond her sufferings and my own irreparable losses. The fields of Holland were empty, her roads were practically without traffic, all her bridges broken and many towns and villages showing the wounds inflicted by an embittered enemy.

I already knew that the brave persistence of my wife, who had preceded me to Holland by two months, had brought her on the track of our third son. She had followed his path of martyrdom from prisons to German starvation camps and we knew that he was last seen among the dying young men driven along before the approaching Allied armies. Where he succumbed we never knew.

Our second son's fate was still unknown. He had fought the Japanese in Sumatra and was eventually made prisoner. Then a curtain of silence had been lowered between us and for many days to come we would sit and listen in hope and fear to the lists of the dead broadcast daily and we would stand among the silent crowds in front of the printed lists stuck up at the street corners. This anxious waiting lasted for weeks but it ended in relief and great joy, although so many did not emerge from the jungle camps of the Japanese in Siam and Java.

I was not left in Holland for long. I was asked to return to the Dutch East Indies where as a Civil Servant I had worked the greater part of my life. England had been allotted the task of occupying the islands of the Dutch East Indies, of rounding up and evacuating the Japanese troops left there, of collecting their arms and munition, of restoring order and security and then handing over to the Dutch. My task was to try to keep up spirits in the camps and other places where the ex-prisoners, civilian and military, men, women and children, lived, always under circumstances of great hardship and, what was worse, with no proper information about what had happened in the outside world. I had to bring them a message of hope. It was inspiring to tell them of what had happened in the second World War, of what had happened to their home country and to the world and to try to explain why victory appeared to them to be so deceptive.

When a year after their arrival the English left, in October 1946, the Dutch Government took over responsibility and tried to make the last chapter of their rule of the Indonesian peoples a good one. I fear we did not succeed. It became a chapter full of misunderstanding and frustration. The day came when Dutch official relations with Indonesia were broken. I had preceded by some months the last of my countrymen who had been rulers in the land and who now returned to Holland. There I was asked to organize an Arabic section for our world broadcasting system in Hilversum and this task brought me back on the Arabian scene. I was convinced that no new voice speaking Arabic could hope for listeners in the Middle East if that voice did not come from men who knew Arabia and who spoke with a background of personal knowledge of what had happened and was happening there. So before 'going on the air' I wanted to see the countries that were at war with the Zionists and had suffered most from it. How was I to carry out my plan?

I bought a small car and got permission for my youngest son, who was then serving with our Royal Marines, to drive it to Egypt. There we could see whether we could go on or not. We crossed to Tunisia and were soon driving through lands of ancient culture where the Roman legions had been followed by the hosts of Islam pushing westwards on their way to conquer the whole of North Africa and so on to Spain. The traces the Romans had left behind were impressively beautiful, but ruins. Islam, however, since its advance more than twelve centuries before, had never lost its grip on the character of the land or the heart of its people. No Mussolini, no Rommel, no Montgomery had changed that in the least. Mussolini had left in some of the coastal towns vain-glorious imitations of Roman magnificence. He had rebuilt the two thousand miles road of which greater men than he had been the architects and repairers. Mussolini's imprint on this land of antiquity and possible future greatness was transient and his attempt to reclaim this once fertile land from encroaching desert, by means of Italian settlers, was failing under the relentless pressure of those 'fathers of deserts', the beduins. The reversion of this land to sterility was the beduin revenge, their answer of hatred to everything Italian founded, as it was, on injustice to themselves, the true owners of the land.

In Egypt our journey came to a stop: there was no question of our driving further. Leaving my son in Cairo I flew high over the ways followed by the Jews when Moses led them through the wilderness and landed safely on the tiny aerodrome of Transjordan near its capital 'Amman. There on the terrace of the Philadelphia Hotel I had the good fortune to meet an old Jerusalem friend, Ruhi Pasha Abdul Hadi. In 1942 he had been Adviser to the British for Palestinian affairs and now that he was a refugee in 'Amman he had been made Minister of Foreign Affairs to King 'Abdallah, son of the Husain who had fled the Hejaz on the approach of the Wahhabi invader. Ruhi Pasha arranged for me a meeting with the Ruler of what was now the

Hashimite Kingdom of Jordan, so at last I had an opportunity of meeting the only one left of Ibn Saʻud's contemporary Hashimi adversaries. As soon as I had spoken one sentence in answer to the King's graceful welcome he knew that I came from the Hejaz.

"How is it that you speak the language of my birthplace?" he asked, looking at me intently.

"I was ten years in Jedda, Your Majesty."

"Why?"

"I was the Netherlands' representative there."

"Were you in Jedda when my father or when my brother was King there?"

"I went to Jedda shortly after Ibn Saʻud's entering the town." It would not be well to put into print my interlocutor's lack of appreciation of his family's arch-enemy. My answer being an inarticulate question mark the King went on to explain why my government had made a gross mistake in not siding with his brother, the late King Ali. Then he continued:

"Tell me all about it. How is he managing the country, he the Bedu?"

I said what I felt and he was much too interested in talking about his country to resent my doubtless patent sympathy with an Ibn Saʻud he did not personally know. At dinner the conversation finally came to an end where silently I had hoped it would, when the King addressed his Minister saying:

"Ya Ruhi, has this Dutch gentleman any wishes you know of?"

Knowing that I had understood what had been said, Ruhi Pasha looked at me.

"Yes," I said, "I have one wish. I ask Your Majesty's permission to go to Jerusalem."

"Granted," replied the King. And then with a sudden change of expression:

"You meant the Old City, did you?"

"Yes, Your Majesty."

"Not the Jewish New Jerusalem?"

"That too, Your Majesty."

"And I thought you were our friend?"

"That is what I am. But I am charged to study this great problem. I shall only understand it having seen and heard both sides."

"I have no power to bring you to the New Jerusalem."

"I know. I only ask your permission to try to get there and yet be sure you will let me return to the Arab side." And that was the end of it and the start of my visit to the brand-new Republic of Israel.

During my second stay in Jedda, during the second World War, I had twice made an official journey to Palestine which gave me an opportunity of becoming acquainted with its tragedy and with the men who played a role in it. Now in Tel Aviv I was fortunate again in meeting an old friend from war-time Jerusalem, Moshe Shertok, now His Excellency the Minister of Foreign Affairs, Moshe Shareth. He invited me to lunch in one of the hotels overlooking the wide, sandy beach of Tel Aviv and there we sat with Mr. Eban, the Israeli Representative to the United Nations. For more than half an hour Mr. Shareth asked me question after question about what had happened between my country and Indonesia.

"You will excuse me if, belonging to a young independent state, we are inclined to give our sympathy to the Indonesian side?"

"Of course I will. Mine are there too," I replied. "But I came here to ask questions, not to be questioned. Am I to have no chance?"

My first question was how it had all come about, and then: "What now, Mr. Shareth?"

"You mean the refugee problem?"

"Yes. I think it is your most urgent problem, for you the question 'to be or not to be'. You of course know the Arab proverb [Moshe Shareth was born in Palestine and grew up there as a boy speaking its language as well as his own mother-tongue]: *al jar qabl ad-dar*—first the neighbour and then the house—that proverb is full of wisdom. You said just now that you were an oriental people that long ago reached nationhood in this country

and then being driven away by force had started on a two-thou-
sand-year peregrination throughout the world. And you added:
now we have come back to where we started, to live here for
ever. Did you realize the full weight of such a statement?"

With a smile Mr. Shareth answered:

"I think so. But tell me, what are you thinking of?"

"I was thinking that he who claims to originate from and for
ever to belong to this part of the world must be willing to take
upon himself his share of the burden of the Arab nations living
here."

"That is just what I meant."

"Well then you agree that it is all-important for you to be
accepted by them and openly do away with expressions such as
being a bridgehead of the West?"

"That is my conviction."

"In that case there is the refugee barring your way."

Mr. Shareth then gave his explanation of the situation, that it
was not the Jews who were to blame but the Arab leaders who
ordered the Palestinians to move away from the Jews so that in
the coming battle they might not be killed with them.

"About the cause of the tragedy I may have a different opinion
but what matters for you is that the problem is there and it
could easily become a festering sore of hatred on your land
frontier."

"How would you handle the problem, Mr. van der Meulen?"

"Why ask me? I am not a Jew. You are and so you are responsible."

"I know that only too well and I don't shirk it."

"Then why ask me that question?"

"Because you must have had problems of mass suffering in your
civil service in Indonesia. Tell me what you suggest."

I gave the answer: "The first thing to do in my opinion is to
declare publicly that you are very sorry for the sufferings you
caused to your Arab neighbour."

"But it is not our fault; it was the nations of Europe who drove
us here pressing us into this last place of safety."

"I know, Mr. Shareth, and I bow my head in shame for what we, the Christian nations of Europe, did to the Jews. You are right in blaming us. But don't try to tell the Arabs. They don't know world history. But they know you and panic-stricken they took to flight after what was done in Deir Yasin and other places. Tell them that that is a cause of grief to you and ask their permission to try to make good what you did to them."

"We cannot take them back, their houses have been wholly filled by all those Jews who are now streaming into Israel. And will not take them all back; they would be a fifth column. We can only take Christian Palestinians and members of families that are half with us and half in the refugee camps."

"Why accentuate religious differences!"

"Because Muslim Palestinians will always be loyal to their brother Muslims."

"If you think you cannot take them back, ask to be allowed to help them."

"In what way!"

"Let your cleverest men make a plan for their resettlement and you be the first to make a substantial gift to put the plan into execution."

"We! We are bankrupt; we have no money."

"Give the money that will be given you, give of your poverty and the greater will be the impression upon the Arabs and upon the whole world."

King 'Abdallah let me return to Old Jerusalem and from there I made my way to 'Amman. I had a long talk with Ruhi Pasha and according to the promise I had given the King I told him what I had heard and seen in Israel and what might help to heal the breach between the two.

And then I returned to Holland where in Hilversum a small team started talking to listeners in Arab speech. But the time came when my heart urged me to go once more to the Arabia of the Wahhabis to see with my own eyes whether my premonitions had come true. I also wanted to see what was happening in the

Hadhramaut and Aden Hinterland, that most picturesque part of Arabia where its old history is engraven in Sabaean script on the walls of the rocky wadis and where the ruins of the famous cities, the capitals of the five kingdoms of Arabian antiquity that once flourished along the incense road, are to be found, the Unknown Arabia of my explorations.

I realized that it might be difficult to get a visa for entering the Sa'udi kingdom now that I was no longer in government service. So I decided to go and see my old Arabian friend Sheikh Hafiz Wahba who has been Ibn Sa'ud's Ambassador in London for many years. Would he recognize me? Of course he did. He welcomed me as an old friend and though he must now be quite fluent in English we talked Arabic and I relished finding myself back again in the atmosphere of confidence of the days when we first met in Muhammad Nasif's house in the Jedda of 1926. When I ventured to ask whether it would be possible to visit His Majesty now that old age and weakness were weighing heavily on him the answer sounded like music in my ears: "Of course you must go and you will always be welcome. This very night I will write a letter to the King telling him of your proposed visit."

And so the door to Sa'udi Arabia was again open to me and soon I was on my way. Not to Jedda, the Red Sea port of entrance, but to the Persian Gulf gate of Dhahran with al Khobar as its harbour. What interested me most was the switching over of Sa'udi Arabia's centre of gravity to its east side. There I would find the leaders of Aramco, most of whom I had met in 1944-5 and who had again invited me to see how their work was progressing. When I went ashore in this new Sa'udiyya in the beginning of February 1952 it was in the good old-fashioned way, landing from a sailing dhow with auxiliary motor, in which my companion on this occasion, Bram Drewes, a student of Arabic of Leyden University, and I crossed from Bahrain island where a Dutch steamer had dropped us. We found a warm welcome in Dhahran, a quickly expanding oil town and the headquarters of the oil company, the Aramco. I was fortunate enough to find the Amir Faisal in town. Assisted by Hafiz Wahba he was leading political discussions with a British mission that had come over to discuss ownership of a strip of desert the Sa'udis disputed with Sheikh Shahbut of Abu Dhabi, the ruler of one of the small coastal territories that had made a treaty with Great Britain long ago. The Amir Faisal welcomed me and told me that when the discussions were over he would return to ar-Riyadh and inform his father of my wish to visit him. I well understood that I must be patient and only hoped that I had not come too late for a last audience with the King.

It was not weary waiting in a place like Dhahran where I was the guest of a friend of war-time days, the capable young American Arabist Dr. George Rentz. I was back in Sa'udi Arabia and that was enough for me. The prospect of meeting the King in his capital, of seeing the Crown Prince and of renewing my contact with the centre of Wahhabism, was more than sufficient for the time being and the only question that remained was whether Allah would give us, and the King, the blessing of health. In the meantime we had not a moment, for American hospitality, backed by the Aramco desert transport facilities, was opening for me a new Arabia with wide and unexpected horizons. What I had seen at the end of 1944 and the beginning of 1945 had been only a foretaste of what now opened before my eyes.

14

The Americans in Arabia

DHAHRAN had grown considerably since I last saw it in January 1945. The first women from America were then about to take possession of the first bungalows built there. Nearly all the men lived together in long wooden barracks divided by a passage into two rows of double rooms. An air-conditioning installation kept the rooms warm during the brief winter and cool during the sweltering heat of the long summer. Some thirty miles to the north of Dhahran, on the sandy cape of Ras Tanura, a great refinery was under construction, the small one in Dhahran having proved quite incapable of coping with the ever-increasing flow of oil. Ras Tanura reached out into deep water and quays had been built where big ships could tie up alongside. But these quays soon proved to be insufficient for the enormous quantities of material imported to keep pace with Aramco's extension programme. Groups of prospectors had moved inland probing the country northward, then westward and finally southward where they discovered what was to be the greatest oil deposit ever found in one single field. Two factors spurred on these activities: the call for oil from the Middle East to help in bringing about a final decision in the war, and Ibn Sa'ud's urgent need of money. During the war his income from the pilgrimage had shrunk to nearly nothing.

His expanding administration required more and more money though it was as yet not more than a patriarchal system on to which a few ideas of Western origin had been grafted. It produced results that were not good to beduin and quite inacceptable to Western eyes. The trustworthy Wahhabi administrators had proved to be below standard in the Hejaz and had been recalled to

Nejd. As rulers of the desert they were adequate enough but the Hejaz proved too difficult for them to handle and the moral dangers to be found there too great for them. Thus, after 1926, the first year in which he had had to rule the difficult Hejaz with its touchy pilgrim problem, Ibn Sa'ud realized that he must bring in more experts from outside. From Egypt, Syria, Iraq, the Lebanon and Palestine he got physicians, military officers, administrators and technical men for the motor transport, condensing plants, etc. On the whole he was poorly served by these men and they were a heavy drain on the finances of the state. Not all the blame, however, should be laid on them as they got little help from the local inhabitants and the Nejdi élite looked down upon them as a very poor kind of true believer. This drove them to look to the King for support and led them to cling together. They soon had a monopoly of the medical services and as doctors to the ruling families found opportunities to fortify their position.

The Syrians also succeeded in penetrating into the Financial and Foreign Departments. Some of them were capable, energetic and worthy men. The outstanding Syrian among them was Sheikh Yusuf Yasin, who originally came as a young man from Lataqiyya to ar-Riyadh in about 1923 and was intended to be the teacher of the young amirs. His ability and integrity soon took him to the post of personal adviser and secretary to Ibn Sa'ud. He had served the King faithfully and well right from the early days when conditions were difficult and life was hard; and when, while he was away on a political mission, he learnt of the death of his King, he was so overcome that he fainted. Sheikh Yusuf seemed to us Europeans moody and morose and fanatically anti-Western. For us he was hard to deal with. We were glad to know that above him was a man much milder and wiser, a man free from any anti-Western bias. And so it often happened that the King decided in our favour when we, the foreigners, had clashes with Sheikh Yusuf. But I, for my part, gladly condone any harshness I may have met with from the Sheikh because I saw in him a rock of moral strength in a sea of corruption. So far as I know,

Sheikh Yusuf Yasin was an exemplary family man and a man who was not to be lured by the snares of luxury. If only the same could be said of his compatriots and of the Lebanese who presented themselves for work in the Sa'udi administration!

Ibn Sa'ud knew that many of them were intriguers and self-seekers rather than supporters. Sometimes he gave vent to his fury. When we heard of this in Jedda we received it with great satisfaction, but we knew that the King could not do without these men, and they, alas, knew it too. This foreign element in important, and even in confidential posts was a constant source of weakness both administrative and financial. The Syrian—as the foreign Arab element in the administration soon came to be styled—was naturally uncomfortable in the trying climate of Sa'udi Arabia and in its backward society. So most of them tried to put aside as much money as possible, and as quickly as possible, and quit this land of desert exile.

Everyone in Sa'udi Arabia knew quite well what was happening. Far too great a part of the income of the country found its way to the fashionable resorts of the Middle East where the men who served Ibn Sa'ud found profitable investment for the money they had filched from him and his poor subjects. It is common knowledge that in Cairo, Beirut, Damascus and elsewhere, enormous blocks of the most expensive buildings belong to Sa'udi officials.

It is not only the Syrians who caused leaks in the state treasury. Hejazi officials who had learned their lessons in the days of the Turks and of King Husain, and Nejdis of not too stern a Wahhabi conviction, were very ready to follow their example. The pilfering by officials of Sa'udi nationality, however, was less detrimental to the country as it took them some little time to learn how and where to place their money abroad. When Wahhabi fervour began to retreat to the desert whence it had come, Sa'udi officialdom became more and more infected by the spreading disease of corruption. And when the money from the oil began to flow the chances of grabbing it grew also and in big towns like Cairo public rumours spread exaggerated stories of the apartment buildings in the garden quarters of the town set up by ʿAbdullah as-Sulaiman and his favourites. In the smaller towns of Lebanon and Syria the taxi-drivers told me more factual tales of those compatriots who had left the country for Saʿudi Arabia not very long before and who were now the happy owners of beautiful houses built along the shore of the Mediterranean or in the mountains of the Lebanon. So long as such stories are more admired than scorned, public censure of this behaviour of Saʿudi officials will not help in curing the disease.

The more the money leaked away, the greater became the demand for it and the stronger the pressure of the Saʿudi government on Aramco to step up their output. Aramco's prospectors soon approached the borders of the British Protected Sheikhdoms along the Persian Gulf coast and the northern fringe of the ʿOman territory and the quest for oil made frontier conflicts inevitable. A difference at Abu Dhabi was followed by the more serious one of Buraimi oasis claimed by the Saʿudis as convincedly as by the Masqat authorities.

Originally Ibn Saʿud's need for financial assistance had only fallen on Great Britain, the Western Power that in the first World War started giving him a monthly subvention. When the second World War started British assistance had to be resumed. It was no longer a question of small, but of large, sums of money and of shipments of food as well. One can imagine with what bitterness my British colleagues saw that a great part of their relief was drained away from the country it was meant for and added to the private possessions of the leading Saʿudi officials. They pressed for effective control but their representations led to little result other than increased dislike of the British instead of gratitude for what Great Britain did for the country.

Once before the King had tried to reorganize his Finance Department. At his request the Dutch Bank had found an expert who was asked to prepare a scheme for a thorough reorganization. He was given full powers of investigation and started to draw up a budget for the state. Those were dark days for the Saʿudi officers of finance. When the expert started to explain to His Majesty that the basis of all sound national finance was the rigid separation of the income of the Royal Family from the income of the state the whole scheme was abandoned. The King would not submit himself to any control, no one should know what he was doing with his money. So after half a year of hard work a sadly disillusioned financial expert took his leave and there was great rejoicing in the Finance Department at his departure. A mortal blow to the most powerful and cleverest man in the Sa'udi government, to 'Abdullah as-Sulaiman himself, had been warded off by the King who was not willing to pay the price without which no sound financial base could be laid.

The next attempt at reform came from the British. When in the beginning of the second World War the aid in money and kind was rising month after month the British Minister in Jedda demanded the dismissal of Sheikh 'Abdullah's right-hand man, the Lebanese Najib Salha. Without this man who was fully versed in modern book-keeping and who was responsible for financial contacts with the outside world, Sheikh 'Abdullah as-Sulaiman would have been greatly handicapped. The British Minister insisted so Najib went into the wilderness which in his case meant Egypt. And there he continued working for His Majesty's finances and for 'Abdullah as-Sulaiman's and his own. The process was more circuitous but the results were the same. Nothing was changed for the better.

The discovery of gold and oil and the advent of the Americans meant that 'Abdullah as-Sulaiman was out of danger and beyond reach. He was not much younger than Ibn Sa'ud, in uxoriousness he was nearer to the Sa'udis than to Yusuf Yasin and he did not believe in Wahhabi abstention where whisky was concerned, yet he was a hard worker and full of new ideas at a time when the King was losing his vigour. No one could now stop him from calling back from exile his clever former assistant Najib Salha, but the latter preferred the flesh-pots of Egypt. And he was useful there for the private financial transactions of both of them.

'Abdullah as-Sulaiman, second only to the King in power, was an exceptional man. He was content to remain in the background but was virtually financial dictator. He built palaces for the King in nearly all the important places in the state. Huge compounds they were of impressive massiveness. Wherever there was water ʿAbdullah as-Sulaiman would start an experimental garden. He was the right man to further Twitchell's activities, to make full use of the latter's technical abilities and to win him over to his own plans. He did the same later with the engineers of Aramco and the American State Department's specialists who started the agricultural experiment of Al Kharj. Wherever new ideas were abroad in the land one could be sure of finding ʿAbdullah as-Sulaiman. He was a man who knew no fatigue, who grew with the miraculous growth of Ibn Saʿud's administration and who was admirable as the servant of a King whose financial acumen was that of a beduin. He was endowed with the genuine Arab gift of accommodating himself to all circumstances of life but he was not strong enough to withstand two enemies who unexpectedly came his way; money and whisky. And a Wahhabi he certainly was not.

Yusuf Yasin and ʿAbdullah as-Sulaiman were thus the two men to whom the greatest tasks in the administration were given. Only two of the King's sons were moved to the foreground: Saʿud, the Crown Prince, and Faisal, the second surviving son, who was made his representative in the Hejaz and whom he used to send abroad on political missions. Saʿud he kept near him and gave him charge of the Nejd. Only reluctantly and towards the end of his life were these sons given real responsibility. Then younger sons were drawn into the picture but I myself only met one of them, Amir Mansur, who became Saʿudi Minister for War and as such was posted in Taif where he commanded a small regular armed force. The foreigners in the country never dealt with one of the Amirs deputizing for the King; their business if they had any, was with the Finance Minister Sheikh ʿAbdullah as-Sulaiman or with the King's Secretary for Foreign Affairs, Sheikh Yusuf Yasin.

The Americans who were providing the principal source of income of the country were now receiving the greater part of Saʿudi official attention. They were more fortunate than the rest of us in their dealings with the two Saʿudi key-men. Theirs was, of course, not a difficult task. They brought the money, the men and the machinery to set the country on its headlong rush. The man who was in the American vanguard was Colonel W. A. Eddy, whose second fatherland was Syria, who spoke her language and who had known as a schoolboy several of the Syrians now serving Ibn Sa'ud. He had opportunities that no British Minister in Jedda had ever had and Colonel Eddy knew how to make good use of them. The American advent into Sa'udi Arabia was unlike any other. No other country had ever produced a Crane with a Muslim-Arab hobby. No other nation had had a Twitchell to rediscover Arabia's gold and set oil flowing to the ends of the earth. America found a fortune in the poorest country of the world and shared the proceeds. The Americans found the task they accepted in an unknown country testing but most attractive.

In Jedda I had seen Eddy and his men at work and had admired their forthrightness. I had seen the men of the gold-mine and with my wife had enjoyed a treat—rare for those of us who lived in Jedda—of motoring two hundred and fifty miles into the forbidden interior to taste of their bountiful hospitality.

With the development of the eastern part of Ibn Sa'ud's land the Americans made the overland route from Red Sea to Persian Gulf a *darb an-nasara*—a road for Christians. They built the landing-grounds and with air travel did away with the distances and much of the heat and dust of Arabia.

Aramco started her work with imported labour. Under American supervision camps, refineries, tank farms, etc., were built by Italians with unskilled labourers imported from Iraq, Persia and India. Gradually as conditions permitted the men from other countries were replaced by Sa'udis and so American contacts with the local population increased, the more so as the range of the Company's activities spread out into the interior. Ibn Sa'ud's original aim of isolating foreigners and thus creating a sort of sanitary cordon around his people to prevent any deterioration of their belief and morals came to nothing. Restrictive practices were swept aside in the sharing by two nations of a common task.

Aramco had three departments working to smooth the

company's way and as a guest of Dr. George Rentz, the Head of the Research Department, I was able to see what his department was doing. He and his men were the scholars, the Arabists in the broad sense of studying the people, their language, history and social conditions. And what golden opportunities they had! From the far backsands of the desert they had visitors with whom they could talk the whole day long if they wished. Their guests from the interior were treated with the respect due to men who are in possession of invaluable knowledge. In Aramco's hospitality these men had better fare than they had ever met with before and each, in addition, received a monetary gift. Here the systematic study of Arabia was, for the first time in the long history of the country, being done at home, and in an air-conditioned home at that. Here I met men from the remote wadis of the Hadhramaut: Manhalis and Sai'aris, 'Awamir and Murris to meet whose tribes I, years before, had had to travel for months over the mountains and rocky plateaux of the Aden hinterland. It was good for us both to meet and talk about their homeland and, after the conditions prevailing in 1931 when I first visited their country, to sit in perfect peace and safety and not to be bothered by flies, fleas, bugs nor heat. Even more thrilling was it for me to find here sheikhs of tribes I scarcely knew of by name and who talked to me about regions then unknown to the West and of remote beduin dialects. In their daily talks with these men Rentz's able assistants pieced together the information they required of the as yet unexplored regions into which Aramco wished to penetrate. Draughtsmen were busy drawing maps and adding those local features which give a map of the unknown parts of Arabia its real value. Here too were compiled facts never before studied about important parts of Sa'udi Arabia like Al Hasa province, and territories such as the inner regions of 'Oman bordering on the southern Sa'udi frontier, hitherto beyond Western exploration. All these publications were produced bilingually in the Latin and the Arabic script, thus fulfilling a triple purpose: first of preparing the ground for Aramco's operations, second of providing the Sa'udi administration with invaluable information and third of furthering the pursuit of learning. Besides collecting its own information on the spot this department kept in close contact with orientalists and scholars the world over and had assembled an admirable specialist library. Books or manuscripts required for study were often micro-filmed and all modern resources pressed into service. Even the ungrateful Sa'udi could not be blind to the value of this priceless work of Aramco's Research Development and as one result men like George Rentz had no difficulty at all with Sheikh Yusuf. The tables were turned by these Americans: on many a political problem the Sa'udis could not do without their superior knowledge.

The second department that helped to smooth Arabian-American contacts was that of Public Relations. The work of this department was of a more superficial character than that of the other two and so far as I could see it relied very largely on them.

The third was the Training Department, under Harry Snijder's capable leadership. It had a double task: the technical training of Arabs so that they might usefully work alongside Americans and the teaching of Americans to work in co-operation with the Arabs. For me who had performed similar duties in the Dutch East Indies it was a particular pleasure to see what the Training Department was doing and how they set about their task. I shall not soon forget my visits to the 'school' where the first sorting out of local applicants for employment was in progress. They were for the most part raw bedu from the desert attracted by reports of the marvels that could be seen and the high money that could be earned. In a large room there were sitting together boys of sixteen and men of forty and all were given a fortnight's instruction. At the time of my visit their two Palestinian teachers were teaching them to read and write. The lessons were conducted with the utmost good humour in which the whole class shared. As they worked the teachers began a first sorting of their human material and the men only fit for unskilled labour would be sent out to work. Those more fitted for skilled employment would be retained for further instruction. Here a cross-section of the nomad and oasis population was being given a chance to acquire a new standard of living. A great responsibility indeed rested on the men of the Training Department.

The other side of their work was the training of Americans to co-operate with Arabs and live contentedly in their country, and the promotion of ties of mutual trust and sympathy between the two nations. I was specially interested in the method used for teaching Arabic to Westerners. The system favoured was the so-called 'natural' way of learning to speak a language as a child learns its mother-tongue. In my view this is wrong. An adult has more ways of storing his memory than a child has and with an adult all approaches should be used. I suggested that all the students who were really interested in the language and wanted to learn more than the bare minimum should be taught in an adult way.

"Do not," I said, "start telling them that Arabic is easy, that it is not necessary to learn to write it, that all that is required is to memorize a few stock phrases. Tell your students that Arabic is a difficult language, that it must be understood grammatically and that one must be able to read it in order to get the fullest benefit out of the privilege of living in Arabia."

I received an attentive hearing and was told that the Training Department would go deeper into the matter for both Americans and Arabs. The Department, I knew, took a very serious view of its responsibilities and was even then considering plans by which Arab trainees would be sent beyond the borders of Saʿudi Arabia into the universities of the Middle East and even further, into the centres of learning in the West. For the American employees the matter was not one of national interest but important none the less if they were to be successful in Saʿudi Arabia. The Training Department kept in contact with me and, much to my gratification, invited me again to Dhahran in the middle of 1954 for discussions on the question of future lines of study for the keener Americans.

Aramco's work of geographical exploration in Arabia had for me a special interest, because so far back as 1931 I had myself been a pioneer in this field in the Hadhramaut which is in south-west Arabia. So the Aramco explorers were kindred souls to me and I went to Dhahran hoping to hear of their experiences and to see something of the work they were doing. When I arrived in Dhahran most of them were absent because their working season was in full swing. I was fortunate enough to be invited to visit them in action both in the south and in the north. The two trips that followed were for me the highlights of my stay with Aramco. Geologist Carr took me a good one-day drive to the first camp south of the wells of Jabrin. We reached the camp two hours after sunset but there was no danger of our missing it, as a powerful electric lamp on a high pole announced the site from the far distance. Half of the camp lived in caravans and half in tents. As a guest I was given the best type of sleeping accommodation, which was on top of a double-deck aluminium caravan. It was a fine room and, of course, had electric light. It was screened against flies during the day and mosquitoes at night; it was air-conditioned and I did not sleep on a camp-bed but on an American patented mattress. The men in the camp worked five weeks at a stretch and were then taken by plane to Dhahran for a week's holiday. I sat with them until midnight answering their questions and telling them what Arabian exploration had meant for me when with my friend Professor Von Wissmann I had trekked with half a dozen camels walking in front or following them, but always on foot through an Arabia that was far more romantic than the land of Ibn Sa'ud. The next morning I had the use of their shower-bath wagon and then, sitting in the shade of an awning attached to the kitchen wagon, ate a choice of American food. It was difficult indeed for me to realize that I was on the very border of the Empty Quarter that Bertram Thomas had crossed for the first time only twenty years before. We were actually near the eastern border of the Dahana desert that here changed its name to Duhaina which means the little Dahana; southwards it ended in ar-Rumaila—the little sands. When I sat in my sleeping-room I looked out over a faintly undulating land of reddish sand sprinkled with patches of white gravel. Here and there were small bushes that showed as small, dark tufts sparsely scattered over the empty land. Overhead spanned a bleak sky so thick with blown dust that one could stare at the sun with the naked eye as through a heavy veil. Wind, blown sand, heat and silence was what the day promised. Driving deeper into the great desert we saw no animal life. Once in 1939 coming from the southern coast of Arabia and travelling with Von Wissmann and his assistant through a land from which life seemed to have retreated, my companions and I had said to each other: there in the distance must be the Rub' al Khali. We had not then the means to venture further ahead. Now I was driving southwards towards that same Rub' al Khali as guest of the American oil company.

At intervals of about fifty miles we passed a solitary herdsman keeping watch over widely dispersed camels. Grazing was sparse and hard to find for it rained here only about once in every three years. Then the desert would quickly be covered with green and camels would come great distances for the grazing. Even small boys would then be given ten to twelve camels in their charge. Mr. Carr once saw such a year of abundance in the Duhaina. He asked such a boy where his tribe was and the boy answered that he did not know.

"What do you live on?"

The boy pointed to his head and on his head was an inverted wooden bowl. Into that bowl he milked one of his camels and that would be his food and drink for weeks on end. As we passed those solitary herdsmen I could not help wondering what it must be like to be alone for hours of endless watching in an empty and lifeless land. Every day the same as the day before and as empty and silent as the days to come. What would be in his mind? What would be in mine in such circumstances?

In the next Gravity Meter camp I met Mr. Gerhard the geologist in charge of the group of camps working in the Rub' al Khali. The Gravity Meter is a very sensitive instrument registering the transmission of vibrations caused by the artificially induced explosions used in oil prospecting for indications of subsoil structure. Mr. Gerhard took me south to the spot where Philby had stood as the first Westerner to be guided by beduins to the 'burnt city of the desert'. Al Hadida—the Iron—was comprised of two big meteoric craters. When the meteor hit the ground its great heat had melted the sand and reduced it to caked black lumps.

I had driven with Gerhard a hundred miles over high dunes of reddish sand, all crescent-shaped with steep gradients of 30° facing south. The slopes to the north, whence we came, were gentle. At a short distance behind us there followed a Dodge breakdown car. We would drive at full speed to reach the crests of the half-moons of sand and then turn sharply so as to avoid toppling over on the other side. Whenever we stuck in the sand the breakdown car would halt, hitch a steel cable to our car and then pull us out.

In camp at night the talk always veered towards the topic of America's increasing involvement in Arabia. Gerhard was a man with experience in many other Eastern countries, and he could make comparisons. For him and for his fellow-workers the real problems were not those of the technical processes connected with oil but the problems of America's attitude towards Arabia, her coping with the poverty and backwardness of the country. These talks, not, alas, around a camp-fire, nor in the presence of the natives of the country, revealed to me some of the uneasiness that was growing among these men in the front line. They knew better than the men in Dhahran how Arabia reacted to America's experiments and in them I saw grounds for hope.

I flew back to Dhahran in a small plane that serviced the camps of the Empty Quarter using flat strips of gravelly desert as landing-grounds. The desert no longer offered serious obstacles to American motor vehicles and air transport obviated even the danger of breakdowns and losing one's way. And so the greatest sand waste of Arabia, the Empty Quarter, is losing its significance as a natural dividing zone between the countries bordering on it. Sa'udi Arabia was annexing the bulk of those sands where no man could live and no others could go to protest. America was the instrument of Sa'udi penetration because she wanted to know whether these sands too were floating on oil.

The American exploration of the innermost parts of Arabia had eliminated the dangers and hardships that were formerly inseparable from them. Viewed from the American camps the desert lost its menace, its all-enveloping immensity and silence, its nearness to eternity. The desert was being tamed and losing its grim soul and the beduin desert-dweller was passing out of existence.

Silence fled from the desert with the heavy purring and thudding of motors that worked day and night. Water was no longer the life-blood of the traveller and scarcely the *rahmat Allah*— the blessing of Allah. A huge tank-wagon stood arrogantly in the middle of each camp like an enormous panzered water-bag. Even the heat that used to strike man and beast dumb seemed to be kept at arm's-length in these camps. The smell of the motor replaced that of the camel. Formerly the camel had helped mankind to overcome his fear of the desert and together they turned it into a dwelling-place for both of them. The intruders from America had no use for the camel and no fear of the desert. The Arabia of old they were pushing inexorably aside. Before their advancing host the characteristic Arabia retired with its beauty, its poetry, its grandeur and, let us hope, part of its sufferings too.

My visits to the north took me to different country and showed me a different side of the American oil activity. We travelled day after day over a road that had been built when the first trans-Arabian pipe-line was under construction. This time we did not sleep in camps but in houses arranged in compounds around pumping stations. At night these stations were an impressive sight with all their lights shining far into the desert. Day after day we drove alongside the pipe-line which is surely the most hideous if perhaps not the least essential concomitant of oil operations. The pipe is not buried but generally rests two or three feet above the surface of the desert, on metal or concrete supports. The pipe with the road alongside it and the supervising 'plane on its daily tour of inspection from the air have cut clean through the desert's independence. The pipe, heedless of age-long desert customs and rights, now dominates life in these grazing grounds of the Shammar, the tribe of Ibn Sa'ud's once formidable opponents, the Rashids. The tribal life still went on and I passed many beduins mounted on their camels with their tents and other belongings and followed by the boys with the herds of small cattle, sheep and goats, and with their privileged women riding under canopies that they call *hawdaj* or *maqsar*. Compared with the men in the south, the men of the Shammar were tall and attractive-looking. They lived in a generally cooler climate, in much more fertile country with long, wide, sloping wadis green with vegetation.

It was the end of March and they were gradually moving towards their summer quarters in the north. The pipe could only be passed at intervals where a mud ramp was built over it but any inconvenience the pipe-line caused to the bedu was more than compensated by the stations of drinking-water built for them and their herds wherever the company was itself in need of water for its men and machines. The five pumping-stations along the pipe-line between the Persian Gulf and the Jordan frontier have become centres of attraction for the nomads in summertime. But the sites of these unfailing watering-places were chosen for the convenience of the oil company and not that of the beduins, and often the good grazing grounds are far away from them. Still, around a pumping-station like Turaif, the farthest to the west and only a few miles from the Jordan frontier, the summer of 1951 saw three thousand beduin tents pitched. Because of these concentrations of beduins around the water reservoirs of the T.A.P. line (the Trans-Arabian Pipe line as it is called) the Sa'udi government were able to intensify its control of the beduins and to start welfare work among them. The government leant heavily on the men of the T.A.P. line which is a branch organization of Aramco, and induced the company to build offices and houses for the Sa'udi officials. From what I saw of the building that was going on around Badana and Turaif I thought that Sa'udi officials working in the shade of the T.A.P. line were to be congratulated. The schools for beduin children and for the youth of the quickly expanding villages that sprang up close to the pumping-stations were built to a standard pattern evolved by American and Arabs in co-operation. Perhaps the standard was too high, too American, too far above nomad requirements. I myself would have preferred to see mud buildings in the local

o   199

manner that enriched past centuries of Arab architecture. T.A.P. line changed the life of the neighbouring nomads abruptly, too abruptly. Even the style of dress which had not changed substantially for ages was now being discarded. New food made its appearance and was welcomed by people who had hitherto only known the monotonous desert diet. More disturbing was the birth of a spirit of unrest and discontent. For all his novelties the bedu had to pay by speeding-up the tempo of desert life and by increased efforts to get the money to buy them. And the money was never enough, for prices soared unceasingly.

Our party was so absorbed by all we saw along the pipe-line road and around the bustling pumping-stations that little time was left for visits to the nearest prospecting camps. Here they were not of leading importance, the pipe-line was. I tried to see as much as possible of the land and its population. Whenever I met them mounted on their camels, fanned out in a disorderly manner as they advanced through the desert, the Shammar had no time for foreigners. From the height of their well-fed, tall mounts they looked down upon the man who walked over to them. Their women wondered with amusement what I was going to photograph while I ran to keep pace with the long strides of the camels. What they must have expected happened. I picked out a young woman proudly seated on cushions among the brightly coloured straps of her *maqsar*. A bride elect of the sheikh? When she saw me coming she jumped down lithely from her high seat, fell, was quick on her feet again and off among the marching camels, to the accompaniment of laughter from the other women. I had to be content with the photograph of the empty shell.

Once, with Hans Helley, the young leader of the party, I left the pipe-line and rode across country towards the black dots of a Shammar camp. Dismounting, we slowly approached on foot, announcing our arrival by discreet coughing. A little boy, taking his courage in both hands, brought us to the big tent, a much larger 'house of hair'—as the beduin calls his tent woven from goats' hair—than those usually seen in the south. The reception was as always in the desert.

"*Ahlan wa sahlan, ya ajnabi*"—"You are welcome, O stranger."
Even the women joined in the general activity to make us feel
comfortable, spreading sheepskins over camel-saddles for us to
lean against and bringing in butter that just had been made from
goats' milk. We accepted gratefully and shut our eyes to the
goats' hair with which the gift was liberally adorned. Our host
flung some dried camel dung on to the fire and pounded coffee
beans, while the little boy who had had the courage to bring
us to the tent was praised by the sheikh and sent to invite the
men from the other tents to come and join us. He was a smart
little boy by beduin standards and had the nice pet name of
Khufaiyef which is a diminutive of *khafif*—light: we might have
called him 'little feather'. When I asked him to pose for his
photograph, his courage suddenly left him and tears began to
appear in his eyes. Fortunately a small present served to overcome
this moment of weakness. When his photograph had been taken
he was told by his father to greet "*ash-shaiba*—the greybeard"
properly. 'Little feather' came nearer and kissed not only the
greybeard—that was I—but every member of the party. His warm
young lips touched our cheeks in turn and we had to overlook
his dirty nose. After the butter came the coffee and then to
finish up with a long draught of buttermilk before we went our
way again.

Several times we went off the beaten track to view the remains
of *mahfuras*—reservoirs formerly built to catch rain-water. We
saw also the ruins of what long ago may well have been fortified
places guarding grazing grounds in the broad wadis. The most
impressive of the ruins we saw were at Duqra, twenty miles
south of Turaif. There the surrounding wall of a *mahfura* still
stood to a height of twenty feet. The eliptical reservoir itself
measured two hundred and forty feet in length and one hundred
and sixty in breadth. Nearby we saw the ruins of a huge building,
one hundred and twenty feet wide, the lower part of whose walls
of tall hewn blocks of stone was still standing. Behind it a great
spread of ruins could be seen. For archaeologists this north-west
tip of Sa'udi Arabia seems to offer a great field of exploration.

The last day of this excursion brought me to the farthest point of Sa'udi territory. The boundary with Jordan has not yet been fixed but may well be an outstanding landmark called the *Tell al Hibr*—the Ink Hill—a hill covered with black boulders, perhaps an old volcano. As I climbed over the boulders I noticed that in places the shiny black face of the rock had been scratched with characters that were clearly legible. There were a number of these graffiti but few when compared with the abundance of such inscriptions in the west and south-west of the Peninsula.

We flew back to Dhahran in Aramco's regular service-plane, landing at every pumping-station and even at the nearly forgotten Ras Misha'ab, the sandy cape on the Persian Gulf coast, where during the building of the T.A.P. line the huge iron casings thirty inches in diameter, were landed by means of an aerial steel cable. Only a remnant of the former settlement was left.

The sun was setting when we approached Dhahran and in the fading light I saw innumerable mounds breaking the flat surface of the desert. They were not simple sand dunes but man-made monticules, tumuli, as are to be found on Bahrain island. I had also seen them on the hillsides of Wadi Al Kharj, the next goal of my investigations during my stay with Aramco. The air transport of the company had opened up a vast field of research in eastern Sa'udi Arabia. Sa'udi Arabia had opened its doors wide to the men who were discovering and producing her oil. They were given an opportunity for further exploration of the country on a scale hitherto unknown and they gladly seized the opportunity presented to them. But that was not all. The more they got to know the people in whose midst they had to work the more they realized that they had, too, a humanitarian task to perform and in this their people at home, their Government would have to join for much of Sa'udi Arabia's future depended on it. Al Kharj was the first proof of America's wider understanding of her responsibilities in Arabia. In 1944-5 I had seen how Aramco and the State Department had started out. I was very anxious to see what progress they had made and so I now turned my face towards Al Kharj, the American experiment with water and agriculture.

15

Agriculture and Water

BACK IN DHAHRAN I did not find awaiting me the expected invitation from the King to visit him in ar-Riyadh. I was in no hurry but cherished the hope I would not have to leave the country without having seen the King, the Crown Prince and ar-Riyadh as a town of oil prosperity. One thing more I had in my mind and that was, before continuing my journey to south-west Arabia, to see again Al Kharj, the American agricultural experiment, fifty-four miles to the south of the capital. In January 1945 I had been the guest of the men sent out by the American State Department to show the Arabs what mechanized farming could do even with desert soil if water could be pumped to it. I had good and bad memories of that trip and of the hardships I had suffered between Dhahran, and Al Kharj and ar-Riyadh. My Ford wagon had fought a stiff battle with the high sand dunes of the Dahana desert and often I had had to join in the fight. The red hue that sunset threw on the sands had seemed to me not entirely earthly and not inappropriate to the struggle. I was not reluctant to see the Dahana again, this time not to struggle with her but to ride as her victor, as a passenger on the Sa'udi railway.

It was an early spring morning when Bram and I stood near the *sikkat al hadid*—the iron road—on a spot where later a station was to be built, on the outskirts of Dhahran. We were elated at the prospect of the journey but our elation did not last long. A sand-storm had been blowing throughout the night, the air was thick with dust, no sun was to be seen and with a grey sky of mourning above us, we stood unprotected in the open and shivered. We knew that the train had already left Dammam, its starting point.

For more than an hour we waited, ashamed to go back to the friends who had told us how foolish we were to think of travelling by rail. Finally we heard and then saw the train coming. It advanced very slowly indeed. In front of the green-and-white striped diesel engine a sort of snow-plough on wheels had been adapted for sand ploughing and in a car behind the engine rode a group of men with shovels and spades. As we made our way to Abqaiq, the second centre of oil activity, visibility was very poor; we moved in constant fear of running into too much sand for the plough. When that happened, the workmen descended and cleared the rails by hand. We, inside, were not very happy. There was dust everywhere. We could not even see the desert but we tried to be as patient as Arabs in similar circumstances. Hours after Abqaiq we arrived at Hufhuf, the great oasis, but saw very little of it. Usually Arab travellers on a train like to pass the time in eating and drinking. This day we all seemed to be down-hearted for there was little eating and drinking and less talking. Nose and mouth covered against the dust, we sat crumpled up in protection against the cold wind. In a big southward bend we set out for Haradh and there we halted. All the passengers got down and washed their hands, arms, faces and feet with the water that flowed from an iron pipe and could not be turned off. After ablutions, prayers were said and we all climbed back into the train and set off again for Al Kharj in the neighbourhood of which we arrived about midnight. If no one had been there to meet us we should have had to curl up beside the tracks. Fortunately a car was waiting for us and soon carried us off to a shower-bath and a clean room in an American home. My second contact with Al Kharj had begun.

Two things had impressed me during my first visit in 1945: the monuments of the past and those of a very modern present. Both were still there and I was now better prepared to meet them. The Americans had brought here their best machinery and their know-how and money was not lacking. The monuments of antiquity around Al Kharj were still waiting to be explored and yield up what secrets they might have. I knew now that these remains were much greater in number and far more varied than I had suspected seven years before.

In May 1942 the United States Agricultural Mission headed by Twitchell had, after the meeting with Ibn Sa'ud, gone to Al Kharj, guided by Sheikh 'Abdullah as-Sulaiman. He had himself started the Al Kharj experiment some years before by importing Iraqi agricultural engineers. One of them was still there when Twitchell arrived. 'Abdullah as-Sulaiman had also secured the co-operation of some engineers and geologists from the oil company and work was begun in the optimistic expectation that it could not fail. An earlier attempt made in ancient days had come to grief because of diminishing water supplies. Near the great water-holes of Al Kharj and in the neighbouring desert one could still see the remains of irrigation ditches, one deeper than the other and even the *qanat*—the underground water conduit of Persia—that had been tunnelled through the limestone over long distances, many feet deeper in the earth than the deepest ditch. The ancient Arabs had seen all these efforts come to naught and the cultivation of Al Kharj had stopped.

'Abdullah as-Sulaiman was convinced that modern machinery would succeed where the ancient Arab had failed. Motor pumps would make the water flow into the irrigation ditches and then Al Kharj's former prosperity would return. The water holes of Al Kharj were very impressive, especially the 'Ain Dhila', a deep square well with perpendicular sides, cut in the edge of Wadi Al Kharj. Looking down on its dark, shiny mirror one could well understand the urge to bring water to the arid plains above. 'Ain Dhila' and 'Ain Samha, 300 feet each in diameter with water 420 feet below the surface, were a miracle in Al Kharj. Umm Ghisa in the plain, a mile to the west, was only forty-five feet deep and much less impressive.

I had the good fortune to meet Muhammad al 'Uthman as-Subai'i who in 1940 had been taken by 'Abdullah as-Sulaiman from their common native village al Khabra near 'Anaiza and brought here. Muhammad as-Subai'i told me that British engineers had brought the first motor pumps and that once the pumps had been got working they were left in the care of the Iraqi. They pumped the two ancient wells of 'Ain Umm Ghisa and the 'Ain Samha but the water level sank and the foundations of the pumps gave way having been laid too near to the border of the 'Ain. When two years later the Americans took over it was decided to concentrate on the 'Ain Dhila' which was situated a little way uphill in more solid limestone. Aramco provided geologists in B. A. Brancamp, Tom Barger and L. M. Snijder and field engineers Brown, Perry and Holbard. Aramco also advanced money, brought and installed machinery and made the water flow again in the British-built main channel.

That is what Twitchell's State Department Mission found. They were seized with the same facile optimism that had inspired those who had worked at the experiment before them. On return to Washington the Mission persuaded the State Department that this was America's opportunity to make an official contribution to the nation in whose land was the oil that might be of decisive importance to the Allied war-effort. In those days England was making a great effort to bring wheat and rice to Sa'udi Arabia and so stave off starvation. If wheat could be grown within the country it would release urgently needed Allied sea transport and be the surest means of providing food for the local population. The project seems to have been adopted without much investigation, as Twitchell puts it in his *Sa'udi Arabia*: 'A most efficient and able group of practical agriculturists loaned by the United States Department of Agriculture was sent. They have directed an immense amount of construction along lines of the most approved American practice.'

In January 1945 I had met these ten or twelve men then fully occupied in trying to irrigate and cultivate Arabian desert on American lines. It was a feasible project although difficult and of doubtful wisdom. If the object was to produce as much wheat as possible in the shortest possible time, this indeed was the way to do it. The demands of the Allied war no doubt acted as a spur but if the experiment was to go farther and be a way to help Arabia, to show her how her agriculture could be raised to a higher level, this, surely, was not the right way to go about it. War-time is no time for adequate preparation or deep study. The quick and simple way was to imitate what had been done and done successfully in the desert lands of America. And that was what I saw happening in Al Kharj in January 1945. But in the spring of 1952 the guiding principle of the experiment had, so far as I could see, not been changed and that was inexcusable.

After the initial set-backs that are to be expected when foreign methods are used in a country with entirely different conditions, most of the difficulties seemed to have been overcome. Twitchell, whom I knew as a sober and prudent man, wrote in his book: 'Mechanization at Al Kharj has proven practical. In 1945 there were 1,452 workers on the farm; in 1949 this number was reduced to 742 but production was increased.' Elsewhere Twitchell wrote: 'In 1951 cash value of the harvest exceeded the costs of the operation.'

In January 1945 the Americans lived in a mud-built house near 'Ain Dhila' where the motor pumps raised water for the irrigation of the neighbouring plain. Now in 1952 the American centre had been moved seven miles away to better soil where two flat plots of mixed loam and sand were being cultivated. Twenty miles to the south-west the third and most fertile plot of all got its water from the Khafs Dughra well. A total of 3,500 acres was under cultivation and it was said that with the water available a total area of eight thousand acres could be irrigated. With Joe Clark Smith and his wife Winon, a young couple deeply interested in the problems of poverty and backwardness of the Arabian culti-vators of the soil, I made a trip every day through the cultivated parts and in the surrounding country. This American pair was making an effort to learn the two foreign languages that were their daily stumbling blocks in Al Kharj: Arabic first and then French. What French people were doing here will soon be seen. I drove through every section of the plantations. Bersim—lucerne—the staple fodder for the four hundred Sa'udi cows and for the two hundred odd royal horses, together with Sudan grass and wheat, covered the greater part of the fields. Cabbages, onions, tomatoes, green peas, carrots, beet, different varieties of melons, egg-plants and potatoes made up the rest. Wide stretches of tomato and egg-plants seemed dead: the cold had killed them or nearly done so. There were nearly 20,000 date-palms of sturdy growth. These trees do not bear fruit until their sixth year and on each of those that were not much older I counted eight to nine clusters of blossom. Later the number may rise to fifteen. The pollination, as usual in Arabia, was done artificially, a cluster of blossoms of a female tree was cut open with a knife and a small bundle of flowers from the male tree introduced before the place was bound up again with fibre.

An experiment in poultry raising was shown to me with special pride. The year before three thousand chickens had been supplied to the Royal Court which also took 250 eggs daily. The number of both eggs and chickens was soon to be doubled. Incubators were working at top speed and a first generation of turkeys was being raised successfully, the eggs being flown over from America.

There were scarcely any labourers to be seen in the cultivated fields of Al Kharj. The American principle of doing the work with machines instead of men had been followed here. When I asked Joe Clark he agreed it was a mistake and said that he tried to let as much work as possible be done by men and women. The only men who had their houses in the plantations were the guards who patrolled the fields on horseback during the night keeping away thieves and preventing Arabs from letting their camels stray on to the greenstuff. When we wanted to talk to Arabs Joe, his wife and I had to drive to a headman's house or to the incubators where young Hadhramis from the Aden Protectorate were in charge. The guards, too, were not local: they had learned their job in the army of their home country, Jordan. The stories they told in front of their American bosses often smelt a little anti-British and they appeared to see no inconsistency in declaring their great pride in being sons of *Abu Hunaiq*—the father of the small chin—Glubb Pasha, the man who made the Beduin Legion the best Arab armed force of the Middle East.

Joe Clark took me to as-Saih, the most prosperous of the villages

of Al Kharj district, to the house of an Arab whose name was
'Abdallah bin Muhammad as-Sama'il and who styled himself
Wazir of Amir Sa'ud al Kabir, an uncle of the King. I had already
met him in the house of his lord, seven years before. He had made
good use of the chances offered to him by the presence of the
Americans and the prosperity that followed in their train. We
had coffee and tea and every one of our party was presented with
a package of 200 excellent American cigarettes. Joe got two.
Thanks to our host I was invited to the house of Muhammad, the
son of the old Sa'ud al Kabir. Him, too, I had met seven years
before and in memorable circumstances. He was then returning
from Mecca where he had accompanied his mother to perform
the pilgrimage. Both of us had difficulties because of the rain.
I passed a car in the distance and saw it getting bogged in the
mud. Walking over to lend a hand I was welcomed by a tall, fine-
looking man who was helping his driver to clear the car. He
was Muhammad and a moment later he came over to help us
when we got stuck. Here he was again, recognizing me at once
and inviting me to go to al Hayathim, another Al Kharj village,
where he had a garden and a big house. He himself could not go
but the wazir of the family knew all about it and would show us
the trophies of the hunting expedition from which he had just
returned. When I asked him about his trip he told me he had taken
twenty desert motor vehicles, which is the new way of hunting,
and that he had ranged even as far as the wadis bordering on the
Rub' al Khali. The white oryx—*wudhaihi*—was the game they
went after. They had killed forty *baqar al wahsh*—wild cows—
as the white oryx is also called by the Arabs. The white oryx
belongs to the antelope family and is the tallest animal living wild
in desert Arabia. This sturdy, snow-white, animal with its black
blaze and black feet and its long, slightly curved horns is the most
beautiful representative of Arabian animal life. When I heard
what Muhammad said I could not help showing my repulsion at
such butchery and said: "You could not eat half that number
even if you had a big party. You must have thrown away at least
half of the kill." He did not deny it but his face continued to beam

with the satisfaction of the successful hunter. Then as if to console me he said: "This time we caught some alive. Come and take a picture of them in my garden."

I listened to more hunting stories. The year before their party had killed sixty-four oryxes and of course far more than a hundred gazelles. Looking out of the window I saw that behind the Amir Muhammad's three cars was a pick-up at the back of which was fixed a horizontal wooden bar bound with sack-cloth. Eight hunting falcons with leather caps covering their heads and eyes were perched on the bar into which their sharp claws dug firmly. How ugly this modern combination looked and yet how picturesque it had been in the days when the falcons were carried on the leather-clad arms of the falconers mounted on Arab horses. In those days oryx and gazelle and other game had had a chance. Hunting had then meant a struggle of endurance between man and game. It also meant a contest in alertness and in the sharpness of the senses of the hunted and the hunter, be it a horse, falcon or that forebear of our modern greyhound, the *saluqi*. Years before, in Jedda, I had seen the beginning of this motorized slaughter when the *effrenjis*—the foreigners—started the dangerous and exciting sport.

When first in Jedda I used to drive aimlessly in the desert, and as soon as I was far away from the beaten tracks, saw herds of gazelle fleeing before my car. In later years the herds had become small groups. The gazelle was fighting a losing battle for the Hejazi, as now the Nejdi, alas, had learnt the *effrenji* lesson only too well. In Muhammad ibn Saʿud al Kabir's garden I admired his six white oryxes, the few that escaped alive from his royal hunting expedition. How long, I wondered, will it be before the white oryx departs into Arabia's past to join there the many other species of fauna that once lived and now live no more in the Peninsula? In Muhammad's garden I also took some pictures of the *waʿal*—an ibex or wild goat—a typical animal of the rocky mountains of west and south Arabia that I saw here for the first time from nearby. He at least cannot be followed with motor cars and may well survive the oryx.

I have to thank Joe Clark and his wife Winon for other encounters in the Al Kharj of their days. They introduced me to the
French mission, twelve men sent out in advance of others who
were to build a factory for small arms and ammunition and a
military town which they called a 'cité militaire'. In the townlet of
al Kharj the extensive former royal palace had been turned into
barracks. The Sa'udi government seemed to be planning new
military headquarters to be built much nearer the capital than the
existing headquarters in Taif and both contracts had gone to a
French firm. An Alsatian, Dr. Peltz, with his wife and little
daughter were special friends of the Clarks and were soon mine
too. Dr. Peltz was deeply interested in the country and its people
and he proved to have a sharp nose for antiquities. Before we went
to see his discoveries I was shown the lay-out of the officers'
quarters of the future Sa'udi army. The work in progress centred
round the well which had to produce the water for the workers
and their machinery. In the plan even a modern swimming
pool for the army officers and the factory engineers was included.
What was told about the factory reminded me of the Imam of the
Yemen's similar small-arms factory for San'a. It is understandable
that Arab Governments should wish to make their own weapons
but they would be better advised not to play with such useless
toys. Much cheaper and better small arms and ammunition can
be bought from countries where these highly perfected industries
have existed for many years. It will take many years to train
beduins into skilled workers and even then the factory will be
entirely dependent on foreign countries for its raw material.
The experience of the Imam in San'a ought to have served as a
warning.

I was glad to turn with Dr. Peltz to vestiges of Arabia's past.
Together we went to Jebel Farzan near the village of Sulaimiya
whose date-groves seemed to be fighting a losing battle with the
sands. There was scope for archaeologists at Jebel Farzan. Stone
monuments in different shapes lay all around the foot of the
Jebel—mountain. There were caves in the mountain, flint imple-
ments and fossilized fragments of ostrich shells were lying about

in the caves and along the foot of the Jebel were easily recognizable. From the top of the Jebel one looked out over varied traces of former human habitation. The most impressive was a double underground irrigation canal cut in the limestone for a distance farther than the eye could reach. The manholes surrounded by excavated rubble stood out in distinct lines in the light of the sunset. The source of the water that must once have flowed through these qanat was at the foot of Jebel Farzan itself. One qanat soon branched off and was lost to view but the other stretched across the wide plain in a great easterly bend. We found by measurement that the conduit lay at a depth of from 48 to 50 feet and the distance between the manholes was approximately 40 yards. The manholes were very wide and a trickle of water could be seen flowing on the rubble below. On our way to Jebe Farzan we had passed a newly built qanat with square masonry manholes. We were told it was an extension of one of the old qanats and had been built in the direction of Al Kharj by the order of the Minister of Finance. The work had been stopped when the expected water did not flow through the tunnel.

We spent another day seeing the horses of the King and the cows. Most of them were kept in large enclosures with mud walls near the Khafs Dughra farm where the food for the animals was grown. Arabs were in charge of both horses and cows and the latter were very small and thin. The horses were in better condition but interest in them seems to have declined with the advent of the motor car as a handier means of transport. The horses each had one foot shackled to a chain and were feeding from long troughs made of mud bricks. In a special enclosure we were shown some very old mares said to have been used by Ibn Saʿud himself when he rode to war. The stories told us by the grooms seemed a little exaggerated for they quoted ages much higher than the twenty-five or even thirty years that we consider the normal life-span of a horse. The royal sport of horse-racing, once practised by all the Amirs, was dying out and the horses at Al Kharj seemed to be kept on for sentimental reasons. Interest in the breeding of pure Arab horses now seems to be the prerogative of the West. It was in England, America and Holland, when they visited those countries, that the sons of Ibn Sa'ud could see this finest product of their country. At home the competition of the motor-car was proving deadly. Having nearly exterminated the beautiful wild animals of the desert, the Arab is now apparently content to see the domesticated horse disappear. Before long they may only survive for them in poetry and Arab tales.

We heard little, and did not enquire, of the military plans of the Sa'udis. The matter was regarded as secret and respected by us as such. The agricultural experiment was public property and so much more open to discussion. Started hastily in wartime it was now due for overhaul and replanning for peacetime conditions. The Americans responsible, in this case the men sent by the State Department to follow up Aramco's initial efforts, seemed to have their doubts. I sensed their approval when they listened to the criticisms I made at their invitation. Fundamental truths that I had learnt from experience with similar plans in the Dutch East Indies had been ignored at Al Kharj. Nature is a jealous mistress. As the British learnt from their ground-nuts failure in East Africa and their disastrous experiments in Queensland, Australia, schemes for agricultural development in any country can only succeed if they satisfy local laws of nature. Introducing American methods in the heart of Arabia is fundamentally wrong and will only continue so long as American money (even if it is oil money made by Americans in Arabia) is paying for it, so long as American machinery does the work and American know-how is its driving force. This type of experiment is often superficially successful but breaks down in backward countries whenever one of these three conditions is not fulfilled. These experiments do not take root in Arabian soil. In Al Kharj for instance the Americans did not attract the Arab agriculturist but pushed him aside. They wanted large, open spaces for their machinery and any small farmers that happened to be in their way were asked to settle elsewhere. So the American plantations became royal, princely and plutocratic interests. 'Abdullah as-Sulaiman, the royal family and the few 'nouveaux riches' alone profited by it and became the owners of this new type of Arabian 'garden'. Into the largely democratic Saʿudi Arabia Americans helped to introduce a feudal type of society such as Europe discarded hundreds of years ago. Instead of serving the interests of the governing few, Al Kharj should have been the el dorado of a new type of Arab peasant. The American experiment should have been applied to creating a new landed peasantry, an Arab smallholder: it is based on what is good for Americans in America. Its leaders ought to try to reshape it into a plan based on what is good for Arabia and for Arabs living in Arabia.

It is interesting to compare Al Kharj with a similar experiment tried by the British in south-west Arabia and started at about the same time as the American project. At Abyan on the shore of the Indian Ocean about fifty miles east of Aden there was a large stretch of fertile soil that had been left waste by earlier inhabitants who were probably decimated by fever and by local wars. Years ago I had myself passed through the coastal portion of this wide wadi and wondered why land apparently so fertile had so few living on it. This land was watered by rains from the nearby mountains of the Yemen. Before starting the experiment the Aden Government put the political situation in order and created security in the country. Next they enquired as to who were the rightful owners of the land. After ensuring that the profits of any agricultural development would not go to a Sultan and his family or to any other privileged class but to those who actually tilled the soil the scheme was put into operation. A number of small dams were built and the water from them led through irrigation channels. Human labour was employed and no machines. People from surrounding tribes who were willing to work were allowed to do so but no one was allocated more land than he and his immediate family could work. Anti-malarial precautions kept the place healthy. Agricultural experts gave advice and distributed good seed and the population increased from three to sixteen thousand. As the soil proved to be very suitable, cotton-growing was introduced with marked success and soon the tribesmen were earning more money than they had ever seen before. This might have encouraged laziness and led them to stop working until their profits were consumed so it was decided that only one third of the profits should go to the workers, another third would be set aside as a reserve for years of failing crops for slumps in the cotton, and the remainder would be used for purposes of research. Instead of the sinking water-level of Al Kharj, the water-table here is rising steadily thanks to careful administration. Abyan's problem is how best to dispose of their surplus water. Al Kharj's problem is how in the future they can face their diminishing supply. At Abyan the problem may cause some technical difficulty in the way of construction of an aqueduct carrying the surplus water to other arable land but at Abyan the British curbed from the start the Sultan's efforts to direct the profits into his own pockets. The experiment was directed by a 'Wadi Abyan Authority' representing three separate parties: the Aden government, the Sultan and the cultivators themselves.

Water lies at the bottom of many of the problems of Sa'udi Arabia. Experience had taught the Americans at Al Kharj not to pump from the three pits more than the apparent water inflow. At first the water-level in these pits had sunk alarmingly but later it became almost stabilized at a much lower level when the pumps were drastically slowed down. The water-table, however, was gradually sinking. The high salt content of the water had proved to be detrimental to soil and to crops and to overcome this fresh desert soil had had to be introduced as a surface covering.

The American geologists knew roughly where Arabia's subteranean rivers flowed and having drilled to the requisite level they would astonish the Arabs by bringing up a spout of sweet water a yard or so above the ground and the supply seemed to be endless. To the Arabs this was the blessing of Allah. The American rightly feared that the water would be squandered and allowed to run off as waste to the sea (these artesian wells being generally near the shore) or would form pools and breed malaria mosquitoes. The Arabs in charge promised that the water would be turned off after use but the Americans soon discovered that it was running day and night. Why cut off a divine blessing? The bounty of Allah was boundless, water was Allah's gift, so let it flow. American talk about *huma*—fever—merely showed that they were unbelievers. They, the Arabs, knew better than that because it was God who sent diseases and He gave health. So artesian wells flowed in many parts of the country. What began as a blessing turned into misfortune. Waste water turned the fields and date-groves into swamps, malaria inevitably followed and the coastal oases saw their populations dwindle and their green belts of fields and gardens become desolate.

Elsewhere American enterprise was better rewarded. They brought pure drinking water in closed conduits from the Wadi Fatima to Jedda and set drinking places for the beduin along the T.A.P. line. In the oases and the towns the big owners of property were helped to improve their estates. They were shown that by digging deeper wells they could bring more water to the surface. The actual raising of the water no longer depended on human or animal effort. Motors never tired and soon the thump of motor-pumps and the gurgling of a continuous stream of water was to be heard in the gardens of all the rich. The gardens of the great landowners were thus extended and prospered, but poorer cultivators who could not afford a motor-pump were left to struggle with an ever-lowering water-level. They could no longer raise sufficient water for their needs and their gardens began to wither.

The rich Arabs of the towns saw new prospects opening before them. They too would pay for American expert advice about water. All members of the royal family and all those who held high official office could count on receiving special attention and so teams of well-drillers were soon busy in and around ar-Riyadh. Water was provided for men and camels at public drinking-places inside and outside the town. The surrounding tribes soon learnt that ar-Riyadh could in future be depended on for water. This first necessity of life being thus assured, the King in his widely-famed generosity would take care of the second necessity: food. So they gave up the struggle for life in the desert and set their tents near the walls of the town and of the palace with the ever-flowing water and the food distribution centres near-by. The town spread far out into the desert.

The rich then found it imperative to get away from these poverty-stricken, evil-smelling, unhygienic hordes of desert people who so polluted the ground they lived on that ar-Riyadh stank. So they started to build houses on the desert plateau. They were now no longer tied to the vicinity of the old wells, for the Americans would provide water and the Americans did what the men in power, the men of influence and riches, asked them. On patches of desert gravel these men built their new houses and put mud walls around them as soon as the drillers had made sure that water could be raised with pumps. Then within their walls the desert would disappear, for water makes the desert of Arabia blossom everywhere, even when its surface is strewn with gravel.

American drillers and motor-pumps bought from the West made possible the new Riyadh that defies the desert. When I was in the capital directly after my visit of Al Kharj I asked the leader of a driller team what they thought of it.

"We? We obey orders. From His Majesty, from the Princes and the *Wazirs*—Ministers. It has nothing to do with us."

"But what about the future? What about the water-table of this desert plateau on which the capital is built?"

"During the last two years the water-table appears to have sunk more than thirty feet, but thank God," the man added, "thirty wells more and I leave this God-forsaken country for good."

I heard the voice of his conscience and I did not find it very reassuring.

Some days later I met one of the King's advisers and asked him whether he was not aware of what appeared to be an imminent danger.

"We know," he said, "that the water reserves under the desert around ar-Riyadh are perhaps being tapped too heavily, but if it should become difficult to raise enough water we can always build a pipe-line from here to the Euphrates or the Tigris. There is plenty of water there and as the Americans built that huge pipe of thirty inches from the Aramco oilfields to as-Sa'ida [Sidon] on the Mediterranean, which is much more than a thousand miles away, why should not they build a much smaller pipe over a far shorter distance to bring an abundance of water to this town and enough even to raise the subterranean water-level again?"

Happy the man who can be so irresponsible and naïve!

The responsible authorities of Aramco fearing ultimately a catastrophe gave repeated warnings to the Saʿudis. Such warnings, backed by the weighty arguments they used, would have convinced anyone with a background of Western learning but were entirely without effect on the uncomprehending Arab. Aramco then felt that something drastic had to be done to bring home to the Arabs the dangers of the situation and not only to the leaders but to the whole nation down to the meanest beduin. Americans are masters of mass suggestion and have wide experience in putting across ideas. A very American solution was found in an idea that would have worked perfectly in America. Why not in Arabia? Mankind is the same all over the world and particularly where, as here, a primary human need was at stake. So it was decided that experienced American camera men should visit Saʿudi Arabia and make there an educational film on *al miya*—the water. Technically the job they did was a good one and from a point of view of popular scientific exposition of the water problem they produced an able piece of work. It was not easy to persuade the King to give permission for a film to be made in the land of Wahhabism, a film intended for showing to his Wahhabi subjects, a film, moreover, with musical illustrations in the land of ʿAbd al Wahhab who had regarded modern music as an invention of the devil and a film centred round the Royal House and thereby showing the royal approval. But with tact and patience the Americans overcame all difficulties and after two years' hard work they completed the first film made in Saʿudi Arabia and intended for her people. If it proved a success the film with Arabic and English commentary might well spread its benign influence to the neighbouring Arab countries.

The film was very American, readily comprehensible to movie-minded and film-trained spectators. But the average Saʿudi is incapable of understanding what flashes on the screen before his eyes. Nor can he understand a metallic voice speaking literary Arabic with which he is completely unfamiliar. Scientific explanations of rain sinking into the soil, gathering in places and being brought to the surface elsewhere are entirely beyond him He believes, and his is still that stubborn Wahhabi conviction, that Allah has directly to do with His greatest blessing for the Arab, the water He gives him. The man who tries to shake his belief attacks the foundation of his life. The Arab will have to learn one day, perhaps very soon, but the teaching will have to be done with the wisdom and patience of the man who understands what is in the heart of the Sa'udi Arab. He will find there a wisdom he himself may have forgotten: *al 'ajalu min ash-shaitan wa as-sabaru min ar-Rahman*—haste is from the devil and patience from the Merciful. Let us hope too that nature, in supplying water, will be patient with her erring children in Arabia.

16

The Last Audience

THE INVITATION to visit His Majesty in al Murabba'a palace in ar-Riyadh reached me when I was still enjoying to the full the many opportunities that Al Kharj offered. Yet it was the hope of securing this invitation that had chiefly brought me to Sa'udi Arabia, so it was with delight that I learnt that my hope was going to be fulfilled. On Sunday, 2nd March 1952, Joe and Winon Clark drove Bram and me the fifty-four miles to ar-Riyadh. We saw in the distance the places known to have been the former favourite camping-grounds of Ibn Sa'ud when he could allow himself a little relaxation. In talking to us, the foreigners, and to leading Hejazis he liked to tell of the good healthy life one lived in tents and in the open, fanned by the pure desert breeze, drinking warm, frothy camel's milk out of wooden bowls and eating with it dates and some handfuls of mutton and rice. That simple and unvaried diet of the desert, he claimed, did him a lot of good. Sitting in front of his tent he had found rest in looking at his camel herds as they were driven past by herdsmen he knew and with whom he would exchange greetings and information about the numbers and condition of the animals.

We drove through the Wadi Hanifa, which is a shallow depression between Al Kharj and the capital, and from time to time mounted the slightly higher plateau to avoid wide bends in the wadi below. The nearer we got to ar-Riyadh the scarcer the vegetation became. This was not the work of nature alone but of man. The people of the capital had needed firewood—much firewood—and so they had stripped the desert clean, first near the town and then further away in an ever-widening circle. We saw some caravans bringing firewood to the market in front of the town wall. I remember having seen a lonely lorry in the desert near Jabrin wells, two hundred miles to the south. We had gone to the men to ask why they were there so far away from the track and had been told that they came from ar-Riyadh and were gathering firewood. There were eight of them.

"How can that pay, such a distance by lorry?" we had said.

"Back in the town with our lorry piled high with firewood we shall be paid more than six hundred Sa'udi riyals for it." We decided that the appetite of the town, even for firewood, must have grown beyond measure.

The first sight we had of modern ar-Riyadh was two sets of radio masts indicative of the changes that had taken place. The next unexpected sight was of a drilling rig and an American camp of motor vehicles. We had a talk with its leaders. There were four of these water-drilling units working in the desert around the town. When they struck water at a favourable depth wells were dug, motor pumps installed and gardens laid out. Longing for a well and a garden of one's own had, we were told, spread like wildfire among the wealthy classes of ar-Riyadh.

The town, when it eventually came in sight, was colourless in the haze of fine dust that filled the air. Though a *salat al istighath* —a special pray for rain—had been held by royal command throughout the whole kingdom, the blessing of the much-belated rains had not descended yet. The grey outline of the big fort that rose above the horizontal lines of the flat-roofed houses, gradually took shape and was followed by the long, low blocks of al Murabba'a palace that stood apart in the desert at some distance from the town. The track we had been following changed into a better one leading by the terminal of the railroad, parallel to the eastern wall but distant from it, to the landing-ground. A brand-new concrete airport building of the type one finds all over the world was being given a local touch by a mosque that was under construction near it. The mosque had an elegant minaret and thereby flouted the Wahhabi tenet that a mosque should not have a minaret but that a raised corner of the roof should be used for the 'azan—the call to prayer. It was the first, but not the last, contravention of Wahhabi sternness in the modern additions to the capital. Opposite the entrance to the aerodrome on the other side of the broad asphalt approach road was a large American-built contractor's camp, at that time run by the Baker Company. The Sa'udi military guard at the gate of the camp let us pass for the camp was to be our lodging during this visit to the capital. The camp looked exactly like all other camps, that is to say utterly practical and tasteless. Long, low, concrete sheds parallel to each other stood in front of large store-houses which in turn led to vast dumps of rusty machinery and heavy material. The administrative and residential quarters were very attractive with air-conditioned bedrooms, a mess-room and offices. Thanks to Joe Clark, Bram and I were made very welcome at this un-expected introduction to ar-Riyadh that even from a distance was now unfamiliar to me.

I made my first excursion that same afternoon with the Americans of Baker Camp who although they had to work with the Royal Court did not come into contact with al Murabba'a palace for the King preferred not to be disturbed by foreigners. When we drove along the walls of the old palace quarter I no longer recognized it. It seemed to me that the mud wall with its recurrent bastions had been extended and now enclosed a much vaster space. Through a gap in a new east wall could be seen a concrete building with brightly coloured exterior, rows of balconies and the usual tasteless exaggerations common to all modern villas in the Middle East. The old wall, which had lain farther back, had been demolished and with this new villa in front the original palace buildings were pushed into the background. Sadly, it seemed to me, its crenellated crest now cut the sky-line and its bands of almost dog-tooth ornament cast their shadows on those massive, sober walls, relic of the traditional, aristocratic, Nejdi style. In front of the villa was a garden full of bushes and young trees, a patch of exuberant green speckled with flowers. Garden and villa were in violent contrast with the aridity of the rest of the Murabba'a compound and seemed to offer themselves mutely to the criticism of the passer-by. The palace quarter was now a silent monument to the rift between the strength and dignity of the old and the tawdriness of the new.

The road, in a wide curve, avoided the old palace and then reached the fringe of the town as it spread out towards the desert. There was a square lined with the houses for younger sons of Ibn Saʻud all of the same dimensions and all built in the good old style; and in a corner of the square a mosque that conformed to Wahhabi ideas having an elevated roof-corner and no minaret. This most pleasing remnant of the old was in the corner nearest the old town. Opposite, on the desert side of the square, the new town palace of the Crown Prince, *Al Hamra*—the Red One—had been built by a modern Syrian architect. The next house again was modern, the villa of a guest and protégé of the King, Rashid Gulaini Ali, former leader of the 'Golden Square' in Iraq. Midhat Sheikh al Ardh, the private Syrian physician of the Royal Family, whom I had met several times in Jedda, lived in the next villa. And then we were in the open again, on our way to an-Nasriyya palace, built by the order of the Crown Prince on the desert plateau that stretched above the depression of the Wadi Hanifa in which ar-Riyadh itself lay. This palace, too, was surrounded by a high mud wall that neatly cut off a large patch of the desert. We drove up to the outer gate where the guard asked for our credentials.

The Americans had no difficulty in getting permission to drive on, for their work took them daily within the compound. Inside we drove along a straight avenue with young tamarisks planted in shallow ditches through which water flowed. At the end of the avenue was the inner wall and having passed through a gate we found ourselves in a garden with bushes, flower-beds and lawns separated from the avenue by a sports field where young amirs were playing football. A white mosque with a minaret painted in bright colours and adjoining it a school for the princely children were built along the end of the playground. A further gate led to the vegetable garden and the cowsheds of the imported American Holsteiner cows. Further off, but still within the walls, were two wells, huge square pits cut in limestone. They had been enlarged and deepened several times because of the sinking water-level. The new palace with its surrounding gardens of more than a hundred acres required so much water that it was difficult to cope with its growing needs. The depth of the pits was, so I was told, then between twenty and twenty-two *qamas*. A *qama* is the distance between the tips of the middle fingers of a man's out-stretched arms, so that twenty *qamas* would be roughly a hundred and twenty feet. We went down a steep tunnel to a space that had been cut out of the rock in the side-wall of the pit near the water-level. There stood the motor pumps that brought the water to the surface. Nearer the palace skilled Syrian labourers from Damascus were cutting limestone brought in from the mountains into the big slabs used for paving the floors of the palace. They had almost finished the great banqueting hall that had a length of one hundred and ninety yards and had already entertained two thousand guests at one sitting. The old King was famed for his hospitality; he fed thousands of guests a day but in places spread over the whole town. His son was following his example but in a modern manner.

Before leaving these vast living quarters of Saʿudi Arabia's future ruler, we had a look at the extensive servants' quarter. Here the black servants of the palace, originally slaves imported from Africa, lived with their families, a total of about five hundred people. The toilets used once to be covered with faeces and the kitchens black with flies. Now my American guides showed with pride the modern sanitary arrangements they had installed with the entire approval of the Amir Saʿud. No flies even in the meat kitchen, no stench in the toilets, and a crowd of curly-headed black children playing on clean pavement in front of the rows of spotlessly-white concrete houses.

We left the Amir Saʿud's palace and drove through a new part of the town eastwards of old ar-Riyadh. Here was great building activity, partly in mud bricks in Nejdi style and partly in lime-stone blocks cut from the rocks near the town. Schools, mosques, houses for the rich, shops for the men who had flocked from far and near to the town of soaring prosperity were being built and lent, to me, an unfamiliar air of activity and optimism to the town which only a few years before I had known as a place of austerity where the 'azan would silence all worldly activity five times a day. Beyond the town, bordering on the emptiness of the desert, were beduin camps. Some of their occupants had had difficulty in making a living and, finding abundant water and the King's free food in the capital, had settled down to a life of indolence. Others had heard of the new prosperity of the town and had come to get a share of it by trading or by working as labourers. These beduins formed the wide, poor and unsavoury fringe around ar-Riyadh which they fouled with habits inoffensive in the vast spaces of the desert but intolerable in the confines of a town.

Public hygiene is one of the major problems of Arab towns. Homeless dogs are the street scavengers and these wretched animals are a familiar sight throughout the East. The dog is unclean according to Islam and strict Muslims will not touch it, not even with the foot to give it a kick. The Arab looks on the *saluqi* alone with kindness. But he will curse all other dogs and hurl lumps of clay and stones at them. That may perhaps be the reason why one sees everywhere maimed and limping dogs with broken legs.

As ar-Riyadh increased in prosperity more and more waste food was thrown into the streets. The army of mongrels grew in number and as a nuisance. Their nocturnal fights made life in town unbearable, so it was decided to get rid of these pests. Since no Muslim will kill an animal simply because it barks the dogs were not shot or poisoned, but in the desert at some distance from the town high, square, mud enclosures were built. At the entrance to each enclosure was posted a town official who paid three Sa'udi riyals for every dog delivered to him. When we visited these pounds the guards told us that between four and six thousand dogs had passed in. I looked through the crack between gate and mud wall and saw a host of fly-pestered dogs. For long I could not take my eyes off these suffering animals. There are other creatures that suffer in these lands. I cannot help seeing before me those bravely trotting little donkeys, disappearing under fantastic loads or carrying on their backs two grown-ups. What is their reward? Untended sores, loud curses and prods with a stick in their tenderest parts. When I asked one of the government officials about the dogs he told me that they were given water and old dates and would doubtless die when their time came.

When I had first known ar-Riyadh in December 1944 it was a town of little more than fifty thousand inhabitants. Its population in 1952 must have increased to nearly two hundred thousand and there seems to be no limit to its expansion. As I prepared to meet the man whose life-work had led to all this I understood better than ever why the King and most of the Amirs preferred to live at a good distance from the crowd.

Next morning, 4th March 1952, an aeroplane with the new Chairman of Aramco and some of his advisers arrived for the Royal audience and we were all of us collected by car from the aerodrome and taken to the guest-house opposite al Murabba'a palace. It was the building in which I had stayed seven years before. The exterior brown mud wall had now been painted in bright colours and the entrance made wider so as to appear more impressive to guests from the West who came here and enjoyed Sa'udi hospitality. The interior of the building was furnished in the manner then passing out of favour in the Middle East with plush, heavily gilded furniture, mirrors and imitation oriental carpets soon, no doubt, to be replaced by tubular furniture and chromium plate.

We all changed into Nejdi dress and then settled down for a long wait. Nobody told us or could tell us exactly how the King's health was. So we waited for the call to come, passing the time in drinking bitter coffee with cardamum from small cups with no handles. George Rentz had come from Dhahran with the Chairman of Aramco and they had brought with them an Arab interpreter. In the same plane came Sheikh Hafiz Wahba, Sa'udi Ambassador in London, who because of the death of King George VI had been obliged to break away from the talks on the Abu

Dhabi frontier dispute. Now back from the royal funeral he had to report to Ibn Saʿud and so preceded us into the palace.

When at last word came that His Majesty was ready for us we walked out of the Guest House and crossed the road to the original mud-built part of the palace. In the courtyard were what seemed to be innumerable glittering Cadillacs but otherwise the place had not changed much. I passed again along familiar corridors and climbed familiar mud stairs. Along the stairs and corridors were palace guards, some westernized in dress and some still wearing the loose attractive garb of the beduin.

Beduins squatted on the floors in wide mantles of varying shades of brown with strips of embroidery in gold thread down the front and on their knees rested curved silver-sheathed swords. The beduins seemed to expect us to greet them first and on the whole paid scant attention to the foreigners. As in former days I felt that a *nasrani* was not welcome in this stronghold of Wahhabism. I could only hope that the reception of the King himself and of the two sons with whom I had been most in contact, would be as warm as before. I was shown into the room of his Majesty's Secretary and had the pleasant surprise of finding there the man I had last met in Marat when we had sat on a rug in front of his tent and discussed together the Palestine problem. While we were talking in walked another old acquaintance, Sheikh Yusuf Yasin, who had given even longer service to his royal master than Rushdi Bey.

Sheikh Yusuf, after a youthful experience of political exile in Malta where he could reflect on his rash anti-British agitation against their Palestine policy, had gone to Ibn Saʿud in 1923 in search of freedom and an opportunity to work in an independent, entirely Arab environment. So here together were two men who neither liked nor respected the Nejdis and were neither liked nor respected by them, but who were bound to the King and served him faithfully and well so long as he lived. It was they who took us into the audience-chamber and for me there could have been no happier reminder of former audiences. But when I entered the hall I saw a change. The King at the far end no longer rose from his seat in welcome. Only the guards in Western uniforms saluted. The beduin Sheikhs near the entrance silently moved backwards to make room but gave no greeting. No one rose from his seat because the King could no longer do so. He sat in what seemed to be an invalid carriage. The sparse, curled beard and the few locks of hair that peeped from his head-cloth were black—but dyed. The once graceful, slender hands had now become stiff and wrinkled, the face more set, the gaze weak and lustreless. But it was his voice that disappointed most. The voice was still kindly but the music had gone out of it. That noble voice was now no longer raised to address, over one's head, the men who lined the walls. It had in the old days been the King's habit to draw his people into the conversation by way of instructing them; this custom had formerly made every audience dynamic. Now the King had only strength enough to make himself understood to us. And perhaps he did not find the same inspiration in talk with the Aramco men as he had found in former days when religious and political questions were brought up for discussion. Or had the Wahhabi ideal lost its force for him who had seen it retreat in the face of modern politics and finance and irreligion?

The Aramco representatives were placed on the King's right hand. I was asked to sit on his left. Bram found a place farther down the line along the wall and the Arab interpreter brought by the Americans knelt at the King's feet. After greetings and the usual compliments I saw the King looking, it seemed to me, very feebly at me. When I asked whether he recognized and remembered me he answered that he did but I was not convinced. A silence ensued and then the leading American seemed to think it incumbent on him to do the talking which of course he did through his interpreter. The King's replies were considerate, sometimes ironical and often surprisingly to the point, but tired. The American seemed well-prepared and said things that might have been acceptable to his compatriots but were often inappropriate to the Sa'udi environment. I remember one passage where he said he had just been seriously ill for the first time in his life but God had granted him recovery and he saw how great were God's gifts to men. He saw with new freshness how wonderful this world was, how beautiful the fair sex and then he understood that what really mattered in life was not money, not success but religion; it was religion that counted most. The King was completely unimpressed by what his visitor doubtless thought was a successful venture at Wahhabi levels and said to the interpreter: "Tell him that if he had been a Muslim he need not have fallen ill in order to understand what matters in life. We knew that long ago!"

I got the impression that the King was not interested in the conversation. He had talked with Westerners many times about many things. Often he had been keenly interested in the men who spoke and in what they said. I had many times heard him turn the conversation round to his principles of belief or to his political views. Then what he said had interested both foreign listeners and his own people. But the problems connected with oil had come late in his life and were not part of the great idea for which he had worked. They were not part of the scheme of his life, the scheme that with the help of Allah he had accomplished. When the Americans came and produced oil much at first seemed easier. These new people from the West were less complicated than the British. They had stuck to their own affairs and did not interfere in his. The ground on which he had met the British was a difficult one: that of politics. The Americans met him on a commercial ground where problems seemed to be few. Even so, difficulties had arisen, new and unexpected problems of a type with which he was not familiar. The King made no mention of this; he was polite to his visitors; he answered their questions but asked none himself.

When I left the audience-chamber of Ibn Sa'ud I felt, for the first time, unsatisfied. The unfailing spring had failed. I heard nothing new, no sparkling comments, no vigorous views on Arab-Muslim policy or the affairs of the outside world. The audience-chamber was no longer a place of inspiration for his people. The voice that used to resound there no longer raised an echo in the hearts of men. Before long it would be stilled. Ar-Riyadh was waiting for that moment and out of respect due to the great old man it waited in silence.

We took leave of the King. Uniformed officers from near the entrance took us back to the private secretary's room. The beduin bodyguard paid us no attention. They had not been trained to do so and seemed tired of these ceremonies. Their King would die when his day had come according to the will of Allah. And foreigners they did not like, why be kind to those unbelievers? In the audience-chamber I had seen very few wearing the white *Ikhwan* strip wound on the top of their head-cloths. The *Ikhwan* had clearly declined, not least in importance.

In Rushdi Bey's room I returned to the full life of day. Time had gone back for me in the audience-chamber in the presence of the man who for me had been great. Now he seemed to belong only to the past. As I was with Rushdi Bey the Amir Faisal came in and with a smile stretched out his hand towards me. I had twice accompanied the King's second son on official trips through Holland. He had finished the talks on the frontier dispute of Abu Dhabi that had dragged on for weeks in Dhahran and would soon return to his duties in the Hejaz. His smile and handshake also reminded me of days gone by when with young and wondering eyes he had entered the world of the West. He, too, had then believed that his was the greater gift, the fulfilment of Allah's special promise to them who were His most faithful servants. Alone I walked down the stairs, away from what once had risen victoriously and was now almost extinguished in the hushed Murabba'a palace.

JEDDA

THE CROWN PRINCE IN HIS OFFICE IN AR-RIYADH

17

A Visit to Amir Sa'ud

FROM al Murabba'a palace Bram and I drove back to the American camp. There a message from the Royal Court followed me borne by a young Ethiopian who brought greetings from His Majesty and said that he and his Chrysler car were at my disposal for the duration of my stay in the capital. After the audience the private secretary had handed me an invitation to stay in the royal guest-house. He explained that it was not an order and that I was completely free to stay where I was or to move into the guest-house. It was a difficult choice as both places had advantages but as the guest-house would mean official control of all my movements I decided to remain in the American camp where nobody took any notice of me. In the afternoon I drove in my newly acquired car to an-Nasriyya palace. The Ethiopian drove through the desert rounding al Murabba'a palace from the north at a respectful distance from the wall and without even touching the outskirts of the town we came upon the metalled road to Amir Sa'ud's new abode.

The tamarisk avenue behind the principal gate still lay through bare land, but even that row of young trees had a story behind it. Not so long before the avenue had lived for a few days only. It was when King 'Abdallah of Jordan had visited the former enemies of his father and brothers. Amir Sa'ud had then called in the assistance of the Americans of Al Kharj whose own irrigation ditches were lined with thousands of tamarisk trees. They said that the uprooting and transport through fifty miles of desert, even if it were done at night time, would kill most of the trees. The Amir replied that he would be content if they lived only for the few days of the royal neighbour's visit. So an avenue of green trees came into being overnight. Now I drove through the second avenue on the same spot. These were taking longer to materialize but were expected to live for many years longer. At the gate of the inner wall I was met by an officer who asked me to leave the car and walk with him the rest of the way. I was very glad to do so for it was into a real garden that we walked. What is more beautiful than a garden in a desert and who can blame an Arab prince for taking a pride in his garden? With American help a continual flow of water was now irrigating the former desert soil that surrounded the palace and under the expert care of Indian gardeners flowers, bushes and lawns grew in a very short time out of the plantless desert. The Amir Saʿud had visited America and had seen how attractive gardens with swimming pools and fountains can be in lands that are green and rich with vegetation. How much more beautiful are they in Arabia!

The officer who accompanied me insisted upon my walking slowly so that I might be the more impressed. In front of us two very tall men in Arab dress were walking with an officer when suddenly, contrary to the custom of the country, they turned round and heartily laughed at the surprise I had in recognizing them as two Americans from Aramco. Near the palace we were led to a mosaic paving where armchairs had been placed. On one side was a blue-tiled swimming pool brimful with clean water and on the other the palace façade. Sitting there awaiting the arrival of our host I understood why Arabs use the same word for garden as for paradise. A typical addition in Arab taste were the different kinds of birds kept in cages that hung from long poles near the pool. Wild birds would not come until the bushes had grown to the dimensions of trees but the caged birds ensured that even at that early stage one need not be without bird song.

The Amir Saʿud soon came walking towards us from the palace and was followed by a small number of Arab guests. I was glad to see among them Sheikh Hafiz Wahba. Rashid Gulaini Ali and Jamal al Husaini, a brother of the ex-Mufti of Jerusalem, were pointed out to me by Sheikh Hafiz. The Crown Prince came straight up to us, first greeting the Americans and then, turning, he welcomed me with a smile and a kind reference to our former meetings. We were invited to sit down, Americans on the right and I on the left of the host. The open air, the declining sun, the beauty of the garden, the gurgling of the water overflowing from the pool and the bright face of the Amir, all encouraged animated conversation. The interpreter of Aramco did not fit into this intimate circle so he went off with the assistant to the Chairman of Aramco for a business talk inside the palace leaving the Chairman himself with us. He now had to depend on Sheikh Hafiz or on one of the others to translate for him. The Amir's first question to me was if I had ever been there before?

"Yes, Your Highness," I replied. "At the end of 1944."

"And what did you see here then?"

"Nothing but sand and gravel, not even a single blade of grass."

"You are right. So it was only a year ago. But now look around you and see this palace and the garden. Do you like them?"

I said it was beyond my power of description, as indeed it was. All the talking was in Arabic except for the moments when Sheikh Hafiz or one of the others who knew English translated for the American. The atmosphere of the party was most lively. There was a freedom and frankness, a feeling of relaxation among friends, there were jokes and stories and round after round of laughter. It was a side of Arab life that we in the West only know of from the literature of the peoples of the East.

In due course the Amir invited us to follow him to a lawn surrounded by flowering shrubs where long tables with fine linen table-cloths, plates and cutlery were laid out in Western fashion. The Amir and his entourage to which we now belonged took their seats at the first table while the officers and officials took seats at the other tables. A conventionally dressed Italian waiter stood behind the Amir's chair and on the other side of the table a Syrian waiter served the guests. I had already been told that Amir Saʿud liked good food. He gave abundant proof of his tastes at this tea-party where the choicest examples of Middle Eastern and Western cooking were laid before us, the Amir himself announcing each dish with a few words of commendation. We had a small glass of soup to start with followed by spaghetti and a meat sauce, then slices of cold meat with cheese biscuits and a Turkish dish with youghourt. Then came Syrian sweets and nougat (not made in Syria, the Amir told us, but by his own cooks). Then we had Indian candied fruits and after that Turkish Delight. Next cake appeared and oranges. The drinks served were tea and tinned fruit juices. I have doubtless forgotten some of the courses although I believe I tried every one of them. The meal progressed slowly leaving time for table-talk which was an innovation in Sa'udi Arabia: the former practice was to eat quickly and without talking.

At the other tables conversation proceeded in whispers but ours tended to be noisy. Our fellow-diners included political refugees from other Arab countries and former enemies of Sa'udi Arabia itself detained in the capital. Some were renowned humorists and clever at mimicking foreigners, others storehouses of ancient lore, of the rich literary and historical sediment of centuries of Arab culture. These were the modern equivalents of the jesters formerly common to oriental as to western courts. Sheikh Hafiz, although he had lived thirty years of his life in British surroundings, showed his mastery of Arab wit and humour. In that garden in the desert one forgot the outside world and the passage of time and although nothing was served after the sun had set the talk went on.

Suddenly we, the two Christians present, realized that the hour for the sunset prayer had drawn very near and hurriedly started to apologize for not having retired earlier. With a smile the Amir asked us to be seated again and to stay just a little longer. Darkness began to close in on us from the surrounding bushes. The Amir gave an order that was unintelligible to me. The man disappeared and some moments later, while we waited in silence for the sign to break up the party, hundreds of coloured electric bulbs burst into light. Their number increased as we watched and spread noiselessly all over the garden until they reached the farthest end of the garden where was the palace and opposite the private mosque. The minaret suddenly rose up flood-lit out of the dark. The minaret was in all colours: blue, yellow, green and red; the palace walls were in orange. Not a word was said as we watched this sparkling mantle spreading ever wider until we seemed to be sitting in a garden covered with flowers of light. The Amir sat there, himself radiant with satisfaction at the impression made on us. He now gave the sign that permitted us to leave while he and his Arab guests and the officials moved in the direction of the mosque to perform their sunset devotions. We Christians made our way to the inner gate, outside which the motor-cars were parked. From the top of the minaret a modern loudspeaker started to rend the air with a metallic roar that Allah was most great. It reminded me of the raucous voices of those Wahhabi patrols that must at that moment have started on their rounds of the streets of ar-Riyadh beating up the people for prayer. Or did that already belong to the past?

The reality was that in the garden of an-Nasriyya we had witnessed not a return to an Arabian Night of Harun ar-Rashid but a demonstration that what should have been the last bulwark of Wahhabism was in full retreat from advancing materialism. And not a fighting retreat either! Here in the desert, where the West was breaking through the Wahhabi defences that had protected the last remnant of romantic Arabia, the future ruler of the country still seemed to believe in methods of days that were irrevocably gone. His style was a copy of that of his father with its weaker sides magnified. Not because his father disposed single-handed of the income of the state had he the right to do the same. In his years of vigour his father had been stronger than money and though he failed near the end of his life it was not on splendour or luxury that he spent. His father could still rule in Old Testament style. The son would rule a country that has drifted far away from those days and forsaken the Wahhabi bedrock on which it was built.

Beyond the gate in the outer wall I was back in the desert and in it there were the beduins, dozens of them distinguishable in the glare of the thousands of electric bulbs and the flood-lit walls of palace and mosque. Light enough to shine on their wasted nomad bodies and on the dirty threadbare mantles that clad them so thinly in the cold desert night. Light enough to see their startled faces. There was amazement on those faces but not only that: there was scorn too. These beduins had awakened. They had begun to see what life might be for others and doubtless to hope that for them, too, some other way of living might be possible. They knew their own misery, they must surely yearn for a different existence far from fear and poverty, an existence fit for human dignity. Those of them who had worked as coolies in the oil-fields would never again feel at home round the camp-fires of the desert. How long will they remain in astonished admiration of their rulers who take the money from the oil and use it for building palaces and watering large and wonderful gardens? How long will the beduin be content to stand in the desert at the outer gates of those gardens and have only a distant view of the luxury inside? Was the future ruler on the wrong tack and too far removed from his people to understand that not only had his own position fundamentally changed but that of his people too? A gulf that formerly did not exist had appeared between the ruling dynasty and the ruled and every day it grew wider and deeper. The twenty five thousand electric bulbs in that princely garden consumed, according to trustworthy technical information, power enough to meet all the requirements of a small desert town. And electric bulbs were only one princely extravagance.[1]

Back in ar-Riyadh the streets were completely deserted. The adult male population had gathered for evening prayer in the mosques or hidden at home behind carefully closed doors and shutters. For me it had been a day of contrasts. In the morning I had seen for the last time a man I had once admired for his strength, respected for his wisdom and liked for his sincerity.

[1] It is reported that this new £4 million palace has since been demolished to make room for a £10 million substitute.

All this now seemed near to disappear. The country waited and in Murabbaʿa palace sounds were muffled. Soon the man and his greatness would belong to the past and Saʿudi Arabia would have to find its future salvation, or damnation, without him.

From the past I had turned to the present, from the mud-built abode of the King to the garden, the running water and the floodlit an-Nasriyya palace of the Amir. But if I said no more I should be doing the present ruler of Saʿudi Arabia great injustice. This garden meeting was by no means the only contact I had with Amir Saʿud. It had always been a pleasure to meet this brightly-smiling Amir with his frank, open manner. He loved life and the many good things it showered on him. His father had chosen him to be ruler of beduin tribes and oasis dwellers and had kept him nearly all his life near to him in the desert surroundings of ar-Riyadh. Was it because the King feared that his eldest surviving son might become an easy victim of the snares that would surround him in his contacts with the outside world? Or was it because of the positive qualities for beduin rulership he found in him? Ibn Saʿud's second son, Faisal, was chosen for contacts with the outside world, that part of the ruler's task that is most mistrusted by the true Wahhabi. Their father had made the choice and both sons obeyed. And both were loyal to their father and to each other even when the time came for Saʿud to be King. Then Saʿud showed wisdom and greatness of character by giving the second place in the kingdom not to his eldest son but to his brother Faisal. He made him Crown Prince. That is another side of the man we watched in those days when responsibilities were denied to him although his suffering father was no longer capable of carrying them himself. Saʿud may well have found the waiting irksome. He may well have wanted to prepare for the task that lay ahead of him. And it may well be that Ibn Saʿud's failure to prepare for his sons' and his country's future set the son off on the wrong foot.

It was late enough before Ibn Saʿud allowed this son to leave the country and have a look at the outside world. Faisal had started travelling abroad in 1919 at the early age of fifteen but it was many years later before Sa'ud got even as far as Egypt. In 1943 Faisal had preceded his brother to America. But when in December 1944 I was the Amir's guest in ar-Riyadh he was still full of the impressions gathered during his first trip to the United States in that same year. Some years earlier, just before the war, he had also been in the European countries of importance to Sa'udi Arabia and what he told me about the impressions he had taken home with him of the political leaders and their countries proved that he had been a keen observer. But his foreign travel was badly arranged. As prospective ruler of the new Arabia Sa'ud ought to have had the chance of acquiring more knowledge of the outside world than is possible for a Crown Prince on a state visit. What he then saw may have been impressive, even beautiful, but it was superficial. The foundations of Western culture remained hidden from him. How could he have avoided the notion that all he saw that was attractive could be bought with money and that the money that now poured in to his father would one day pour in to him? Yet has wealth ever brought happiness? I felt that Sa'udi Arabia was losing its spiritual sheet-anchor of the faith of its fathers and I was sad at the parting of the ways.

The remainder of my short stay in ar-Riyadh was crowded. The King's car gave me the opportunity of seeing nearly all the interesting sites of Wadi Hanifa in the neighbourhood of the capital. Every morning I used to drive out to the narrow oases down both sides of the wadi bed. The number, the length and the solid structure of dams to hold the water whenever the *sail*—flood— would sweep down from the Tuwaiq mountains surprised me. Motor pumps had partly taken the place of the traditional screeching pulleys with which men and animals used to pull up the leaking leather water-bags, from the wells below. The oasis gardens of the rich now had tiled pools and were better irrigated than ever before. On the borders of the pools I sometimes sat and chatted with the gardeners. They told me the same story that I had heard in town and on the plateau: that of the sinking water-level. Here in the chain of oases the lower level spelt tragedy for those owners of date-gardens who could not afford to buy a motor. I found more uneasiness than hope in the Wadi Hanifa for the rich were fewer than the poor.

One day I went to Dhar'iyya, where the great Sa'ud had made his pact with 'the Sheikh', the founder of Wahhabism, Muhammad ibn 'Abd al Wahhab. The birthplace of Wahhabism was, this century and a half later, the symbol of its death struggle. The ruined town had not been rebuilt, and those crumbled mud walls were all that was left of its forts, the palace of the Sa'uds and the houses of the other great men of Wahhabism. Dhar'iyya is only a few miles away from the new ar-Riyadh and had been built in the Wadi Hanifa at a place where there was a wide strip of gardens. I was astonished to find so much left of the buildings that had been exposed to rain—and sand-storms for so many years. People working in neighbouring gardens came running to point out to me where the houses of Faisal and of Sa'ud as-Sa'ud had been and where the Jiluwis had lived. Some parts of houses that were left intact showed a difference in architecture from that of to-day. The windows were quite small triangular holes, without wooden frames and arranged in triangular groups of six or in wide bands that ran the length of the building. The walls were very strongly built. The houses were forts and during the Egyptian campaign under Ibrahim Pasha had had to withstand for months the heaviest bombardment with field-guns ever directed against a Sa'udi town. Opposite the original Dhar'iyya a lower site of ruins was pointed out to me. There, I was told, the town of the slaves had been.

For long I climbed and pondered over the ruins and found them more impressive than I had imagined. To me the ruined town of Dhar'iyya was the memorial of the defeat of the men who had set out from there on their first mission. I had seen its revival and, now in ar-Riyadh, its second defeat. Wahhabism was in ruin. The capital, bigger, wealthier and richer in palaces than any town in Central Arabia had ever been before, was witness of a ruin that was greater, immeasurably greater, than that first ruin because this time the ruin was spiritual.

18

The Last Visit

IN THE SUMMER of 1954 I was again drawn to that quickly changing Arabian Kingdom. Ibn Sa'ud had died. Only a few years before Wahhabism had still held undisputed sway but I had seen it gradually retreat before the American advance. The struggle between the two parties, none the less decisive for being unavowed and, certainly from the American side undesired, had been an unequal one. On the Wahhabi side a spiritual force, a creed and on the American side open materialism. It was a ranged battle and the Americans had no inkling that they were fighting. Yet they were. Their very presence in Arabia meant attack on Wahhabism. Neither of the two parties is to be blamed for not having foreseen the far-reaching consequences of their encounter, certainly not the Americans who had had no earlier experience to guide them. The Arabs, particularly those with a knowledge of past Wahhabi history, might have remembered Ibrahim Pasha and had a foreboding of coming disaster. D. G. Hogarth once said 'the fantastic spirit of Nejd has boiled up and over more than once, none of its past ebullitions has, for obvious reasons equally operative today, enjoyed any but very brief life. I see nothing in the circumstances or constituents of the present Wahhabi expansion to promise it longer life than has been enjoyed by earlier Nejdean ebullitions. These, to take only one test, have not prevailed in Mecca for ten years on the average. Just conceivably the masterful and sagacious personality of the Sultan, Abdul Aziz Ibn Sa'ud, may prolong this last domination: but for myself I expect him to find, not less quickly than his forebears, that Mecca, Taif and Medina are so many Capuas sapping the fervour and

fortitude of his fanatics, and that he has overreached the limits
of one-man rule. . . . I prophesy therefore that Arabia is not in for
more than a decade at most of Wahhabi domination outside
Nejd. . . .' Hogarth's prophecy has not been fulfilled in the letter,
but in the spirit . . . ? Wahhabi domination has outlived the
decade, and Hogarth too, but were there none among its stalwarts
who with the advent of the Americans did not foresee the end of
another 'very brief life'?

During my last visit to Eastern Arabia I had seen Wahhabism in
full retreat and with nothing spiritual to take its place. It is safe
to assume that here was a gap that the Americans never anticipated and to which they had never even given a thought. The
captains of the oil army had so overrated the intolerance of Islam
—and particularly that with a Wahhabi imprint—as to be willing,
if not eager, to leave all outward appearance of their own faith
at home. Once the backbone of Wahhabism was broken a spiritual vacuum took its place.

I had seen the beginning of this process and was anxious to see
how it had progressed. I had heard vague stirrings on this subject
among the Americans both at home and out in Arabia. As soon
as I had landed on Dhahran airfield from 'the Flying Camel', one
of Aramco's twice-weekly service of Constellations between
New York and Dhahran, I was met by a request from the
Personnel Department for a lecture the following Sunday
evening. It was to be held in the Cinema which was usually
available for meetings of a serious character. I had just returned
from a gathering of Muslim and Christian representatives from
all over the world so I gave a talk on the discussions there and
tried to keep away from the subject of American responsibilities
in Sa'udi Arabia. In the discussion that followed the questions
put to me showed that my audience was very much alive to these
responsibilities and I was forced to express an opinion which I did
quite frankly. When, at last, the discussion was stopped at my
request, the chaplain of the near-by air base begged me to go to
the officers' mess there and talk again on that subject or any other
that I might choose. It was difficult for me to refuse and so in the

middle of a hot summer day in Dhahran, and that means a really hot day, I stood in the air-conditioned hall of the mess in front of a hundred officers and spoke of the meeting of Muslims and Christians and of the factors involved. How they listened, those officers to what I, a foreigner, had to say! And how afterwards, in their questions, they tried to probe to the heart of the problem! What I had feared might happen, did happen, and I had to answer, there and then, questions about America's—not only Aramco's—direct responsibility. Taxing though they were, these contacts gave me much comfort and hope in the following days of my visit during which I saw much that was disturbing.

I went to see what had become of Al Khobar, the neighbouring Arab fishing village on the coast. I had seen Al Khobar grow into a shopping centre for the Americans of Dhahran. Its growth had now continued along the shore and towards the desert. The streets had been straightened and the houses changed from mud into limestone or concrete buildings. Agencies for air- and sea-travel, banks and restaurants had taken the place of the former primitive *qahwas*—coffee-houses—the money-changers' shops, the bakeries and the fruit-stalls. The place had become a small town with no desert character, no smells, no dirt, no flies and no simplicity.

Dammam, the terminus of the Sa'udi Railway with a pier that stretched out into the sea farther than the eye could reach, was equally unrecognizable. Large plots had been surrounded by walls and the building of houses begun within them. The Arab speculators seemed to have great expectations of Dammam. An electricity plant was already built and working. 'Abdullah as-Sulaiman, the omnipresent, was of course in the forefront of this development and he had built a considerable number of modern villas hoping to attract Americans to live away from Aramco with its eternal oil. His prices were extravagant but he seemed to be heading for success because Aramco's living quarters, too, were not cheap. On the outskirts was a modern dairy farm, again the property of the Finance Minister. The price of milk, butter, eggs and rabbits was prohibitive except for oil-employees but they would certainly buy his products as well as the vegetables and fruits raised in gardens that stretched one after the other all along the road to Ras Tanura. One building in the *suq*—bazaar—of Dammam had my special sympathy. It was the first Aramco Department that had moved away from Dhahran oil-town, the Research Department, which certainly serves Aramco better the farther it stands away from the oil and the nearer to the Arabs.

Then came the day when I was allowed to go back to my starting-point in Sa'udi Arabia, to Jedda. I travelled in a four-engine Constellation of the Sa'udi Arabian Airways with one long stop at ar-Riyadh. There the plane filled up to the last corner where still a negro servant boy or girl could squat on the floor. Astonished to see so many negro women of the common type among the crowd that boarded this very expensive means of transport I asked the Arab steward how they could afford such a method of travelling. "They belong to the royal court and all of them travel free," he whispered.

The sun had set when we approached Jedda. Our plane had followed a course far to the north of Mecca to avoid flying over holy territory. So I saw only the barren mountains of the Hejaz until the shore was nearly reached and we headed south to Jedda. The landing-ground I had known ten years before then lay a mile and a half from the town, now a new modern town that had spread far beyond it into the desert in all directions except the west where the sea is. Jedda had grown so much that it was difficult for me in the gathering darkness to recognize in it the shape I had known. When I left the plane I stood on the runway of a modern airfield and walked a little dazed towards the neon lights ahead of me. Only the heavy, damp heat reminded me of the Jedda I had known of old. And that impression was merely a passing one for the airport buildings and the Aramco staff-building where I was received as a guest were air-conditioned and muffled against outward noises so that I could not even hear whether Jedda's familiar sounds were still there or not.

What a difference there was between the Wahhabi Arabia I had first met here in 1926 and oil Arabia now! The old town had been torn to pieces. Its walls had been used for the building of the pier and in the place of the wall an asphalt road for motor traffic now encircled the old town. There was no more that sharp separation between a well-protected walled-in living place for townsmen and the hostile desert of the roving beduin tribes. The new Jedda fanned out far into the desert seeking space and air and meeting it with the great gift of the piped water from the Wadi Fatima, thirty miles away, that changed its wastes into gardens.

In the narrow lanes of old Jedda I found again the familiar smells of the years gone by. The houses were in decay except only where modern shops and offices had been built on to some existing premises. I followed once more the dusty streets that twisted between high houses whose tops leaned over to each other. The wooden balconies with torn and tattered shutters, still protected in semi-obscurity the antiquated family-life that was preparing to flee into the open, to the new houses, full of light, that lay outside in the desert.

I was just in time to say farewell to the Jedda that was passing away. The little town, bordering on holy territory, had prospered on religion and given reverential lip-service to its blessings, welcoming the yearly influx of pilgrims, fleecing them with devout appraisal, then, when on their way home they passed once more through the streets of Jedda tired, weak and shorn of their worldly possessions (but assured of heavenly merits) looking despisingly on them and trying to get rid of them as soon as possible. Those were the weeks when hordes of fleas would invade our houses and armies of flies feasted on dirt and diseased humanity. The penniless stragglers left behind would be repatriated by the foreign legations and shipping companies and then Jedda would tidy up her streets and houses and turn to feasting on the spoils the pilgrimage had brought them.

As I plodded through the dust and sniffed the odours I tried to remember how often I had seen these empty lanes crammed with exhausted families of pilgrims over whose bodies one prudently stepped with the aid of a flashlight. For centuries Jedda's streets had been the first stage of that possibly greatest of all human dramas called the *hajj* but now a new dawn had appeared. The Holy Land of Islam no longer depended on the income from the *hajj*. How poor was that income now compared with the profit from the oil! During that year of my visit the government had stopped taxing the pilgrims, partly out of shame as a country grown so rich and partly because the number of pilgrims had fallen so low that it was scarcely worth while to collect the taxes. A pilgrim town had been built by the government in the desert, south of the old town where once Nakatoo had stood, the village where the black slaves lived. The pilgrim-town was near the new pier so that the pilgrims could go directly to and from the ships that brought them. The type of pilgrim too had changed. He no longer came from Western ruled colonial lands, but from Independent Muslim states. The pilgrims from the two greatest Muslim states shrank to numbers unheard of before: in periods of economical stress the amount of money allowed for pilgrims to take out of the country was very restricted.

When I visited one of my best friends among the pilgrim-sheikhs I heard long stories of the falling numbers of pilgrims and of increased control by their governments resulting in ever diminishing profits from ever increasing work. The three sons of the pilgrim-sheikh were no longer in the traditional family business. They worked one in trade, one in a bank and one in a government office and made a much better living than they could ever hope from the pilgrimage.

I went to the Qa'im Maqam's office in the same old building with still the same primitive equipment and many well-known faces. Here little had changed except that the pay was now several times what it had formerly been. The administration of the town seemed to have stayed still while everything else had changed beyond recognition. The Qa'im Maqam gave me some figures and although I knew him to be a staunch Wahhabi I found it difficult to credit what he said. Half a million inhabitants?

"Do you realize," the governor said, "that the built-up area of the town now stretches two miles to the north, three to the south and two to the east?"

This Sa'udi administration had no system of registration and no means of assessing the size of the population but even if it was no more than two hundred thousand then a tenfold increase had taken place in the nine years of my absence. The Jedda I now saw was no longer the Town of the Consuls nor was it any more a town of pilgrimage, the gateway to Mecca. It had gone over to something more remunerative than religion and such soul as it had ever had was lost in the pursuit of oil-wealth.

SA'UDI-ARAB EMPLOYES RETURNING TO THEIR LIVING QUARTERS IN
THE OIL TOWN OF DHAHRAN

THE ARABIAN AMERICAN OIL COMPANY'S STABILISING UNIT AT DHAHRAN

19

Ibn Sa'ud's Inheritance

IBN SA'UD died on 9th October 1953. He himself who had started with nothing, left to his heirs a great state and an enormous personal income. His father had had no land he could call his own and he himself had first relied on the generosity of others to supply his daily wants. At Ibn Sa'ud's death the territory over which he ruled was greater than had ever before been seen by the House of the Sa'uds and the riches were such as had never even been dreamt of in the whole of the Arabian Peninsula. The outside world was largely benevolently disposed towards the Sa'udi state and even those neighbours, the Hashimites in the north and the Imam of the Yemen in the south, who looked on jealously had long since been quietened. Outwardly all seemed hopeful and bright but within its borders the country was in a state of anarchy and even within the intimate circle of the ruling family potential forces of disintegration were clearly visible.

The founder of this new great Arabian state had been strong in his own strength. After winning over the desert tribes of Nejd he moved towards and overran the Hejaz, the Holy Land of Islam. In the Hejaz the Wahhabis reached their Western limits at the shore of the Red Sea. Northward they met a stern 'so far and no farther' in the territories of Transjordan and of Iraq that were then under British mandate. Southward was the only direction left open for Sa'udi advance and before long 'Asir, the small buffer state of the Idrisis, was gathered into the fold. A short war with the Imam of the Yemen had ended happily in a peace of Arab friendship and Muslim brotherhood, and the appointment of a frontier commission that fixed and demarcated the frontier between the Yemen and Sa'udi Arabia.

The remainder of the southern frontier seemed to be protected well enough by the greatest sand desert of Arabia, the so-called *Rubʿ al Khali*—the Empty Quarter. No beduin could live within the fringes of that immense sand waste. No regular caravan routes crossed it and no enemy would ever dare pass through it for a *ghazu*. The *Rubʿ al Khali* seemed to be one of the best natural frontiers known to the world and nobody at that time dreamt of finding oil in such inhospitable land. In 1930 Bertram Thomas succeeded in crossing *'ar-rimal'*—the sands as the local Arabs generally call that great desert—and in 1931-2 he further explored the region. Experience tended to stress rather than diminish the importance of the *Rubʿ al Khali* as a safe border-line on the south of the Wahhabi state. Eastwards, towards the Gulf of 'Oman and the Persian Gulf, habitable land took the place of the sands. Here, where frontiers had been left undefined, difficulties were to be expected and did not fail to arise as soon as prospecting for oil moved in that direction. Then the barrenest desert became fruitful of disputes. Sheikhs and Sultans in the disputed areas were naturally inclined to look for profits for themselves and England who had for long given protection to these potentates found herself bound by old agreements and undertakings to defend local rights against the increasing pressure of the Saʿudis covering an Aramco advance. Thus the only undelimited frontiers Ibn Saʿud left to his heirs were with these British Protected territories on the Persian Gulf and the *Rubʿ al Khali* in the South. In the near future the *Rubʿ al Khali* may well prove no natural barrier because oil exploration is not to be halted by purely geographical obstacles. If oil is found there fresh frontier questions are bound to arise. This then is what Ibn Saʿud left territorially to his heirs and with a perspective of material prosperity such as no ruler in Arabia had ever seen before him.

Following the example of Arabia's greatest son, the Prophet of Islam, Ibn Saʿud had used a force that was both religious and political. Once his state had expanded it proved impossible to keep it shut off from the outside world. Nor did Ibn Saʿud wish that it should be. With him there was no reluctance to follow the way he took. He was not driven, he drove. He sought friendship with England and her countrymen, and with the Dutch who then still ruled what was called the Dutch East Indies and sought the services of their medical, financial and geological experts. That the Americans later got away with the great profits his land had to offer was not thanks to his but to American activity.

Ibn Saʻud was the first Arab ruler to send his sons to Europe and later to America to strengthen relations with the governing powers there and to prepare the way for the introduction of European and American help into his country. During the second World War England even in her darkest days did not leave her friend to fend for himself in his difficulties but kept famine from his doors and supplied the money to keep the wheels of state turning. It was England, too, that sent the first military mission in 1942 to teach young Saʻudi officers the use of the small mechanized weapons supplied to the country and to help build up the nucleus of a modern armed force. In due course the American nation, prepared by a wise President, was ready to take a share—and how generous a share—in defending the world against totalitarianism and so America took over a growing part of British responsibilities in Saʻudi Arabia.

Then, alas, approached that ever-increasing cloud that came between him and the British and led Ibn Saʻud to draw away from the old friend and pass over to the new. The Palestine problem could no longer be contained within the British mandate and its darkening shadows spread over neighbouring Arab countries. The friendly attitude of President Roosevelt and the promises he gave in Egypt seemed to Ibn Saʻud to meet his needs and so it was with America that the concluding chapter of his life's work began and the definite form of his inheritance was shaped. The doors of his kingdom were flung wide open and the so-called Christian West streamed in. Ibn Saʻud had hoped that the change would be a gradual one and that he would be able to keep it in check. But the need for money on one hand and the demand for oil on the other forced the pace, much to the detriment of the weaker party, the Arabs. They suffered spiritual shipwreck and being placed in a unfamiliar barque were swept rudderless out to sea. Their distress was obvious but there was no escape for them.

It was among the lower classes, the Saʿudi labourers of Aramco, that the change was most marked. The Americans built gorgeous mosques for them with at least two minarets and loud-speakers to make the call to prayer, oblivious of the fact that to the true Wahhabi even one minaret was an abomination. The Americans tried to give as much time free for prayers and Muslim feasts as the requirements of regular working time allowed but it proved to be very difficult to reconcile conservative beliefs with these new ways. Gradually the Saʿudis began to adopt habits they once held to be sinful. They began to play games and to watch football and baseball matches. They stood on the outward fringes of the crowds at the open-air cinemas. Their *mutawwas* had taught them that all music was a sinful invention, something the Prophet had not known and would never have admitted, but gradually their ears grew accustomed to mechanized music. Many in their spiritual malaise must have yearned to return to their tribes and resume that safe, God-fearing, Wahhabi, desert life that would restore peace to their hearts. But first they had to collect the handfuls of silver riyals due to be paid them at the end of their contract term. Day after day they spent in hard, monotonous work, week after week they lived in wooden or concrete sheds far from their wives and children. The food they had in the Aramco canteens was cheap and substantial, much better than what they were used to, but it was unfamiliar and, to them, taste-less. Homesick though they were, they bore all these hardships for the sake of money. With money one could do everything. Money meant happiness: that, at least, is the conviction of the man who has never had any.

At the beginning of the American invasion the riyal still retained its purchasing power but there was not very much in the Arabia of those days that a tribesman could buy. Camels, perhaps, and sheep, but then one had to stay at home and look after them. One could buy a second wife. The simple man in the desert is monogamous. His struggle for life is hard and his faithful companion in all his hardships is his wife. She quickly loses physical attraction and the man's fancy may often have made him yearn for the days when she still had the charms of youth but the old way of life gave him no hope of a young wife for his pleasure in addition to the old companion who ordered his tent for him. The silver Aramco paid him for his months of toil was enough to buy a young bride but with her arrival he would soon find that peace departed from his tent.

There appeared in the markets Western goods that appealed to the men of the desert although they did not make his life happier or easier. As the flow of money increased the value of the riyals declined and the wages paid by Aramco had to be increased. Once the wages were doubled by order of the King who with his advisers was convinced that most of the difficulties caused by the rise of prices would then be overcome. Aramco experts warned them of the more likely result but in the end they were forced to comply with the order. Then, as Aramco had predicted, prices rose in sympathy and for those outside the orbit of the Company the rise of the cost of living was calamitous. The Saʿudi Government could not understand what had happened and thought that the merchants were responsible. The merchants were ordered to bring their prices down and heavy punishments were inflicted on them, with the result that goods were no longer put on sale. Life that formerly, when nearly every one was poor, had been so simple had now become excessively complicated although many people now had money.

The experts of Aramco knew the underlying causes and could have given useful advice to this inexperienced government and in fact did so but when the advice was not accepted they could only rigidly follow their declared policy of non-intervention in the internal affairs of the country. In the new Arabia, fast becoming submerged under the income from oil, the Minister of Finance was left alone and was soon completely out of his depth. He had his own ways of managing and for those he wanted no Western advice. Who was to blame for the complete failure of the Finance Department? Was it the King who entrusted his Minister with a task he must have known to be beyond his capacity? Was anybody else available? Could the King have called in a foreigner, even an Arab foreigner, for a task in which the intimate life of the whole royal family was so deeply involved?

Are the Americans to be blamed for the scale on which the millions poured into one of the poorest countries of the world were swept out again in private hands? Could they not have done something about it? Who is to say that they did not tell and warn the King? But was that enough? They well knew that Ibn Sa'ud had never been interested in the details of finance, that neither he nor his advisers could stop the rot and that it could only be done if they did it for him. But then they would have overstepped the limits of their self-imposed policy of non-interference. So they continued paying their gold into the hands of an inexperienced child! American criticism had been too rash and too outspoken on the overseas administration of the so-called colonial powers for them to change their own course quickly. Perhaps they tried, perhaps they hoped that their expert advice might some day be followed. Aramco encouraged the execution of great public works under its own control, or, what was better, under that of trustworthy American firms directly financed from the royalties to ensure the proper use of at least a part of the income from oil. Thus the costly project of the railway line connecting the Persian Gulf at Dammam with the capital was completed in record time. Although it can never pay, the money invested in the railway was not completely squandered. Jedda, the harbour on the Red Sea coast, was given an excellent pier alongside which big ships could load and unload. The town wall of Jedda was pulled down and asphalted roads were built around the town. Great modern aerodromes were built near ar-Riyadh, Jedda and Dhahran. Al Kharj's agriculture experiment was launched with the help of Aramco and then financed by the government from the oil royalties. Contracting American firms built roads, hospitals, electric plants and various public buildings but this way of putting part of the oil royalties to a safe and generally good use came to an end. There was a limit to the scope of Public Works and in any case the Sa'udi officials who handled the country's money preferred to be completely free.

It was not only in the Finance Department that a very low standard of integrity prevailed and the responsible chiefs had neither the qualifications nor the attributes of character indispensable for such a task. Even if the other Departments had been good they could not counterbalance the shortcomings of that key Department. They were not good although sometimes they were better than the Department on which they all depended for their wages and their means. The root of the trouble was the principle, on which Ibn Sa'ud insisted, that the income of the state was the personal property of the ruler.

Nor was it only in its administration that the weakness of Sa'udi Arabia was exposed. The moral basis proved to be deficient. When the Hejaz was conquered the full rigour of Wahhabi doctrine had to be mitigated for that country. Yet in the form Wahhabism took in the Hejaz it was still far from being acceptable by Western or even enlightened Middle East standards. For instance the administration of justice based upon Qur'anic precept may survive in secluded desert communities but not in countries that have opened their doors to the West. Punishments that take the form of mutilations in public are too barbarous and too closely associated with conceptions of revenge and deterrents now historically remote to be acceptable in any modern state. Nor is such jurisdiction tolerable for a foreigner living temporarily within the state. The solution reached in the case of American offenders who had, for instance, killed by accident was that with the connivance of the Sa'udi authorities the culprit was quickly sent out of the country before local law could reach him.

In the early days of their contacts with the Americans the Sa'udis welcomed foreigners at public executions. But by 1952 when I visited the country again they were barely tolerated and it was strictly forbidden to take any photographs or films of these proceedings. Clearly the leaven was working but the Government did not take the step of cutting loose from principles and practices that belonged to times gone by. As a result class justice grew up: the backward part of the population remained subject to Qurʿanic jurisdiction while westernized groups and foreigners came more and more under a humaner system. I found in 1952 the Americans in Dhahran, in the province of Al Hasa notorious for the severity of Ibn Jiluwi's jurisdiction, in suppressed revolt against the treatment of Saʿudi subjects in their midst. It had recently happened that a Saʿudi servant had stolen a dollar and was sent to the police for correction. Although the man admitted the theft, promised never to repeat the offence and begged for mercy, his hand was chopped off. As usual the wound was dipped in boiling *samn*—sheep's milk butter—but an infection developed and the man died. The lenient American, who had only wanted to have the man taught a lesson, was horrified and the whole community so deeply moved that it was decided never again to report Saʿudi subjects to their police. The Saʿudis soon became aware of this and a marked deterioration in their conduct was the result. In the old Arabia next door, in the oasis of Hufhuf, the old system still flourished and in 1952 one could often see swollen hands and feet from which the blood was dripping stuck up for the edification of believers as they left the mosque on Fridays. Beatings with sticks were a lesser form of public correction, female culprits being put in a sack so that their bodies should be unseen by the executioners. The high-water mark of the public administration of justice were the decapitations performed by Jiluwi's herculean black executioner.

Ibn Saʿud had spoken with conviction of his system of justice when I first met him. He then referred to the special difficulty of forcing beduins into obedience to Allah's laws once and for all and claimed that he had succeeded in enforcing obedience. His system, cruel though it was, had worked. He did not believe in any other because his he derived from the *Qurʿan*. And so he has left to his heirs as a prominent part of a disintegrating Wahhabism a jurisdiction that is moribund.

Ibn Saʿud had ruled as a patriarch against the democratic background of the nomad life in the desert. He showed himself fully capable of ruling in this manner but towards the end of his life the weakness of his system was exposed. The task was too great for one man. Ibn Sa'ud either did not realize it soon enough, or he lacked the wisdom to change when his faculties weakened and the task grew more complicated. He surrounded himself by a group of assistants who were not of his own calibre and who were never able to do more than execute detailed orders. No responsible team was prepared to take over the task when he was no longer there. Many felt that his sons were not admitted into his full confidence or given a real share of responsibility. Again too many men from neighbouring Arab countries and too few Sa'udis were used in the centre of government. None of the Arab foreigners felt any sense of responsibility to the future. All were convinced that their own interests and those of their children did not lie in Sa'udi Arabia but in their homeland hence their pre-occupation with feathering a distant nest.

The young men of Arabia itself received little or no attention and no adequate preparation for taking a share in the administration of the kingdom. What can be said of a man who created a progeny in whose numbers he took great pride but for whose education he showed little care? And yet to all he gave equally the highly privileged position of royal princes. His five brothers and their descendants shared the prerogatives liberally dealt out to all his kin. Even the kindred clans of the Jiluwis and Sudairis and those belonging to the house of 'the Sheikh' were singled out for favours and honours and in this way the King created privileged classes, a distinction unknown before in desert democracy. Had the forty odd princes been given a good education and had they been set to work at responsible tasks the harm might not have been great. But Ibn Sa'ud was always reluctant to admit his sons to responsible positions save only the eldest two, the Amirs Sa'ud and Faisal who were followed later, as if after much hesitation, by a few of the next in age. Yet all the Princes were given the means of living royally which meant a heavy and ever-increasing burden on the country's income. Had they lived as good Wahhabis then again there might have been some curb on them. But they did not do so and we, and the whole country, were told stories of their loose living, in detail. Perhaps the only one who did not know of this was the ageing father yet he saw enough to understand that the blessing of Allah he had so often proudly quoted to us, a numerous progeny, might turn into a curse. This was a problem with which he never dealt. His son Sa'ud, on succeeding his father, had the opportunity of curbing the evil. Why did he not restrict princely prerogatives to a small number of his brothers and make the others work for their living? He did not do so and thus a danger to his own position and to that of the whole dynasty remains.

One man is known to have been outspoken in warning the present King of the dangers hidden in his inheritance. Philby, the only foreigner from the West who had lived in intimate contact with Ibn Sa'ud from 1930 onwards, gave his warning publicly. He must have had weighty reasons for doing so. His most pressing reason may well have been to free himself from any implicit responsibility for what was happening in the land of his hero. Matters had gone wrong for many a year and Philby has too keen and critical a mind not to have noticed what was happening, but he could not go so far as to criticize Ibn Sa'ud in public. He had spoken and written boldly, perhaps too boldly, about the King's enduring significance for Arabia, and it must have been galling for him to see the man he so much admired not only making grave mistakes towards the end of his life, but also failing to secure the realm of his own creation against the storms that were clearly gathering round it. Philby was late in telling the world and Arabia the truth about Wahhabism which shortly after his conversion he, as the Arabia correspondent of *The Near East and India*, publicly confessed to be the essence of his belief. He was late in telling the truth about Ibn Sa'ud's inheritance. Philby waited until his hero had died before he spoke. The subsequent resentment of young King Sa'ud did not in the first place arise from what his father's friend had said but from his speaking publicly.

The late King Sa'ud had rendered Philby a great if not the greatest service. Without Ibn Sa'ud there was less room for

Philby's advice in Sa'udi Arabia. He served Ibn Sa'ud well and Ibn Sa'ud's fame led him to fame; Ibn Sa'ud's success was his success. But Ibn Sa'ud's end looked like Philby's end or at least his end in Arabia. But there is much still to be told. Not perhaps that Philby can fill in any further historical or biographical details about Ibn Sa'ud, but the geographical story has only been told in part. Philby's maps are not complete. Philby must have a vast accumulation of geographical and allied material that still awaits publication and it is in the plaudits of the learned that Philby will find his future acceptance.

Philby was part of Ibn Sa'ud's inheritance. The other foreign, western influence included in Ibn Sa'ud's inheritance was much more acceptable to his heirs and that was the continued presence of the Americans, for with the Americans the welfare of the state and its future had become closely linked. At least so it seemed. The Americans had refrained from criticizing and any advice that contained an element of warning had been clothed in the wrappings of the American principle of non-interference. So long as Philby was there to epitomize overbearing western superiority the American approach could succeed by force of contrast. But now that Philby has gone the Americans are the only western influence left and upon them will fall the odium of the disillusion and the disappointments that will increasingly confront the Government.

What conclusions are we to draw from all this? That Ibn Sa'ud was a heroic figure there is no doubt. He is the hero of this book and he was my personal hero. But do heroes make good rulers? Not this one. The Sherif of Mecca was no hero—at least not on the scale of Ibn Sa'ud—but it is inconceivable that Husain, in the place of Ibn Sa'ud, would ever have led his country into the chaos of which the Sa'udi was guilty. So if we may turn back the pages of history can we say that the record of the Hashimis as rulers is better than that of the Sa'udis and that Lawrence, and not Philby, was right after all?

How long the present dispensation in Arabia will last and what will follow it no one can tell but the outlook is very far from reassuring. And a cloud, no bigger than a man's hand but with an awful warning has already appeared in the economic sky. The Sa'udi state lives on the oil that lies under its sands but the fuel of the future will be nuclear. Within its second decade, the experts assure us, nuclear power will be cheaper than power derived from coal or oil. Nuclear energy has seized the imagination of the whole world with such force as to give research into this new source of power the greatest possible impetus. Progress will almost inevitably be quicker than is now anticipated.

Are we then to expect a slump in oil, as in other existing fuels, within the very near future? If so, happy the countries who have invested their oil revenues productively and thus laid up for themselves a means of subsistence in the future. But what of Sa'udi Arabia which has already anticipated its oil royalties for who knows how many years to build as unstable an edifice as any child's house of cards! Black, indeed, may be its economic future.

And what of its faith that now lies discarded by so many, sold for a mess of pottage? What is the spiritual future of the country to be?

Eefde, Holland, 1956

Glossary

Abu Hunaiq	Father of the small chin (Arabic nickname for Sir John Glubb Pasha)
Ahlan wa sahlan ya ajnabi	You are welcome O stranger (Arab greeting)
'ain	well, spring
akh	brother
akhwan	plural of *akh*, also pronounced, and often spelt, *ikhwan*. Ibn Sa'ud's followers who formed his army and whom he placed in settlements
al	the; the *l* is sometimes assimilated to the initial consonant of the following word, e.g. *ar-Rahman*, the Merciful
Al	family, relationship
al 'ajalu min ash-shaitan wa as-sabru min ar-Rahman	haste is from the devil and patience from the Merciful (Arab saying)
al 'Alamain	the two signs, flags; the two stone pillars marking the boundary of the forbidden territory around Mecca
al 'Aruba	(also pronounced *'Uruba*) belonging to the Arab race
al Hamra	the Red (name of a palace in ar-Riyadh)
al Haramain	the Two Holy Cities of Mecca and Medina
al Hilal al Akhdar	the Fertile Crescent
Allahu akbar	God is most great
Allahu a'lam	God knows best
al Mahad adh-Dhahab	the Cradle of Gold (gold mine near Medina)
al Mu'tammar al Islam al a'la	the Highest Congress of Islam
al Qasr al Akhdar	the Green Palace
al Qibla	prayer niche in mosque showing direction of Mecca; Mecca newspaper edited by the Hashimi King Husain
al Rahmatain	the Two Mercies
Amin	Amen
Amir	Prince, Commander

Amir al 'ahd	Crown Prince
Amir al Mu'minin	Prince, Commander of the Believers (a title of the Khalifa of Islam)
Ansar	helpers, Companions of the Prophet
'aqil baligh	adult male
as-Sa'ih al Iraqi	the Iraqi Traveller (Yunus al Bahri)
as-salat	the prayer, prayer time
ash-Shaiba	the greybeard
Badu	(also *bedu*) Beduin
bait	(plural, *buyut*) house
Bait Ullah	House of Allah (the Ka'ba in Mecca)
baqar al wahsh	white oryx (literally wild cow)
bersim	lucerne
Bilad al Qanasil	Town of the Consuls (Jedda)
buyut ash-sha'ar	tents of goats' hair (literally houses of hair)
dar	house
dar adh-dhiafa	guest house
Darb al Muluk	Road of the Kings (between Mecca and ar-Riyadh)
Darb an-Nasara	Road of the Christians
Daula	Government
dhur'a	millet
dukhn	small-grained millet
effrenji	foreigner
Fatwa	edict of Muslim 'Ulama
ghazu	raid
Hadith	Tradition (of the Prophet)
Hajj	pilgrimage (to Mecca)
hajji	pilgrim, one who has performed the *hajj*

hawdaj	camel litter for women
Hijra	the departure of the Prophet Muhammad from Mecca. The Muslim calendar starts from this event
Hima	territory around Mecca forbidden to non-Muslims
huma	fever
'Ibrat Falastin	The Warning Example of Palestine (title of a booklet by the Palestinian Musa al Alami)
Ihram	ceremonial dress for the *hajj* consisting of two pieces of white cloth worn one round the shoulders and the other round the loins
Imam	Leader in Muslim prayer; more generally leader (spiritual and temporal)
Ingliz	English, Englishman
in sha'a Allah	if Allah wills
iqal	coil worn on the head to keep the headcloth in place
Islam	Religion of the Prophet Muhammad
jabal	mountain
Jabal ar-Rahma	Mountain of Mercy (on the Plain of 'Arafat near Mecca)
Jawi	Javanese
Ka'ba, Bait Ullah	literally the House of Allah; stone building in the inner court of the Holy Mosque in Mecca
Kafir	Unbeliever (not applied to Christians or Jews)
khafif	light (adjective)
Khalifa	One who comes after. Title of the Prophet's successors
Khalifate	Office of the Khalifa
kiswa	black carpet covering for the Ka'ba
kohl	antimony
ma	(plural, *miya*) water
mahfura	reservoir for catching rain-water

261

maqsar	canopy for riding camel
masjid	mosque
Masjid al Haram	Holy Mosque in Mecca
Mazhab	School of Muslim Doctrine
Mecca al Mukarrama	Mecca the Exalted
Medina al Munawwara	Medina the Enlightened
Medinat an Nabi	the Town of the Prophet (Medina)
moya qindasa	condensed water
Mu'azzin	caller to prayer
mushrikin	polytheists
Mutawwa	Missionary of Islam (here, of Wahhabism)
na'am	yes
Nabi	Prophet
Nasrani	Christian (follower of the Man of Nazareth)
Nejdi	Native of Nejd; adjective from Nejd
qabu	prison, vault
qahwa	coffee, coffee-shop
Qa'im Maqam	Governor
qama	measurement of length, distance between tips of fingers of a man's outstretched arms
qanat	underground water-channel (Persian)
qasida	poem, ode
qasr	palace, castle
qubba	cupola, dome
Qur'an	Holy Scripture of Islam
Rahmat Ullah	the Mercy of Allah
Ra'is	Head; Ibn Sa'ud's title for President Roosevelt
Ra'is al Baladiya	Head of the Municipality
Ramadhan	Muslim month of fasting
Rashid	member of House of Rashid
Rashidi	adjective from Rashid
Rasul Ullah	Messenger of God (the Prophet Muhammad)
Rub' al Khali	the Empty Quarter (desert in southern Arabia)
Sa'ida	Sidon

Saif al Islam	Sword of Islam (title of the sons of the Ruler of the Yemen)
sail	flood-water
salat al istighath	special prayer for succour (here for rain)
Saluqi	Arab greyhound
sambuk	dhow
samn	sheep's-milk butter
Sarikat Islam	Union Party of Islam
Sa'ud	member of the House of Sa'ud
Sa'udi	adjective from Sa'ud
sheikh	old man, leader
Sheikh al Islam	official religious leader in a Muslim country
shirk	polytheism
shuqduf	camel litter for pilgrim transport
sikkat al hadid	iron road, railway
suq	market
Tauhid	essential Oneness of Allah
Tell al Hibr	Ink Hill
Tihama	Coastal desert strip along the Red Sea
'Ulama	men learned in religion
'Umm	Mother
'Umm al Qura	Mother of Cities (Mecca); title of official Sa'udi Meccan newspaper
'Ummina Hawa	literally Our Mother Eve. Tomb of Eve at Jedda
'Umra	ritual circumambulations of the Ka'ba
wa'al	ibex, wild goat
wadi	river, dried river-bed
wakil	agent
wali	friend, master, governor, protector, Muslim saintly man
Wallahi!	by Allah!
Wazir	Minister, assistant
wudhaihi	white oryx
Yahudi	Jew, Jewish

263

Ya Sidi!	Oh, sir!
Yemeni	native of the Yemen, adjective from Yemen
zaghrij	(plural, *zagharij*) underground water reservoir
ziyara	visit (here visit to the tomb of the Prophet in Medina)

Index

265

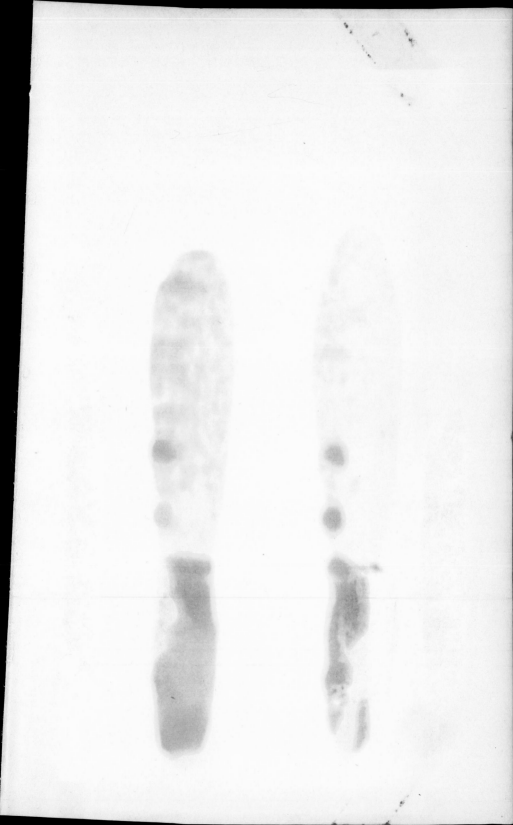